今天
你要提醒自己
你有足够的能力和力量
把满意、爱情和欢乐带进你的生活

唐娜·莱文——《今天是新的一天》

The Most
Influential and Best
Inspirational Voices

听力+词汇+文化

影响你一生的

名校励志演讲

倾听最具感召力的声音　　触摸巨人的美丽心灵　　主编 ◎ 方振宇
听读最地道流畅的英文　　体味世界的励志回声　　编者 ◎ 赵红毅
背诵最闪亮激昂的段落　　收藏灵魂的智慧光芒

海豚出版社
DOLPHIN BOOKS
IPG 中国国际出版集团

图书在版编目（CIP）数据

影响你一生的名校励志演讲：英汉对照 / 方振宇主编 . —北京：
海豚出版社，2010.12

ISBN 978-7-5110-0425-3

Ⅰ.①影… Ⅱ.①方… Ⅲ.①英语—汉语—对照读物 ②演讲—世界—
选集 Ⅳ.① H319.4: I

中国版本图书馆 CIP 数据核字（2010）第 247231 号

书　　名：YINGXIANGNIYISHENGDEMINGXIAOLIZHIYANJIANG
　　　　　影响你一生的名校励志演讲
主　　编：方振宇
责任编辑：董　锋
出　　版：海豚出版社
网　　址：http://www.dolphin-books.com.cn
地　　址：北京市百万庄大街 24 号
邮　　编：100037
电　　话：010-68997480（销售）
　　　　　010-68998879（总编室）
传　　真：010-68994018
印　　刷：北京世纪雨田印刷有限公司
经　　销：新华书店
开　　本：16 开（710 毫米 ×1000 毫米）
印　　张：19.75
字　　数：337 千字
版　　次：2011 年 1 月第 1 版　2011 年 6 月第 2 次印刷
标准书号：ISBN 978-7-5110-0425-3
定　　价：32.80 元

触摸灵魂的声音

对于英语学习者来说，多听多看多练英语演讲是学地道英语的最佳有效途径之一，也是训练语音语调最有效的辅助手段。你不用担心这些演讲是否有语法问题，也不用担心用词是否准确，表达是否到位。因为一些名人的演讲稿通常是字斟句酌精心完成的。此外，通过演讲学英语还可以潜移默化地帮助自己提升对英文的驾驭能力，增强英语的语感和美感。

这是一本英汉对照的世界名人在世界名校演讲的经典之作。本书共收录16篇演讲，涵盖12所世界一流大学，其中有美国的哈佛、耶鲁，英国的牛津，还有中国的清华、北大等。演讲文章皆是从美国最有影响的十大毕业典礼演讲和美国十大最具智慧的演讲之中遴选出来的精品。演讲者来自政治、经济、文化等各个领域，有国家领袖、政治人物、商界精英和娱乐名人等，这些演讲名篇题材涉猎广泛、风格迥异，有的气势恢宏，意蕴精深；有的轻松诙谐，令人捧腹；有的言辞恳切，语重心长。

这些名人在名校的演讲或立足于时代背景下，或从个人自身经历出发，鼓舞人们执着于自己的梦想，奋发向上、积极进取，作出个人应有的成绩，为时代、为国家作贡献。苹果电脑公司首席执行官史蒂夫·乔布斯2005年在斯坦福大学毕业典礼上的演讲，在美国十大最具影响和美国十大最具智慧的演讲排行榜中都位居首位，在演讲中他谈到了他人生中的三个故事，这三个故事不仅在斯坦福大学，在世界各地都引起了强烈的反响。他启发我们，防止患得患失的最好的方法就是记住生命随时都有可能结束，同时要听从自己内心的声音，执着于自己挚爱的事业。著名导演、电影制片人杰里·朱克2003年在威斯康辛大学毕业典礼上的演讲中告诉毕业生，没有人会像自己那样对自己的失败那么在意。你是唯一沉湎于你自己的重要性的人，所以要只管前行。《哈利·波特》的作者J.K.罗琳2008年在哈佛大学毕业典礼的演讲中鼓励毕业生，在未来的人生中要勇于面对失败，要有同情心，敞开心扉关注他人。明星州长施瓦辛格用执着的梦想谱写了人生的传奇，他在清华大学与莘莘学子畅谈理想，并分享自己的成长故事。他告诉清华学子，尽管在自己追逐梦想的过程中会遭受嘲讽和质疑，但是一定要执着于自己的梦想，他用自己的经历启发我们要坚持通过自己的努力去改变生活、改变未来。听他们的声音，你会充满激情；听他们的声音，即使遭遇失败你也会坦然面对；听他们的声音，你会朝自己的梦想迈开坚定的步伐。

随书赠送的 MP3 演讲音频，绝大多数是演讲者的原声音频。这些声音铿锵有力，或给你启迪，或让你感动，或给你温暖，或激发你前行的信念。同时，也让你更有机会品味最地道的英语表达。借音频听演讲，感受现场的气氛，聆听名人之声，感悟世界级人物送给大学毕业生的成功忠告。同时，你可以借此机会跟世界顶级人物学习口语，听他们的声音，模仿地道、原汁原味的腔调。听着他们的演讲，你的心头一定会充满喜悦和激动。

此外，在每一篇文章之后都附有从演讲中提炼出的具有指引性、励志性的名人给我们的启示，方便模仿与背诵。地道实用的英语学得多了、积累得多了，你就能很自然地表达出极为纯正的英语，既能提升你的书面语表达能力，也可以提升你的口语表达能力。

本书是原汁原味的英语集成，是智慧的结晶，是引领你走向成功的声音。让我们聆听、感悟和共鸣，也让我们一起参与到对人生、社会、世界的更深切的思考之中，让我们的心灵因伟大的声音而变得更加丰富和饱满。让我们一起聆听这触摸灵魂的声音，让我们一起携手迈向成功！

时间仓促，以及水平有限，难免有错误和不足之处，希望教育同仁和广大学生朋友不吝赐教。您的意见请直接发往本人信箱：zhenglish@126.com，以便再版时进一步更正、完善。谢谢！

北京千鹤园

Contents

目录

As you begin this new stage of your lives, follow your passion. If you don't have a passion, don't be satisfied until you find one. Life is too short to go through it without caring deeply about something: 当你开始生活的新阶段时，请追随你的爱好。如果你没有爱好，就去找，找不到绝不罢休。生命太短暂，所以不能空手走过，你必须对某样东西倾注你的深情。

As is a tale, so is life: not how long it is, but how good it is, is what matters. 生活就像故事一样，不在于长短，而在于品质，这才是最重要的。

Humanity's greatest advances are not in its discoveries— but in how those discoveries are applied to reduce inequity. 人类最大的进步并不在于其发现，而在于如何用这些发现来减少不平等现象。

Three Stories From My Life
我人生中的三个故事——苹果公司创始人史蒂夫·乔布斯 60

Remembering that you are going to die is the best way I know to avoid the trap of thinking you have something to lose. You are already naked. There is no reason not to follow your heart.　记住自己随时都会死去，这是我所知道的防止患得患失的最好方法。你已经一无所有了，还有什么理由不听从自己的心声呢。

Heal the Children, Heal the World
拯救儿童，拯救世界——流行音乐之王迈克尔·杰克逊 76

In a world filled with hate, we must still dare to hope. Keep hope alive. In a world filled with anger, we must still dare to comfort. In a world filled with despair, we must still dare to dream. And in a world filled with distrust, we must still dare to believe.　即使世界充满仇恨，我们也要勇于憧憬，让希望永存；即使世界充满愤怒，我们也要敢于安慰；即使世界充满绝望，我们也要勇于梦想；即使世界充满猜疑，我们仍然敢于信任。

Cherishing What You Have Now, and Striving for the Future
珍惜现在，把握未来——英国前首相托尼·布莱尔....................104

Be prepared to fail as well as to succeed, because it is failure not success that defines character. 不仅要接受成功，也要准备经历失败。因为是失败而非成功塑造了性格。

Dare to Compete, Dare to Care

Dare to compete. Dare to care. Dare to dream. Dare to love. Practice the art of making possible. And no matter what happens, even if you hear shouts behind, keep going. 要敢于竞争，敢于关爱，敢于憧憬，大胆去爱！要努力创造奇迹！无论发生什么，即使有人在你背后大声喊叫，也要勇往直前。

Everyone Can Be a President

To those of you who received honors, awards, and distinctions, I say, well done. And to the C students — I say, you, too, can be President of the United States. 对于那些表现杰出、获得各种奖项和荣誉的同学，我要说，你们真棒！对于那些 C 等生，我要说，你们将来也可以当美国总统！

Stay True to Yourself

And really when I look back on it, I wouldn't change a thing. I mean, it was so important for me to lose everything because I found out what the most important thing is, is to be true to yourself. And ultimately, that's what's gotten me to this place. I don't live in fear. I'm free. I have no secrets. And I know I'll always be OK, because no matter what, I know who I am. 当我回首这些往事的时候，我一点也不会改变。因为我发现，即使失去一切，最重要的是做真正的自己。最终，我来到了这里。我不再恐惧，我感觉很自在，也不再有秘密，而且我知道一切都会好的，因为无论如何，我知道我是谁。

Follow Your Gut, and You Will Be a Huge Success

Trust your gut to help you stand proudly in your own shoes, as you help others stand in theirs, and I know you will be a huge success. 相信自己的心声，你才能自豪地穿上自己的鞋子走自己的路，如果你也能帮别人走他们自己的路，那你们一定会大有作为。

How to Make Your Dream Come True

But it doesn't matter that your dream came true if you spent your whole life sleeping. So get out there and go for it, but don't be caught waiting. It's great to plan for your future. Just don't live there, because really nothing ever happens in the future. Whatever happens happens now, so live your life where the action is — now. 如果你一生都在睡觉，你的梦想是否实现就无关紧要了。所以，不要等待，要走出去，去实现你的梦想。规划未来是一件好事，但不要只活在未来，因为未来的事情实际上还没有发生。不管发生什么事情，都只是发生在现在，所以要活在现在。

Keep Your Dreams

Some of your families maybe don't believe in your dreams. But let me tell you something, my young friends. Keep your dreams. No matter what, keep your dreams. Don't give up on them, even when you are temporarily defeated or denied. Keep your dreams. 你们的家人也许不相信你们的梦想，但是，朋友们，让我告诉你们，执着于你的梦想！无论如何，坚持你们的梦想。即使你们遭遇暂时的失败或被否定，也不要放弃你们的梦想。执着于你的梦想。

Everything Is Possible

Anything you choose to do is within your reach. How far you go will depend on how high you set your dreams and how hard you work to achieve them. 无论你们想做什么样的事业，你们都可以做得很出色。你们的梦想有多大，你们就能走多远；你们为梦想付出得越多，你们就会越成功。

Challenge of the 21st Century

In the 21st century, your generation must make it your mission to ensure that today's progress does not come at tomorrow's expense. 在 21 世纪，你们年轻一代的使命是必须保证今天的进步发展不以明天为代价。

Each of them, at one point in their life, didn't have any title or much status to speak of. But they had passion, a commitment to following that passion wherever it would lead, and to working hard every step along the way. And that's not just how you'll ensure that your own life is well-lived. It's how you'll make a difference in the life of our nation. 他们中的每一个人，在生命中的某一时刻，都没有响亮的头衔和显赫的地位值得炫耀。但他们有激情，他们追随着这种激情，并在整个过程中努力走好每一步。不仅努力过好自己的生活，更重要的是，努力让自己的国家今非昔比。

Service is the rent we pay for living ... it is the true measure, the only measure of our success. 服务是我们为生活而支付的租金······它是真正的标准，是衡量我们成功的唯一标准。

哈佛大学

校训：**Veritas**（察验真理）

总括

17 世纪初，首批英国移民到达北美洲，在那里开拓自己的"伊甸园"——新英格兰。移民中有 100 多名清教徒，曾在牛津和剑桥大学受过古典式的高等教育，为了让他们的子孙后代在新的家园也能够受到这种教育，他们于 1636 年在马萨诸塞州的查尔斯河畔建立了美国历史上第一所学府，始称剑桥学院。

1639 年，为了纪念建校费用的主要捐献者约翰·哈佛，马萨诸塞议会通过决议，将学院改名为"哈佛学院"。1780 年哈佛学院升格为哈佛大学，此名沿用至今。

哈佛大学是美国最早的私立大学之一，是以培养研究生和从事科学研究为主的综合性大学，总部位于波士顿的剑桥城。

Advice for Graduates

给大学毕业生的几个忠告

Havard University
Commencement Address
Steven Chu
June 4, 2009

背景资料

　　2009 年 6 月 4 日，美国能源部部长朱棣文获得哈佛大学荣誉博士学位，应邀在哈佛大学毕业典礼上发表演讲。出身于华人家庭，成长于美国社会这个大熔炉中，这些铸就了朱棣文既含蓄文雅，又颇具美式幽默的演讲风格。在演讲中，他那诙谐幽默的语言博得台下阵阵掌声和笑声，朱棣文笑称自己名气不够响亮，也非亿万富豪，但至少他是一个"书呆子"。他从亲身经历出发，给哈佛大学 2009 届的毕业生提了几个忠告。

As you begin this new stage of your lives, follow your passion. If you don't have a passion, don't be satisfied until you find one. Life is too short to go through it without caring deeply about something.

　　当你开始生活的新阶段时，请追随你的爱好。如果你没有爱好，就去找，找不到绝不罢休。生命太短暂，所以不能空手走过，你必须对某样东西倾注你的深情。

——朱棣文

姓　　名：	朱棣文 (Steven Chu)
性　　别：	男
职　　业：	美国能源部长，教授
国　　籍：	美国
出生日期：	1948 年 2 月 28 日
毕业学校：	罗彻斯特大学；加利福尼亚大学伯克利分校
成功点睛：	生命太短暂，不能空手走过。 科学家从政的成功典范。
个人成就：	1997 年获诺贝尔物理学奖。

名人简介

　　朱棣文，华裔科学家，诺贝尔物理学奖获得者。1948 年 2 月 28 日出生在美国密苏里州的圣路易斯，排行第二。他的父母是江苏太仓人，现已在太仓创建了朱棣文小学，1998 年曾经访校一次。朱棣文，专业为应用物理（原子物理）；1970 年毕业于罗彻斯特大学，获数学学士和物理学学士；1976 年获加州大学伯克利分校物理学博士学位；任职于美国斯坦福大学，担任该校物理教授和物理系主任。1997 年获诺贝尔物理学奖；2008 年 12 月 15 日，朱棣文被奥巴马正式提名为美国能源部长。

　　朱棣文的个人名言：我们不一定要是天才，但我们知道自己的目标和计划；我们会时常受到挫折，但不要失去热情。

哈佛
大学

斯坦福
大 学

牛津
大学

耶鲁
大学

杜兰
大学

杜克
大学

威斯康
辛大学

清华
大学

北京
大学

亚利桑
那州立
大 学

加利福
尼 亚
大 学

Madam President Faust, members of the Harvard Corporation and the Board of Overseers, faculty, family, friends, and, most importantly, today's graduates,

Thank you for letting me share this wonderful day with you.

I am not sure I can live up to the high standards of Harvard Commencement speakers. Last year, J. K. Rowling, the billionaire novelist, who started as a classics student, graced this podium. The year before, Bill Gates, the mega-billionaire philanthropist and computer nerd stood here. Today, sadly, you have me. I am not a billionaire, but at least I am a nerd.

I am grateful to receive an honorary degree from Harvard, an honor that means more to me than you might care to imagine. As you may have heard this morning, I was the academic failure of my family. Both my brothers have degrees from Harvard. My older brother, Gilbert, after getting a Ph.D. in physics from that other school down the river, got an M.D. Ph.D from Harvard. My younger brother, Morgan Chu, who you've just heard his name today at the Board of Overseers, has a law degree. When I was awarded a Nobel Prize, I thought my mother would be pleased. Not so. I called her on the morning of the announcement, she replied, "That's nice, but when are you going to visit me next?" Now, as the last brother with a degree from Harvard, maybe, at last, she will be pleased.

Another difficulty with giving a Harvard commencement address is that some students may disapprove of the fact that I will borrow material from previous speeches, as well from others. I ask that you forgive me for two reasons.

First, in order to be heard, it is important to deliver the same message more than once.

Second, authors who borrow from others are following in the footsteps of the best. Ralph Waldo Emerson, who graduated from Harvard at the age of 18, noted "All my best thoughts were stolen by the ancients." Picasso declared "Good artists borrow. Great artists steal." Why should commencement speakers be held to a higher

尊敬的福斯特校长，哈佛集团的各位成员，监管理事会的各位理事，全体教职员工，各位家长，各位朋友，以及最重要的各位毕业生们：

感谢你们，让我有机会同你们一起分享这个美妙的日子。

我不太肯定自己是否够得上哈佛大学毕业典礼演讲人这样的殊荣。去年在这个讲台上演讲的是英国亿万身家的小说家 J. K. 罗琳女士，她起初是一个学古典文学的学生。前年站在这里的是比尔·盖茨先生，他是超级富翁、慈善家和电脑痴。今年很遗憾，是我给你们发表毕业演讲，虽然我不是亿万富翁，但是至少我是一个书呆子。

我很感激哈佛大学授予我荣誉学位，这对我很重要，也许比你们想象的更重要。你们今天早上可能听说了，从学术上来说，我在我家很差劲。我的兄弟们都获得了哈佛学位。我哥哥吉尔博特在河下游的那所大学获得了物理学博士学位之后，又在哈佛大学获得医学博士学位；我弟弟摩根，你们在校监管理事会已经听到了他的名字，拿到了哈佛大学法律学位。我本人得到诺贝尔奖的时候，我想母亲会很高兴。但是，我错了。消息公布的那天早上，我给她打电话，她只说："这是好消息，不过我想知道，你下次什么时候来看我？"如今在我们兄弟当中，我最终也拿到了哈佛大学的学位，我想这一次，她会感到满意。

在哈佛大学毕业典礼上发表演讲，还有一个难处，那就是有些毕业生可能有意见，不喜欢我重复前人演讲中说过的话。我请你们谅解我，有两个原因。

首先，为了能让你们听进去，很重要的方法就是重复传递同样的信息。

其次，借鉴他人的作者，正走在一条前人开辟的最佳道路上。拉尔夫·瓦尔多·爱默生 18 岁从哈佛大学毕业时曾经写过这样的话："我最好的一些思想都曾被古人偷用过。"画家毕加索宣称："优秀的艺术家借鉴，伟大的艺术家偷窃。"那么，

热词空间

commencement
[kə'mensmənt] n. 毕业典礼
podium ['pəudjəm] n. 讲台
mega-billionaire
[megə,biljə'nɛə] n. 超级富翁
philanthropist [fi'lænθrəpist]
n. 慈善家
nerd [nə:d] n. 狂热爱好者，呆子
disapprove [,disə'pru:v] vi.
不赞成；不同意
follow in the footsteps of 效仿，借鉴

standard?

I also want to point out the irony of speaking to graduates of an institution that would have rejected me, had I the chutzpah to apply. I am married to "Dean Jean," the former dean of admissions at Stanford. She assures me that she would have rejected me, if given the chance. When I showed her a draft of this speech, she objected strongly to my use of the word "rejected". She never rejected applicants; her letters stated "we are unable to offer an admission". I have difficulty understanding the difference. After all, deans of admissions of highly selective schools are in reality, "deans of rejection". Clearly, I have a lot to learn about marketing.

My address will follow the classical sonata form of commencement addresses. The first movement, just presented, were light-hearted remarks. This next movement consists of unsolicited advice, which is rarely valued, seldom remembered, never followed. As Oscar Wilde said, "The only thing to do with good advice is to pass it on. It is never of any use to oneself." So, here comes the advice.

First, every time you celebrate an achievement, be thankful to those who made it possible. Thank your parents and friends who supported you, thank your professors who were inspirational, and especially thank the other professors whose less-than-brilliant lectures forced you to teach yourself. Going forward, the ability to teach yourself is the hallmark of a great liberal arts education and will be the key to your success. To your fellow students who have added immeasurably to your education during those late night discussions, hug them. Also, of course, thank Harvard. Should you forget, there's an alumni association to remind you.

Second, in your future life, cultivate a generous spirit. In all negotiations, don't bargain for the last, little advantage. Leave the change on the table. In your collaborations, always remember that "credit" is not a conserved quantity. In a successful collaboration, everybody gets 90 percent of the credit.

Jimmy Stewart, as Elwood P. Dowd in the movie *Harvey* got it exactly right. (Now, forgive me, I don't really believe in Jimmy Stewart's story very well, but ...)

毕业典礼的演说者为什么就不适用同样的标准呢？

我还要指出一点，向哈佛毕业生发表演说，对我来说是有讽刺意味的，因为如果当年我斗胆向哈佛大学递交入学申请，一定会被拒绝。我的妻子迪恩·简，曾任斯坦福大学招生办公室主任，她明确告诉我，如果当年我申请斯坦福大学，她会拒绝我。我把这篇演讲的草稿给她过目，她强烈反对我使用"拒绝"这个词。她从来不拒绝任何申请者。在拒绝信中，她总是写："我们无法给你提供入学机会。"我不知道这两种说法到底有什么区别。说到底，那些热门学校的招生办公室主任与其说是"准许他人入学的主任"，还不如说是"拒绝他人入学的主任"。很显然，我需要好好学学怎么来推销自己。

毕业典礼演讲都遵循古典奏鸣曲的结构，我的演讲也不例外。刚才是第一乐章——轻快的闲谈。接下来的第二乐章是送上门的忠告。这样的忠告很少被重视，几乎注定被忘记，永远不会被实践。但是，就像奥斯卡·王尔德说的："对于忠告，你所能做的，就是把它送给别人，因为它对你没有任何用处。"所以，下面就是我的忠告。

第一，每次庆祝你取得成就的时候，不要忘记所有助你一臂之力的人。要感谢你的父母和支持你的朋友，要感谢那些启发过你的教授，尤其要感谢那些演讲拙劣的教授，因为他们迫使你自学。从长远看，自学能力是优秀的文科教育中必不可少的，将成为你成功的关键。你还要去拥抱你的同学，感谢他们同你进行过的许多次彻夜长谈，这为你的教育带来了无法衡量的价值。当然，你还要感谢哈佛大学。不过即使你忘了这一点，校友会也会来提醒你。

第二，在你们未来的人生中，做一个慷慨大方的人。在任何谈判中，都把最后一点点利益留给对方。不要把桌上的钱都拿走。在合作中，不要把荣誉留给自己。成功合作的任何一方，都应获得全部荣誉的90%。

电影《哈维》中，吉米·斯图尔特扮演的角色埃尔伍德P.多德，就完全理解这一点。（请原谅，我并不是很相信吉

热词空间

irony ['aiərəni] *n.* 讽刺；反语；具有讽刺意味的事

chutzpah ['hutspə] *n.* 胆大妄为

dean [di:n] *n.* 院长；系主任

draft [dræft] *n.* 草稿

sonata [sə'na:tə] *n.* ［音］奏鸣曲

unsolicited [ˌʌnsə'lisitid] *adj.* 主动提供的

Oscar Wilde 奥斯卡·王尔德，英国唯美主义运动的倡导者，爱尔兰著名剧作家、诗人、散文家，是19世纪与萧伯纳齐名的英国才子，也是才华横溢的学者。

inspirational [ˌinspə'reiʃənəl] *adj.* 鼓舞人心的；给予灵感的

hallmark ['hɔ:lma:k] *n.* 特点，标志

collaboration [kəˌlæbə'reiʃən] *n.* 合作

"Years ago my mother used to say to me, 'In this world, Elwood, you must be … she always used to call me Elwood … in this world, Elwood, you must be oh so smart or oh so pleasant.'" Well, for years I was smart. … I recommend pleasant. You may quote me on that.

My third piece of advice is as follows: As you begin this new stage of your lives, follow your passion. If you don't have a passion, don't be satisfied until you find one. Life is too short to go through it without caring deeply about something. When I was your age, I was incredibly single-minded in my goal to be a physicist. After college, I spent eight years as a graduate student and postdoc at Berkeley, and then nine years at Bell Labs. During that my time, my central focus and professional joy was physics.

Here is my final advice. Pursuing a personal passion is important, but it should not be your only goal. When you are old and gray, and look back on your life, you will want to be proud of what you have done. The source of that pride won't be the things you have acquired or the recognition you have received. It will be the lives you have touched and the difference you have made.

After nine years at Bell labs, I decided to leave the warm, cozy ivory tower for what I considered to be the "real world", a university. Bell Labs, to quote what was said about Mary Poppins, was "practically perfect in every way", but I wanted to leave behind something more than scientific articles. I wanted to teach and I wanted to give birth to my own set of scientific children.

Ted Geballe, a friend and distinguished colleague of mine at Stanford, went from Berkeley to Bell Labs to Stanford years earlier, described our motives best, and I quote:

"The best part of working at a university is the students. They come in fresh, enthusiastic, open to ideas, unscarred by the battles of life. They don't realize it, but they're the recipients of the best our society can offer. If a mind is ever free to be creative, that's the time. They come in believing textbooks are authoritative, but eventually they figure out that textbooks and professors don't know everything, and

米·斯图尔特的故事。但是……）他说："多年前，母亲曾经对我说，'埃尔伍德…她总是叫我埃尔伍德…活在这个世界上，你要么做一个聪明人，要么做一个好人。'"我做聪明人，已经做了好多年了……但是，我推荐你们做个好人。你们可以引用我这句话。

我的第三个忠告是：当你开始生活的新阶段时，请追随你的爱好。如果你没有爱好，就去找，找不到绝不罢休。生命太短暂，所以不能空手走过，你必须对某样东西倾注你的深情。我在你们这个年龄，是超级的一根筋，我的目标就是非成为物理学家不可。本科毕业后，我在加州大学伯克利分校又待了8年，读完了研究生，获得了博士后，然后去贝尔实验室待了9年。在那些年中，我关注的中心和职业上的全部乐趣，都来自物理学。

我还有最后一个忠告，兴趣爱好固然重要，但是不应是你的唯一目标。当你白发苍苍、垂垂老矣、回首人生时，你需要为自己做过的事感到自豪。你所获得的物质财富和得到的荣誉都不是自豪的源泉。只有那些受你影响、被你改变过的人和事，才会让你感到自豪。

在贝尔实验室待了9年后，我决定离开这个温暖舒适的象牙塔，走进我所认为的"真实世界"——大学。我对贝尔实验室的看法，可以引用别人评价玛丽·波平斯的话，"实际上十全十美"。但是，我想为世界留下更多的东西，而不只是科学论文。我要去教书，培育我自己在科学上的后代。

我在斯坦福大学有一个好友兼优秀同事泰德·格贝拉。他也是从伯克利分校去了贝尔实验室，几年前又离开贝尔实验室去了斯坦福大学。他对我们的动机做出了最佳描述：

"在大学工作，最大的优点就是能和学生们在一起。他们生机勃勃，充满热情，思想自由，还没被生活的重压改变。虽然他们自己没有意识到，但是他们是这个社会中你能找到的最佳接受者。如果生命中只有一段时间思想自由且充满创

热词空间

single-minded ['siŋgl'maindid] adj. 一心一意的，专一的

ivory ['aivəri] tower 象牙塔

motive ['məutiv] n. 动机，目的

enthusiastic [in,θju:zi'æstik] adj. 热情的；热心的

unscarred [ʌn'ska:d] adj. 无疤痕的

recipient [ri'sipiənt] n. 接受者；容纳

authoritative [ɔ:'θɔritətiv] adj. 有权威的，可信赖的

then they start to think on their own. And then, I began learning from them."

My students, post doctoral fellows, and the young researchers who worked with me at Bell Labs, Stanford, and Berkeley have been extraordinary. Over 30 former group members are now professors, many at the best research institutions in the world, including Harvard. I have learned much from them. Even now, in rare moments on weekends, the remaining members of my biophysics group meet with me in the ether world of cyberspace.

I began teaching with the idea of giving back; but I received more than I gave. This brings me to the final movement of this speech. It begins with a story about an extraordinary scientific discovery and a new dilemma it poses. It's a call to arms and about making a difference.

So here's the movement. In the last several decades, our climate has been changing. Climate change is not new: the Earth went through six ice ages in the past 600,000 years. However, recent measurements show that the climate has begun to change rapidly. The size of the North Polar Ice Cap in the month of September is only half the size it was a mere 50 years ago. The sea level which been rising since direct measurements began in 1870 is now five times faster, at a rate now five times faster, than at the beginning of recorded measurements. Here's the remarkable scientific discovery. For the first time in human history, science is now making predictions of how our actions will affect the world 50 and 100 years from now. These changes are due to an increase in carbon dioxide put into the atmosphere since the beginning of the Industrial Revolution. The Earth has warmed up by roughly 0.8 degrees Celsius since the beginning of this Revolution. There is already approximately a 1 degree rise built into the system, even if we stop all greenhouse gas emissions today. Why? It will be decades to warm up the deep oceans before the temperature reaches a new equilibrium.

If the world continues on a business-as-usual path, the Intergovernmental Panel on Climate Change predicts that there is a fifty-fifty chance the temperature will

10

造力，那么这段时间就是在大学期间。进校时，学生们对课本上的一字一句毫不怀疑，渐渐地，他们发现课本和教授并不是无所不知的，于是他们开始独立思考。从那时起，就是我开始向他们学习了。"

我在贝尔实验室、斯坦福大学和伯克利大学教过的学生、带过的博士后、合作过的年轻同事都非常优秀。他们中有30多人现在已经是教授了。他们所在的研究机构有不少是世界一流的，其中就包括哈佛大学。我从他们身上学到了很多东西。即使现在，我周末偶尔还会上网，和还在从事生物物理学的研究组的成员在网络世界里相聚。

我怀着回报社会的想法，开始了教学生涯。然而，我得到的多于我付出的。这就引出了这次演讲的最后一篇乐章。首先我要讲一个了不起的科学发现，以及由此带来的新挑战。它是一个战斗的号令，到了做出改变的时候了。

现在开始本次演讲的最后一章。过去几十年中，我们的气候一直在发生变化。气候变化并不是现在才有的，过去60万年中地球就发生了6次冰河期。但是，最新的测量表明气候变化加速了。9月份，北极冰覆盖的面积只相当于50年前的一半。1870年起，人们开始测量海平面上升的速度，现在海平面上升的速度是那时的5倍。一个重大的科学发现就这样产生了。在人类历史上，科学第一次预测出我们的行为对50到100年后的世界有何影响。这些变化的原因是，从工业革命开始，人类排放到大气中的二氧化碳增加了。这使得地球的气温上升了大约0.8摄氏度。即使我们立刻停止所有温室气体的排放，气温仍然将比过去上升大约1度。为什么呢？因为在气温达到均衡前，海水温度的上升将持续几十年。

联合国政府间气候变化专门委员会（IPCC）预测，如果全世界保持现在的经济模式不变，本世纪末气温上升5度的可能性是50%。这听起来好像不多，但是我要提醒你，上一次的冰河期，地球的气温也仅仅下降了6度。那时，俄亥俄州和

热词空间

extraordinary
[,ekstrə'ɔ:dinəri] *adj.* 非凡的，惊人的，显著的

biophysics [,baiəu'fiziks] *n.*
生物物理学

ether ['i:θə] *n.* 天空；气氛；
【化】乙醚

cyberspace ['saibə,speis] *n.*
网络空间

dilemma [,dai'lemə] *n.* 困境；
进退两难

Celsius ['selsiəs] *adj.* 摄氏的

equilibrium [,i:kwi'libriəm]
n. 均衡

the Intergovernmental Panel
on Climate Change, 政府间
气候变化专门委员会，简称
IPCC，是一个附属于联合国
之下的跨政府组织，在1988
年由世界气象组织、联合国
环境署合作成立，专门负责
研究由人类活动所造成的气
候变迁。该委员会本身并不
进行研究工作，其主要工作
是发表和执行《联合国气候
变化框架公约》有关的专题
报告。

哈佛
大学

斯坦福
大 学

牛津
大学

耶鲁
大学

杜兰
大学

杜克
大学

威斯康
辛大学

清华
大学

北京
大学

亚利桑
那州立
大 学

加利福
尼 亚
大 学

exceed 5 degrees by the end of this century. This increase may not sound like much, but let me remind you that during the last ice age, the world was only 6 degrees colder. During this time, most of Canada and the United States down to Ohio and Pennsylvania were covered year round by a glacier. A world 5 degrees warmer will be very different. The change will be so rapid that many species, including Humans, will have a hard time adapting. I've been told for example, that, in a much warmer world, insects were bigger. I wonder if this thing buzzing around is a precursor.

We also face the specter of nonlinear "tipping points" that may cause much more severe changes. An example of a tipping point is the thawing of the permafrost. The permafrost contains immense amounts of frozen organic matter that have been accumulating for millennia. If the soil melts, the microbes will spring to life and cause this debris to rot. The difference in biological activity below freezing and above freezing is something we are all familiar with. Frozen food remains edible for a very long time in the freezer, but once thawed, it spoils quickly. How much methane and carbon dioxide might be released from the rotting permafrost? If even a fraction of the carbon is released, it could be greater than all the greenhouse gases we have released since the beginning of the industrial revolution. Once started, a runaway effect could occur.

The climate problem is the unintended consequence of our success. We depend on fossil energy to keep our homes warm in the winter, cool in the summer, and lit at night; we use it to travel across town and across continents. Energy is a fundamental reason for the prosperity we enjoy, and we will not surrender this prosperity. The United States has 3 percent of the world population, and yet, we consume 25 percent of the energy. By contrast, there are 1.6 billion people who don't have access to electricity. Hundreds of millions of people still cook with twigs or dung. The life we enjoy may not be within the reach of the developing world, but it is within sight, and they want what we have.

Here is the dilemma. How much are we willing to invest, as a world society, to mitigate

宾夕法尼亚州以下的大部分美国和加拿大的土地，都终年被冰川覆盖。气温上升5度的地球，将是一个截然不同的地球。由于气候变化来得太快，包括人类在内的许多生物，都将很难适应。比如，有人告诉我，在更温暖的环境中，昆虫的个头将变大。我不知道现在身旁嗡嗡叫的这只大苍蝇，是不是就是前兆。

我们还面临另一个威胁，那就是非线性的"气候引爆点"，这会带来许多更严重的变化。"气候引爆点"的一个例子就是永久冻土层的融化。永久冻土层经过千万年的累积形成，其中包含了巨量的冻僵的有机物。如果冻土融化，微生物就将广泛繁殖，使得冻土层中的有机物快速腐烂。冷冻后的生物和冷冻前的生物在生物学特性上的差异，我们都很熟悉。在冷库中，冷冻食品在经过长时间保存后，依然可以食用。但是，一旦解冻，食品很快就腐烂了。一个腐烂的永久冻土层，将释放出多少甲烷和二氧化碳？即使只有一部分的二氧化碳被释放出来，可能也比我们从工业革命开始释放出来的所有温室气体还要多。这种事情一旦发生，局势就失控了。

气候问题是我们的经济发展在无意中带来的后果。我们依靠化石能源在冬天取暖、夏天制冷、夜间照明、长途旅行、环球观光。能源是经济繁荣的基础，我们不可能放弃经济繁荣。美国人口占全世界的3%，但是我们消耗全世界25%的能源。与此形成对照，全世界还有16亿人没有电，数亿人靠燃烧树枝和动物粪便来煮饭。发展中国家的人民享受不到我们的生活，但是他们都看在眼里，他们渴望拥有我们拥有的东西。

这就是新的挑战。全世界作为一个整体，我们到底愿意付出多少来缓和气候变化？这种变化至少在100年内还不会出现。代际责任的观念深深植根于所有文化中。父母为了让他们的孩子有更好的生活而努力工作。气候变化将影响整个世界，但是我们的天性使得我们只关心个人家庭的幸福。我们能不能把全世界看作一个整体，为子孙后代承担起责任？

热词空间

glacier ['glæsjə] *n.* 冰河，冰川

buzz [bʌz] *vi.* 发出嗡嗡声

precursor [pri'kə:sə] *n.* 预兆

specter ['spektə] *n.* 幽灵，恐怖之物

nonlinear [nɔn'liniə] *adj.* 非线性的

thawing [θɔ:] *n.* 融解

permafrost ['pə:məfrɔ:st] *n.* 永久冻土

immense [i'mens] *adj.* 巨大的

millennia [mi'leniə, niə] *n.* 千年期（millennium 的复数）

microbe ['maikrəub] *n.* 细菌，微生物

debris ['deibri:] *n.* 碎片，残骸，（冰川积聚的）碎石

edible ['edibl] *adj.* 可食用的

methane ['mi:θein] *n.* [化] 甲烷

runaway ['rʌnə,wei] *adj.* 失控的；逃亡的

twig [twig] *n.* 小枝

dung [dʌŋ] *n.* 粪

mitigate ['mitigeit] *vt.* 使缓和

the consequences of climate change that will not be realized for at least 100 years? Deeply rooted in all cultures, is the notion of generational responsibility. Parents work hard so that their children will have a better life. Climate change will affect the entire world, but our natural focus is on the welfare of our immediate families. Can we, as a world society, meet our responsibility to future generations?

While I am worried, I am hopeful we will solve this problem. I became the director of the Lawrence Berkeley National Laboratory, in part because I wanted to enlist some of the best scientific minds to help battle against climate change. I was there only four and a half years, the shortest serving director in the 78-year history of the Lab, but when I left, a number of very exciting energy institutes at the Berkeley Lab and UC Berkeley had been established.

I am extremely privileged to be part of the Obama administration. If there ever was a time to help steer America and the world towards a path of sustainable energy, now is the time.

The message the President is delivering is not one of doom and gloom, but of optimism and opportunity. I share this optimism. The task ahead is daunting, but we can and will succeed.

We know some of the answers already. There are immediate and significant savings in energy efficiency and conservation. Energy efficiency is not just low-hanging fruit; it is fruit lying on the ground. For example, we have the potential to make buildings 80 percent more efficient with investments that will pay for themselves in less than 15 years. Buildings consume 40 percent of the energy we use, and a transition to energy efficient buildings will cut our carbon emissions by one-third.

We are revving up the remarkable American innovation machine that will be the basis of a new prosperity. We will invent much improved methods to harness the sun, the wind, nuclear power, and capture and sequester the carbon dioxide emitted from our power plants. Advanced bio-fuels and the electrification of personal vehicles will make us less dependent on foreign oil.

虽然我忧心忡忡，但还是对未来抱有希望，这个问题将会得到解决。我同意出任劳伦斯·伯克利国家实验室主任，部分原因是我想招募世界上一些最好的科学家，来研究应对气候变化的策略。我在那里干了4年半，是这个实验室78年的历史中任期最短的主任。但是当我离任时，在伯克利实验室和伯克利分校，一些非常激动人心的能源研究机构已经建立起来了。

能够成为奥巴马政府的一员，我感到极其荣幸。如果有一个时机，可以引导美国和全世界走上可持续能源的道路，那么这个时机就是现在。

总统传达的信息是，未来并非在劫难逃，而是乐观的，我们依然有机会。我也抱有这种乐观主义。我们面前的任务令人生畏，但是我们能够并且将会成功。

我们已经有了一些答案，可以立竿见影地节约能源和提高能源使用效率。它们不是挂在枝头的水果，而是已经成熟掉在地上了，就看我们愿不愿意捡起来。比如，我们有办法将楼宇的耗电减少80%，增加的投资在15年内就可以收回来。楼宇的耗电占能源消耗的40%，节能楼宇的推广将使二氧化碳的释放减少三分之一。

我们正在加速美国这座巨大的创新机器，这将是下一次美国大繁荣的基础。我们将发明有效利用太阳能、风能、核能的新方法，发明能够捕获和隔离电厂排放的废气中的二氧化碳的方法。先进的生物燃料和电力汽车将会使我们减少对外国石油的依赖。

在未来的几十年中，我们几乎肯定会面对更高的油价和更严厉的二氧化碳排放政策。这是一场新的工业革命，美国有机会成为领头军。当问及伟大的冰球选手韦恩·格里兹基如何在冰上跑位时，他回答说："我滑向冰球下一步的位置，而不是它现在的位置。"美国也应该这样做。

奥巴马政府正在为美国的繁荣和可持续能源奠定新的基

热词空间

enlist [in'list] vt. 征募；使入伍
privileged ['privilidʒd] adj. 享有特权的
steer [stiə] vt. 指导，引导；控制；驾驶
doom and gloom 前景黯淡，无望
daunting ['dɔ:ntiŋ] adj. 令人生畏的
transition [træn'ziʃən] n. 转变；过渡
rev [rev] vi. 加速；增加
harness ['hɑ:nis] vt. 驾驭
sequester [si'kwestə] vt. 使隔离
electrification [i,lektrifi'keiʃən] n. 电气化

In the coming decades, we will almost certainly face higher oil prices and be in a carbon-constrained economy. We have the opportunity to lead in development of a new, industrial revolution. The great hockey player, Wayne Gretzky, when asked, how he positions himself on the ice, he replied," I skate to where the puck is going to be, not where it's been." America should do the same.

The Obama administration is laying a new foundation for a prosperous and sustainable energy future, but we don't have all of the answers. That's where you come in. In this address, I am asking you, the Harvard graduates, to join us. As our future intellectual leaders, take time to learn more about what's at stake, and then act on that knowledge. As future scientists and engineers, I ask you to give us better technology solutions. As future economists and political scientists, I ask you to create better policy options. As future business leaders, I ask that you make sustainability an integral part of your business.

Finally, as humanists, I ask that you speak to our common humanity. One of the cruelest ironies about climate change is that the ones who will be hurt the most are the most innocent: the world's poorest and those yet to be born.

The coda to this last movement is borrowed from two humanists.

The first quote is from Martin Luther King. He spoke on ending the war in Vietnam in 1967, but his message seems so fitting for today's climate crisis, I quote:

"This call for a worldwide fellowship that lifts neighborly concern beyond one's tribe, race, class, and nation is in reality a call for an all-embracing and unconditional love for all mankind. This oft misunderstood, this oft misinterpreted concept, so readily dismissed by the Nietzsches of the world as a weak and cowardly force, has now become an absolute necessity for the survival of man … We are now faced with the fact, my friends, that tomorrow is today. We are confronted with the fierce urgency of now. In this unfolding conundrum of life and history, there is such a thing as being too late."

The final message is from William Faulkner. On December 10th, 1950, his Nobel Prize banquet speech was about the role of humanists in a world facing potential nuclear holocaust, I quote:

础。但是我们不能为所有的问题都找到答案。这就需要你们的参与。在本次演讲中，我请求在座的哈佛毕业生加入我们。你们是我们未来的智力领袖，请花时间加深理解目前的危险局势，然后采取相应的行动。你们是未来的科学家和工程师，我要求你们给我们更好的技术方案。你们是未来的经济学家和政治学家，我要求你们创造更好的政策选择。你们是未来的企业家，我要求你们将可持续发展作为你们的事业中不可分割的一部分。

最后，你们是人道主义者，我要求你们为我们共同的人道主义说话。气候变化带来的最残酷的讽刺之一就是，最受伤害的人恰恰就是最无辜的人——世界上那些最穷的人们和那些还没有出生的人。

在这最后一个乐章的结尾，我想引用两位人道主义者的话。

第一段引语来自马丁·路德·金。这是 1967 年他就结束越南战争的评论，但是看上去非常适合用来评论今天的气候危机。

"我呼吁全世界人们团结一心，抛弃部落种族、肤色、阶级、国籍的隔阂；我呼吁包罗一切、无条件的对全人类的爱。你会因此遭受误解和误读，信奉尼采哲学的世人会认定你是一个软弱和胆怯的懦夫。但是，这是人类继续存在所必需的……朋友们，眼前的事实就是，明天就是今天。此刻，我们面临最紧急的情况。在变幻莫测的生活和历史之中，有一样东西叫做悔之晚矣。"

第二段引语来自威廉·福克纳。1950 年 12 月 10 日，他在诺贝尔奖获奖晚宴上发表演说，谈到在世界面临潜在核战争的情况下人道主义者应该扮演什么样的角色时说道：

"我相信人类不会仅仅存在，他还将胜利。人类是不朽的，这不是因为万物当中仅仅他拥有发言权，而是因为他有一个灵魂，一种有同情心、甘于牺牲和能够忍耐的精神。诗人、

热词空间

constrain [kən'strein] *vt.* 抑制，强迫

hockey ['hɔki] *n.* 曲棍球；冰球

at stake 在危急关头，在危险中

integral ['intigrəl] *adj.* 不可分割的，不可缺少的，完整的

coda ['kəudə] *n.* 结尾部分

all-embracing ['ɔ:lem'breisiŋ] *adj.* 包罗万象的，总括的

oft [ɔ:ft] *adv.* 常常；再三

Nietzsche ['ni:tʃə] 尼采，德国著名哲学家，西方现代哲学的开创者，同时也是卓越的诗人和散文家。

cowardly ['kauədli] *adj.* 怯懦的，懦弱的；胆小的

conundrum [kə'nʌndrəm] *n.* 难题

holocaust ['hɔləkɔ:st] *n.* 大屠杀；毁灭

17

哈佛
大学

斯坦福
大学

牛津
大学

耶鲁
大学

杜兰
大学

杜克
大学

威斯康
辛大学

清华
大学

北京
大学

亚利桑
那州立
大学

加利福
尼亚
大学

"I believe that man will not merely endure: he will prevail. He is immortal, not because he among creatures has an inexhaustible voice, but because he has a soul, a spirit capable of compassion and sacrifice and endurance. The poet's, the writer's, duty is to write about these things. It is his privilege to help man endure by lifting his heart, by reminding him of the courage and the honor and hope and pride and compassion and pity and sacrifice which have been the glory of his past."

Graduates, you have an extraordinary role to play in our future. As you pursue your private passions, I hope you will also develop a passion and a voice to help the world in ways both large and small. Nothing will give you greater satisfaction.

Please accept my warmest congratulations. May you prosper, may you help preserve and save our planet for your children, and all future children of the world.

朱棣文给我们的 启示

First, every time you celebrate an achievement, be thankful to those who made it possible.
第一，取得成就的时候，不要忘记所有助你一臂之力的人。

- -

Second, in your future life, cultivate a generous spirit. In all negotiations, don't bargain for the last, little advantage. Leave the change on the table. In your collaborations, always remember that "credit" is not a conserved quantity. In a successful collaboration, everybody gets 90 percent of the credit.

第二，在你们未来的人生中，做一个慷慨大方的人。在任何谈判中，都把最后一点点利益留给对方。不要把桌上的钱都拿走。在合作中，不要把荣誉留给自己。成功合作的任何一方，都应获得全部荣誉的90%。

- -

If there ever was a time to help steer America and the world towards a path of sustainable energy, now is the time. The message the President is delivering is not one of doom and gloom, but of optimism and opportunity. I share this optimism. The task ahead is daunting, but we can and will succeed.

如果有一个时机，可以引导美国和全世界走上可持续能源的道路，那么这个时机就是现在。总统传达的信息是：未来并非在劫难逃，而是乐观的，我们依然有机会。我也抱有这种乐观主义。我们面前的任务令人生畏，但是我们能够并且将会成功。

作家的责任就是书写这种精神。他们有权力升华人类的心灵，使人类回忆起过去曾经使他无比光荣的东西——勇气、荣誉、希望、自豪、同情、怜悯和牺牲。"

各位毕业生，你们在我们的未来中扮演举足轻重的角色。当你们追求自己所热爱的事业时，我希望你们也会发扬奉献精神，积极发声，在大大小小各个方面帮助改进这个世界。这会给你们带来最大的满足感。

最后，请接受我最热烈的祝贺。祝愿你们前程似锦，也希望你们保护和拯救我们这个星球，为了你们的孩子，以及未来所有的孩子。

热词空间

privilege ['privilidʒ] n. 特权；
优待

compassion [kəm'pæʃən] n.
同情；怜悯

sacrifice ['sækrifais] n. 牺牲；
献身

satisfaction [ˌsætis'fækʃən]
n. 满意，满足

prosper ['prɒspə] vi. 繁荣，
昌盛；成功

preserve [pri'zəːv] vt. 保护；
维持

The Fringe Benefits of Failure, and the Importance of Imagination

失败的额外收益和想象力的重要性

Harvard University
Commencement Address
J. K. Rowling
June 5, 2008

背景 资料

2008年6月5日，《哈利·波特》作者J. K. 罗琳应邀在哈佛大学毕业典礼上演讲。在演讲中，罗琳谈到失败和想象力的重要性。失败让她更好地认识自我，坚定了她做最喜欢、最擅长的事情的决心。她认为，从失败中学到的教训让自己在未来的人生中处于更安全的位置。而想象力让人具备一种"思他人所思，想他人所想"的同情心。罗琳鼓励哈佛骄子在未来人生中，勇于面对失败，敞开心怀关注他人。

As is a tale, so is life: not how long it is, but how good it is, is what matters.

生活就像故事一样，不在于长短，而在于品质，这才是最重要的。

——J. K. 罗琳引语

姓　名：	J. K. 罗琳 (Joanne Kathleen Rowling)
性　别：	女
职　业：	作家
国　籍：	英国
出生日期：	1965 年 7 月 31 日
毕业学校：	英国埃克塞特大学
成功点睛：	人生如同故事的奇迹，逆境中坚持梦想的典范。
代表作品：	《哈利·波特》魔法系列丛书
荣　誉：	英国国家图书奖儿童小说奖，斯马蒂图书金奖章奖

名人简介

　　J. K. 罗琳 (J. K. Rowling)，英国女作家。本名乔安妮·凯瑟琳·罗琳，1965 年 7 月 31 日生于英国的格温特郡。她从小喜欢写作和讲故事，6 岁就写了一篇跟兔子有关的故事。妹妹是她讲故事的对象。创作的动力和欲望，从此没有离开过她。在开始写作《哈利·波特》系列童话的第一部《哈利·波特与魔法石》时，罗琳因为自家的屋子又小又冷，时常到家附近的一家咖啡馆里把哈利·波特的故事写在小纸片上。不过，她的努力很快得到了回报。童话一出版便备受瞩目，好评如潮，其中包括英国国家图书奖儿童小说奖，以及斯马蒂图书金奖章奖。随后罗琳又分别于 1998 年与 1999 年创作了《哈利·波特与密室》和《哈利·波特与阿兹卡班的囚徒》，进一步轰动世界。此后她每创作一部《哈利·波特》小说，都必会引起强烈反响，培养了全世界的书迷。而每部哈利小说也陆续被搬到大银幕上，影迷们从中领略到了罗琳笔下那不可思议的魔法世界。

President Faust, members of the Harvard Corporation and the Board of Overseers, members of the faculty, proud parents, and, above all, graduates:

The first thing I would like to say is "thank you". Not only has Harvard given me an extraordinary honour, but the weeks of fear and nausea I've endured at the thought of giving this commencement address have made me lose weight. A win-win situation! Now all I have to do is take deep breaths, squint at the red banners and convince myself that I am at the world's largest Gryffindors' reunion.

Delivering a commencement address is a great responsibility; or so I thought until I cast my mind back to my own graduation. The commencement speaker that day was the distinguished British philosopher Baroness Mary Warnock. Reflecting on her speech has helped me enormously in writing this one, because it turns out that I can't remember a single word she said. This liberating discovery enables me to proceed without any fear that I might inadvertently influence you to abandon promising careers in business, law or politics for the giddy delights of becoming a gay wizard.

You see? If all you remember in years to come is the "gay wizard" joke, I've come out ahead of Baroness Mary Warnock. Achievable goals — the first step to self-improvement.

Actually, I have wracked my mind and heart for what I ought to say to you today. I have asked myself what I wish I had known at my own graduation, and what important lessons I have learned in the 21 years that has expired between that day and this.

I have come up with two answers. On this wonderful day when we are gathered together to celebrate your academic success, I have decided to talk to you about the benefits of failure. And as you stand on the threshold of what is sometimes called "real life", I want to extol the crucial importance of imagination.

These may seem quixotic or paradoxical choices, but bear with me.

Looking back at the 21-year-old that I was at graduation, is a slightly uncomfortable experience for the 42-year-old that she has become. Half my lifetime

尊敬的福斯特校长，哈佛集团的各位成员，监管理事会的各位理事，各位老师，各位自豪的家长，尤其是毕业生们：

首先请允许我说一声谢谢。哈佛不仅给了我至高无上的荣誉，连日来一想到要发表这个毕业演说所经受的恐惧和紧张，更令我减肥成功。这真是"双赢"。现在，我只需要深呼吸几次，眯着眼睛看看前面的大红横幅，然后安慰自己，让自己相信我正在参加世界上最大的魔法学院聚会。

发表毕业演说责任重大。至少我回想我当年的毕业典礼时是这么认为的。那天致辞的是英国著名的哲学家玛丽·沃诺克男爵夫人（编者注：玛丽沃诺克男爵夫人，教育家，哲学家，存在主义作家，曾先后任职于牛津大学和剑桥大学，终身贵族）。回想她的演讲，对我完成这篇演讲稿有极大的帮助，因为我已完全不记得她当时讲了什么。这让我释然，让我不再担心我可能会无意中影响你们，使你们放弃在商业、法律或政治上的大好前途，转而醉心于成为一个快乐的魔法师。

你们知道吗？如果在若干年后你们还仅仅记得"快乐的魔法师"这个笑话，那就证明我已经超越了男爵夫人玛丽·沃诺克。确定一个切实可行的目标——这是自我提升的第一步。

实际上，我为今天应该给大家讲些什么绞尽了脑汁。我曾自问，在当初自己的毕业典礼上我想要知道些什么呢？从毕业典礼那天到现在的 21 年里我得到了什么重要的经验和教训呢？

我想到了两个答案。今天是个美好的日子，我们欢聚一堂一起庆祝你们在学业上取得的成功。然而我决定跟你们谈谈失败的收益；同时，你们即将迈入"现实生活"，所以我还要褒扬想象力的极度重要性。

这两点似乎是不切实际或自相矛盾的选择，但请先容我讲完。

对于已经 42 岁的我来说，回忆 21 岁刚刚毕业时的情景并

热词空间

overseer ['əuvə,si:ə] n. 监察员

faculty ['fækəlti] n.（美国高等院校或院系的）全体教员

nausea ['nɔ:ziə] n. 恶心，呕吐感

squint [skwint] vi. 眯着眼看；斜视

banner ['bænə] n. 横幅

Gryffindor 葛莱分多（哈利·波特所在的魔法学院）

cast one's mind back to 回想

distinguished [dis'tiŋwiʃt] adj. 著名的；卓越的

enormously [i'nɔ:məsli] adv. 巨大地；在极大程度上

proceed [prəu'si:d] vi. 开始；继续进行

inadvertently [,inəd'və:təntli] adv. 非故意地

giddy ['gidi] adj. 令人眼花缭乱的

wrack one's mind and heart for 为……绞尽脑汁

expire [ik'spaiə] vi. 终止；期满

on the threshold ['θreʃhəuld] of 在……快要开始的时候

extol [ik'stəul] vt. 颂扬

crucial ['kru:ʃəl] adj. 关键性的

quixotic [kwik'sɔtik] adj. 不切实际的

paradoxical [,pærə'dɔksikəl] adj. 矛盾的

bear with 忍受

哈佛
大学

斯坦福
大学

牛津
大学

耶鲁
大学

杜兰
大学

杜克
大学

威斯康
辛大学

清华
大学

北京
大学

亚利桑
那州立
大 学

加利福
尼 亚
大 学

ago, I was striking an uneasy balance between the ambition I had for myself, and what those closest to me expected of me.

I was convinced that the only thing I wanted to do, ever, was to write novels. However, my parents, both of whom came from impoverished backgrounds and neither of whom had been to college, took the view that my overactive imagination was an amusing personal quirk that could never pay a mortgage, or secure a pension.

I know the irony strikes like with the force of a cartoon anvil now, but…

So they had hoped that I would take a vocational degree; I wanted to study English Literature. A compromise was reached that in retrospect satisfied nobody, and I went up to study Modern Languages. Hardly had my parents' car rounded the corner at the end of the road than I ditched German and scuttled off down the Classics corridor.

I cannot remember telling my parents that I was studying Classics; they might well have found out for the first time on graduation day. Of all the subjects on this planet, I think they would have been hard put to name one less useful than Greek mythology when it came to securing the keys to an executive bathroom.

Now I would like to make it clear, in parenthesis, that I do not blame my parents for their point of view. There is an expiry date on blaming your parents for steering you in the wrong direction; the moment you are old enough to take the wheel, responsibility lies with you. What is more, I cannot criticise my parents for hoping that I would never experience poverty. They had been poor themselves, and I have since been poor, and I quite agree with them that it is not an ennobling experience. Poverty entails fear, and stress, and sometimes depression; it means a thousand petty humiliations and hardships. Climbing out of poverty by your own efforts, that is something on which to pride yourself, but poverty itself is romanticised only by fools.

What I feared most for myself at your age was not poverty, but failure.

At your age, in spite of a distinct lack of motivation at university, where I had spent far too long in the coffee bar writing stories, and far too little time at lectures, I had a knack for passing examinations, and that, for years, had been the measure of

不是一件很舒服的事情。21 年前，我一直都在自己的雄心和身边的人对我的期望之间寻求平衡。

我一直深信，自己唯一想做的事情就是写小说。然而，我的父母家境都很贫困，两个人都没上过大学，他们认为我过于丰富的想象力是令人惊讶的个人怪癖，根本不足以让我支付按揭，或者获得足够的养老金。

我现在明白了反讽就像用卡通铁砧去打击你，但……

他们希望我取得高职学位，而我却想攻读英国文学。最后，我和父母达成了妥协，我改学现代语言。现在回想起来，当时双方都不怎么满意。于是，父母的车刚一开远，我就丢下德语，去学习古典文学。

我不记得告诉过父母自己在学习古典文学，他们可能是在我毕业典礼那一天才知道的。我想，他们也许认为，在全世界的所有专业中，不会有比研究希腊神话更没用的专业了，那甚至无法换来一间独立宽敞的卫生间。

在这里我想说明一点：我不会因为父母的观点而怪他们。不要因为父母给你的人生路指错了方向就无休止地埋怨他们。当你到一定年龄，可以自己把握人生时，就应该自己承担责任。再者，父母这样做是希望我不会过穷日子，所以我不能责怪他们。他们经历了贫穷，我后来也一度很穷，所以我很理解他们，因为贫穷并不是一种高贵的经历。贫穷会让人感觉恐惧、有压力，有时甚至让人感觉沮丧。贫穷意味着说不尽的羞辱和艰辛。靠自己的努力摆脱贫穷值得自豪，只有傻瓜才会将贫穷浪漫化。

像你们这么大时我最害怕的不是贫穷，而是失败。

像你们这么大时，尽管我明显缺乏在大学学习的动力，花大量时间在咖啡馆写小说，用于听课的时间很少，但我却有通过考试的本领。多年来，考试一直是衡量我和同龄人成功的标准。

热词空间

strike a balance between
在……之间寻求平衡
impoverished [im'pɔvəriʃt]
adj. 穷困的
quirk [kwə:k] n. 怪癖
mortgage ['mɔ:gidʒ] 抵押
anvil ['ænvil] n. 铁砧
vocational [vəu'keiʃənəl] adj.
职业的
compromise ['kɔmprəmaiz]
n. 妥协
in retrospect ['retrəuspekt]
回顾往事
ditch [ditʃ] vt. 丢弃；掘沟
scuttle ['skʌtl] off 急促奔跑
corridor ['kɔridɔ:] n. 走廊
mythology [mi'θɔlɔdʒi] 神话
executive [ig'zekjutiv] adj. 高
级的
in parenthesis [pə'renθisis]
插入的
expiry date 有效期限
steer [stiə] vt. 引导
lie with 是……的责任
ennobling [i'nəubliŋ] adj. 高
贵的
entail [in'teil] vt. 引起
humiliation [hju:ˌmili'eiʃən]
n. 耻辱
romanticise [rəu'mæntisaiz]
vt. 使浪漫化
distinct [dis'tiŋkt] adj. 明显的
have a knack [næk] for
有……的诀窍

success in my life and that of my peers.

Now I am not dull enough to suppose that because you are young, gifted and well-educated, you have never known hardship or heartbreak. Talent and intelligence never yet inoculated anyone against the caprice of the Fates, and I do not for a moment suppose that everyone here has enjoyed an existence of unruffled privilege and contentment.

However, the fact that you are graduating from Harvard suggests that you are not very well-acquainted with failure. You might be driven by a fear of failure quite as much as a desire for success. Indeed, your conception of failure might not be too far from the average person's idea of success, so high have you already flown.

Ultimately, we all have to decide for ourselves what constitutes failure, but the world is quite eager to give you a set of criteria if you let it. So I think it fair to say that by any conventional measure, a mere seven years after my graduation day, I had failed on an epic scale. An exceptionally short-lived marriage had imploded, and I was jobless, a lone parent, and as poor as it is possible to be in modern Britain, without being homeless. The fears my parents had had for me, and that I had had for myself, had both come to pass, and by every usual standard, I was the biggest failure I knew.

Now, I am not going to stand here and tell you that failure is fun. That period of my life was a dark one, and I had no idea that there was going to be what the press has since represented as a kind of fairy tale resolution. I had no idea then how far the tunnel extended, and for a long time, any light at the end of it was a hope rather than a reality.

So why do I talk about the benefits of failure? Simply because failure meant a stripping away of the inessential. I stopped pretending to myself that I was anything other than what I was, and began to direct all my energy into finishing the only work that mattered to me. Had I really succeeded at anything else, I might never have found the determination to succeed in the one arena where I believed I truly belonged. I was set free, because my greatest fear had already been realised, and I was still alive, and I still had a daughter whom I adored, and I had an old typewriter and a big idea. And so rock bottom became the solid foundation on which I rebuilt my life.

You might never fail on the scale I did, but some failure in life is inevitable. It is

我不会笨到因为你们年轻、有才华并且受过良好的教育，就认为你们从来没有经受过困难或心碎的时刻。才华和智慧并不能使人摆脱命运的反复无常；我也从来没有认为在座的每一个人一直以来都享有优越和满足。

然而，即将从哈佛毕业这一事实就意味着你们很少会经历失败。你们对失败的恐惧很可能与你们对成功的渴望一样强烈。实际上，你们眼中的失败可能在常人看来就是成功，毕竟你们在学业上已经相当成功了。

最终，我们所有人都必须自己判断什么是失败，但是如果你乐意的话，这个世界是非常渴望给你一套标准的。因此根据任何传统的标准都可以说，我在毕业后的短短七年里经历了惨痛的失败：短暂的婚姻闪电般破裂，失业，成为单身母亲。在现代化的英国，我变得极度贫困，只是还没有到无家可归的地步。父母和我自己对未来的担忧，当年都变成了现实。无论按什么标准，当时我都是我所知道的最失败的人。

现在，我不打算站在这里告诉你们失败是有趣的。那段日子是我生命中的黑暗岁月，我不知道我会写出被新闻界称为"童话故事的革命"的作品。我也不知道自己还要在黑暗中走多久，不知道还要过多久才能看到希望的光芒而不是现实的黑暗。

那么我为什么要谈论失败的收益呢？很简单，因为失败意味着剔除那些无关紧要的东西。我因此不再伪装自己，我把所有的精力倾注在对我来说最重要的事情上。如果我真的在其他领域取得了成功，或许我永远都不会下定决心在我确信真正属于我的舞台上取得成功。我得到了解脱，因为虽然我最害怕的事情已经发生了，但我还活着，我还有一个我深爱着的女儿，一台旧打字机和一个了不起的想法。所以人生的低谷是我重新开始生活的坚实基础。

你们也许不会败得像我这么惨，但人生中有些失败是不

热词空间

inoculate [i'nɔkjuleit]
vt. 给……注射预防针
caprice [kə'pri:s] n. 反复无常
unruffled [,ʌn'rʌfld] adj. 平静的
conception [kən'sepʃən] n. 概念
constitute ['kɔnstitju:t] vt. 构成
criteria [krai'tiəriə] n. 标准
(criterion 的复数)
conventional [kən'venʃənəl]
adj. 传统的
epic ['epik] adj. 规模大的，有重大历史意义的
implode [im'pləud] vi. 内爆
resolution [rezə'lu:ʃən] n. 决定；决心
tunnel ['tʌnəl] n. 隧道
stripping ['stripiŋ] n. 剥离；剥脱
inessential [,ini'senʃəl] adj. 无关紧要的
arena [ə'ri:nə] n. 舞台
adore [ə'dɔ:] vt. 爱慕；崇拜
inevitable [in'evitəbl] adj. 必然的，不可避免的

impossible to live without failing at something, unless you live so cautiously that you might as well not have lived at all — in which case, you fail by default.

Failure gave me an inner security that I had never attained by passing examinations. Failure taught me things about myself that I could have learned no other way. I discovered that I had a strong will, and more discipline than I had suspected; I also found out that I had friends whose value was truly above the price of rubies.

The knowledge that you have emerged wiser and stronger from setbacks means that you are, ever after, secure in your ability to survive. You will never truly know yourself, or the strength of your relationships, until both have been tested by adversity. Such knowledge is a true gift, for all it is painfully won, and it has been worth more to me than any qualification I ever earned.

So given a Time Turner, I would tell my 21-year-old self that personal happiness lies in knowing that life is not a check-list of acquisition or achievement. Your qualifications, your CV, are not your life, though you will meet many people of my age and older who confuse the two. Life is difficult, and complicated, and beyond anyone's total control, and the humility to know that will enable you to survive its vicissitudes.

You might think I chose my second theme, the importance of imagination, because of the part it played in rebuilding my life, but that is not wholly so. Though I personally will defend the value of bedtime stories to my last gasp, I have learned to value imagination in a much broader sense. Imagination is not only the uniquely human capacity to envision that which is not, and therefore the fount of all invention and innovation. In its arguably most transformative and revelatory capacity, it is the power that enables us to empathize with humans whose experiences we have never shared.

One of the greatest formative experiences of my life preceded *Harry Potter*, though it informed much of what I subsequently wrote in those books. This revelation came in the form of one of my earliest day jobs. Though I was sloping off to write stories during my lunch hours, I paid the rent in my early 20s by working in the research department at Amnesty International's headquarters in London.

可避免的。人生中不可能没有失败，除非你们活得过于谨慎，这样倒还不如根本没在世上活过，因为在这种情况下，放弃尝试的权利就是你们最大的失败。

失败赋予我内心一种安全感。这种安全感是我无法从通过考试中获得的。失败让我了解了自己，这也是无法通过其他途径做到的。经历失败让我发现我有坚强的意志力，比我想象的更有自律性。我还发现，我拥有比宝石更加珍贵的朋友。

经历了挫折，你变得更加智慧，更加坚强，这意味着你有独立生存的能力。只有经过了逆境的考验，你才能真正了解自己，才能真正知道周围的人所赋予你的力量。这种认识是真正的财富，虽然历经千辛万苦，但这比我以前获得的任何资格证书都有价值。

如果我有一台时光转换器，我会告诉21岁的自己，一个人的幸福在于知道人生不只是一份只有收益和成就的表单。资格证书和个人简历不是你们的生活，虽然你们将会遇到很多与我同龄或年龄比我大的人将二者混为一谈。生活艰辛而复杂，是任何人都无法完全掌控的。谦恭地了解了这一点，你才能从容面对人生的变迁。

至于为什么选择第二个主题——想象力的重要性，你们可能会认为是因为它对我重建生活所起的作用，但事实并非完全如此。虽然我坚持睡前故事对激发孩子的想象力有很大的价值，但我学会了在更广泛的意义上去理解想象力。想象力不仅仅是人类特有的设想不存在的事物的能力，还是所有发明和创新的源泉。毋庸置疑，想象力是最富转换性和启发性的力量，这种力量能使我们与有着不同经历的人们产生共鸣。

想象力使我随后写书有了很多的想法，但对我影响最深远的经历发生在写《哈利·波特》之前。这种影响源于我早期的工作经历。在刚二十几岁的时候，为了付房租，我在伦敦大赦国际总部的调查部门工作，但我可以在午餐时间偷偷溜

热词空间

cautiously ['kɔːʃəsli] adv. 慎重地

by default 由于弃权而输掉

attain [ə'tein] vt. 达到，获得

ruby ['ruːbi] n. 红宝石

emerge [i'məːdʒ] vi. 显露

adversity [əd'vəːsəti] n. 逆境；不幸

qualification [,kwɔlifi'keiʃən] n. 资格（证书）

acquisition [,ækwi'ziʃən] n. 获得（物）

CV [,si: 'vi:] n. 简历（Curriculum Vitae 的缩写）

confuse [kən'fjuːz] vt. 使混乱；使困惑

complicated ['kɔmplikeitid] adj. 难懂的；复杂的

vicissitude [vi'sisitjuːd] n. 变迁；盛衰

gasp [gæsp] n. 喘气

envision [in'viʒən] vt. 想象；预想

fount [faunt] n. 泉；源泉

innovation [,inəu'veiʃən] n. 创新

arguably ['aːgjuəbli] adv. 可论证地

transformative [træns'fɔːmətiv] adj. 变化的，起改造作用的

revelatory ['revələtəri] adj. 启示的

empathize ['empəθaiz] vi. 神会，表同情

precede [pri 'siːd] vt. 在……之前

subsequently ['sʌbsikwəntli] adv. 随后

revelation [,revə'leiʃən] n. 启示

slope off 溜掉

There in my little office I read hastily scribbled letters smuggled out of totalitarian regimes by men and women who were risking imprisonment to inform the outside world of what was happening to them. I saw photographs of those who had disappeared without trace, sent to Amnesty by their desperate families and friends. I read the testimony of torture victims and saw pictures of their injuries. I opened handwritten, eye-witness accounts of summary trials and executions, of kidnappings and rapes.

Many of my co-workers were ex-political prisoners, people who had been displaced from their homes, or fled into exile, because they had the temerity to think independently of their government. Visitors to our office included those who had come to give information, or to try and find out what had happened to those who they had left behind.

I shall never forget the African torture victim, a young man no older than I was at the time, who had become mentally ill after all he had endured in his homeland. He trembled uncontrollably as he spoke into a video camera about the brutality inflicted upon him. He was a foot taller than I was, and seemed as fragile as a child. I was given the job of escorting him to the Underground Station afterwards, and this man whose life had been shattered by cruelty took my hand with exquisite courtesy, and wished me future happiness.

And as long as I live I shall remember walking along an empty corridor and suddenly hearing, from behind a closed door, a scream of pain and horror such as I have never heard since. The door opened, and the researcher poked out her head and told me to run and make a hot drink for the young man sitting with her. She had just given him the news that in retaliation for his own outspokenness against his country's regime, his mother had been seized and executed.

Every day of my working week in my early 20s I was reminded how incredibly fortunate I was, to live in a country with a democratically elected government, where legal representation and a public trial were the rights of everyone.

Every day, I saw more evidence about the evils humankind will inflict on their fellow humans, to gain or maintain power. I began to have nightmares, literal

出去写小说。

在那儿，我在狭小的办公室里看着从集权主义政体偷运出来的信件。写这些信件的人，为了让外界知道他们那里所发生的事情，冒着被监禁的危险，用潦草的字迹匆匆写下他们的遭遇，然后再将信件寄给我们。我看过那些由绝望的家人和朋友寄来的无迹可寻的人的照片。我读过被严刑拷打的受害者的证词并看了他们遍体鳞伤的图片。我打开过目击者的手记，描述了对于绑架和强奸案的审判和处决。

我的很多同事以前都是政治犯，因为他们敢于批判政府，有自己的想法，所以被赶出家门，或被放逐海外。来我们办公室的访客，包括那些前来提供信息的，或想方设法知道那些留下的同志发生了什么事的人。

我永远不会忘记那个非籍酷刑受害者，一个当时还没我大的年轻男子，他因在故乡的经历而精神错乱。在摄像机前讲述被残暴地摧残的经历时，他的身体止不住地颤抖。他比我高一英尺，但看上去却像个孩子一样脆弱。随后我遵照组织的安排护送他到地铁站时，这名人生已遭到残酷摧毁的男子彬彬有礼地握着我的手，祝我未来幸福。

在我的有生之年，我都会记得一件事，当时我正经过一条空旷的走廊，突然听到紧闭着的房门里传出一声痛苦和恐惧的尖叫，那是至今我从未再听过的。那扇门打开了，调查员探出头请我快去给坐在她旁边的年轻男子调一杯热饮料。她刚刚告诉那个年轻人，为报复他对祖国专政的直言批判，他的母亲已被抓走并处决了。

在我 20 多岁的那段日子里，每一天的工作都在提醒我自己是多么幸运，能够生活在一个民主选举的政府领导的国家，人人都享有依法申述与公开审理的权利。

每一天，我都能看到更多有关恶人的证据，他们为了获得或维持权力而对自己的同胞实施暴行。我开始做噩梦，真

热词空间

hastily ['heistili] adv. 匆忙地
scribbled ['skribld] adj. 潦草写成的
smuggle ['smʌgl] vt. 偷运
totalitarian [,təutæli'teəriən] adj. 极权主义的
regime [rei'ʒi:m] n. 政权
imprisonment [im'prizənmənt] 坐牢
testimony ['testiməni] n. 证词，证据
torture ['tɔ:tʃə] n. 折磨；拷问
execution [,eksi'kju:ʃən] n. 处决，死刑
kidnapping ['kidnæpiŋ] 绑架
rape [reip] n. 强奸
displace [dis'pleis] vt. 使背井离乡；取代
exile ['eksail] n. 流放
temerity [ti'merəti] n. 冒失；蛮勇
brutality [bru:'tæləti] n. 暴行
inflict [in'flikt] vt. 造成；使遭受
fragile ['frædʒail] adj. 脆弱的
escort ['eskɔ:t] vt. 护送
shatter ['ʃætə] vt. 摧毁，损坏
exquisite [ek'skwizit] adj. 高雅的
courtesy ['kə:tisi] n. 礼貌
poke out 伸出
retaliation [ri,tæli'eiʃən] n. 报复；反击
outspokenness [,aut'spəukənnis] 坦言相告
democratically [demə'krætikli] adv. 民主地
representation [,reprizen'teiʃən] n. 陈述；代表
evil ['i:vəl] 罪恶
literal ['litərəl] adj. 真实的；不夸张的

nightmares, about some of the things I saw, heard and read.

And yet I also learned more about human goodness at Amnesty International than I had ever known before.

Amnesty mobilizes thousands of people who have never been tortured or imprisoned for their beliefs to act on behalf of those who have. The power of human empathy, leading to collective action, saves lives, and frees prisoners. Ordinary people, whose personal well-being and security are assured, join together in huge numbers to save people they do not know, and will never meet. My small participation in that process was one of the most humbling and inspiring experiences of my life.

Unlike any other creature on this planet, human beings can learn and understand, without having experienced. They can think themselves into other people's places.

Of course, this is a power, like my brand of fictional magic, that is morally neutral. One might use such an ability to manipulate, or control, just as much as to understand or sympathise.

And many prefer not to exercise their imaginations at all. They choose to remain comfortably within the bounds of their own experience, never troubling to wonder how it would feel to have been born other than they are. They can refuse to hear screams or to peer inside cages; they can close their minds and hearts to any suffering that does not touch them personally; they can refuse to know.

I might be tempted to envy people who can live that way, except that I do not think they have any fewer nightmares than I do. Choosing to live in narrow spaces leads to a form of mental agoraphobia, and that brings its own terrors. I think the willfully unimaginative see more monsters. They are often more afraid. What is more, those who choose not to empathise enable real monsters. For without ever committing an act of outright evil ourselves, we collude with it, through our own apathy.

One of the many things I learned at the end of that Classics corridor down which I ventured at the age of 18, in search of something I could not then define, was this, written by the Greek author Plutarch: What we achieve inwardly will change outer reality.

That is an astonishing statement and yet proven a thousand times every day of

实的噩梦，全都和我的所见所闻有关。

同时在大赦国际我也更多地了解了人类的善良，远比我以前了解的多。

大赦国际动员成千上万没有因为个人信仰而受到折磨或监禁的人，去为那些遭受这种不幸的人奔走。人类的同情心引发了集体行动，拯救生命，使那些被关押的人们得以释放。个人的福祉和安全有保证的普通百姓聚集在一起，携手挽救那些与他们素不相识，也许永远不会见面的人。我的参与虽然微不足道，但那却是我一生中最振奋人心的一次经历。

与这个星球上任何其他的动物不同，人类可以学习和理解未曾经历过的事情。他们可以换位思考，能够设身处地去体会他人的感受。

当然，这种能力就像我在小说里虚构的魔法一样，没有邪恶之分。有人可能会利用这种能力去操纵或控制别人，也有人选择用它去了解和同情他人。

而很多人不愿去运用他们的想象力。他们选择舒适地生活在自己经验所及的范围内，从来不愿费心去想想如果生在别处会怎样。他们会拒绝去听别人的尖叫，不愿看一眼囚禁的笼子；对于与自身无关的苦难，他们会封闭自己的内心；他们会拒绝了解这一切。

我可能会受到诱惑，去嫉妒那样生活的人。但我不认为他们做的噩梦会比我更少。选择生活在狭窄的空间会导致不敢面对开阔的视野，那种生活同样会有恐惧。我认为不愿展开想象的人会看到更多的怪兽，他们往往更会感到害怕。而且，那些没有同情心的人会激活真正的怪兽。因为尽管他们自身没有作恶，但他们对于罪恶无动于衷，这已足以使他们成为作恶者的共谋。

18 岁时，为了追寻我当时还无法解释的东西，我踏上了学习古典文学的征途并汲取了许多知识，其中一点便是希腊

热词空间

mobilise ['məubilaiz] vt. 动员；调动

empathy ['empəθi] n. 同情；同感

humbling ['hʌmbliŋ] adj. 微不足道的

fictional ['fikʃənl] adj. 虚构的

neutral ['nju:trəl] adj. 中立的

manipulate [mə'nipjuleit] vt. 操纵；操作

sympathise ['simpəθaiz] vi. 同情

agoraphobia [,ægərə'fəubjə] n. 旷野恐怖；陌生环境恐怖症

willfully ['wilfəli] adv. 故意地

collude [kə'lu:d] vi. 勾结；共谋

apathy ['æpəθi] n. 冷漠，漠不关心

inwardly ['inwədli] adv. 思想上；在内部

our lives. It expresses, in part, our inescapable connection with the outside world, the fact that we touch other people's lives simply by existing.

But how much more are you, Harvard graduates of 2008, likely to touch other people's lives? Your intelligence, your capacity for hard work, the education you have earned and received, give you unique status, and unique responsibilities. Even your nationality sets you apart. The great majority of you belong to the world's only remaining superpower. The way you vote, the way you live, the way you protest, the pressure you bring to bear on your government, has an impact way beyond your borders. That is your privilege, and your burden.

If you choose to use your status and influence to raise your voice on behalf of those who have no voice; if you choose to identify not only with the powerful, but with the powerless; if you retain the ability to imagine yourself into the lives of those who do not have your advantages, then it will not only be your proud families who celebrate your existence, but thousands and millions of people whose reality you have helped to change. We do not need magic to transform our world, we carry all the power we need inside ourselves already: we have the power to imagine better.

I am nearly finished. I have one last hope for you, which is something that I already had at 21. The friends with whom I sat on graduation day have been my friends for life. They are my children's godparents, the people to whom I've been able to turn in times of trouble, people who have been kind enough not to sue me when I've used their names for Death Eaters. At our graduation we were bound by enormous affection, by our shared experience of a time that could never come again, and, of course, by the knowledge that we held certain photographic evidence that would be exceptionally valuable if any of us ran for Prime Minister.

So today, I wish you nothing better than similar friendships. And tomorrow, I hope that even if you remember not a single word of mine, you remember those of Seneca, another of those old Romans I met when I fled down the Classics corridor, in retreat from career ladders, in search of ancient wisdom:

作家普鲁塔克所说：我们的内在修养将会改变外在的现实。

那是一个惊人的论断，在我们生活的每一天里被无数次证实。它在某种程度上说明了我们与外部世界有无法脱离的联系，只要我们活着，就会对其他人的生活有影响。

但是，哈佛大学 2008 届的毕业生们，你们会对其他人的生活产生多大影响呢？你们的智慧、你们应对高难度工作的能力以及你们所接受的教育赋予了你们独特的地位和责任。甚至你们的国籍也让你们与众不同，你们中的绝大多数人都属于这个世界上唯一的超级大国。你们投票的方式，你们生活的方式，你们抗议的方式，以及你们给政府带来的压力，都会产生超越国界的影响力。这是你们的特权，更是你们的责任。

如果你们选择用自己的地位和影响为那些没有发言权的人呐喊；如果你们不仅能认同有权势的人，而且也能帮扶无权势的人；如果你会设身处地为没有你这些优势的人着想，那么你的存在将不仅是你家人的骄傲，更是成千上万因为你的帮助而生活得更好的人的骄傲。我们不需要用魔法改变世界，我们自己的内心就有这种力量：我们拥有想象力，可以让这个世界变得更美好。

我的演讲即将结束。对你们，我有最后一个希望，也是我 21 岁时就有的一个希望。毕业那天与我坐在一起的朋友们现在是我终身的挚交，他们是我孩子的教父或教母，是我处于困境时可以求助的人，是在我用他们的名字给《哈利·波特》中的"食死徒"起名而不会起诉我的人。我们在毕业典礼时坐在了一起，因为我们关系亲密，因为我们共同分享了那永远都不能重来的时光。当然，也因为假想要是我们中的任何人竞选首相，那照片将是极有价值的证明。

所以今天我能送给你们的最好的祝福，就是希望你们能拥有这样的友谊。我希望，即使明天你们不记得我说过的任何一个字，你们还能记得古罗马哲学家塞内加的一句至理明

As is a tale, so is life: not how long it is, but how good it is, is what matters.

I wish you all very good lives.

Thank you very much.

J. K. 罗琳给我们的 启示

Poverty entails fear, and stress, and sometimes depression; it means a thousand petty humiliations and hardships. Climbing out of poverty by your own efforts, that is something on which to pride yourself, but poverty itself is romanticised only by fools.

贫穷会让人感觉恐惧、有压力、有时甚至让人感觉沮丧。贫穷意味着说不尽的羞辱和艰辛。靠自己的努力摆脱贫穷值得自豪，只有傻瓜才会将贫穷浪漫化。

So why do I talk about the benefits of failure? Simply because failure meant a stripping away of the inessential.

那么我为什么要谈论失败的收益呢？很简单，因为失败意味着剔除那些无关紧要的东西。

You might never fail on the scale I did, but some failure in life is inevitable. It is impossible to live without failing at something, unless you live so cautiously that you might as well not have lived at all — in which case, you fail by default.

你们也许不会败得像我这么惨，但人生中有些失败是不可避免的。人生中不可能没有失败，除非你们活得过于谨慎，这样倒还不如根本没在世上活过，因为在这种情况下，放弃尝试的权利就是你们最大的失败。

The knowledge that you have emerged wiser and stronger from setbacks means that you are, ever after, secure in your ability to survive. You will never truly know yourself, or the strength of your relationships, until both have been tested by adversity.

经历了挫折，你变得更加智慧，更加坚强，这意味着你有独立生存的能力。只有经过了逆境的考验，你才能真正了解自己，才能真正知道周围的人所赋予你的力量。

言。我当年没有顺着事业的阶梯向上攀爬，转而与他在古典文学的殿堂相遇，他的古老智慧给了我人生的启迪：

生活就像故事一样，不在于长短，而在于品质，这才是最重要的。

祝愿你们拥有美好的生活。

非常感谢大家。

How to Tackle the World's Worst Inequities?

如何解决这个世界最严重的不平等？

*Harvard University
Commencement Address
Bill Gates
June 7, 2007*

背景 **资料**

　　从哈佛大学辍学30年后，比尔·盖茨终于在2007年获得母校授予的大学学士学位以及荣誉法学博士学位，并在2007届毕业典礼上发表深情演讲，与校友无私分享30年创业的宝贵经验和对人生的心得体会。他总结了前30年的人生轨迹和创业经历，也为自己即将奉献余生的慈善事业拉开了帷幕。他的演讲充满激情和号召力。作为一位成功的商人，一个改变了世界的人，他普视众生，拥有一颗善感、富有同情心和宽容的心灵。在哈佛毕业典礼上，他说："要将同情心化为行动。"

Humanity's greatest advances are not in its discoveries — but in how those discoveries are applied to reduce inequity.

人类最大的进步并不在于其发现，而在于如何用这些发现来减少不平等现象。

——比尔·盖茨

姓　　名：	比尔·盖茨（Bill Gates）
性　　别：	男
职　　业：	微软公司首席执行官和首席软件架构师
国　　籍：	美国
出生日期：	1955 年 10 月 28 日
毕业学校：	湖滨中学，哈佛大学
成功点睛：	以王者的胆识，以预言家的远见卓识，以超人的胆识，把世界引向未来时速之路，把自己置于世界的闪光灯下。
个人成就：	与保罗·艾伦共同创办了微软公司《福布斯》全球亿万富翁排行榜榜首

名人简介

　　比尔·盖茨是美国企业家、软件工程师、慈善家以及微软公司的董事长。他与保罗·艾伦一起创建了微软公司，曾任微软首席执行官和首席软件设计师，并持有公司超过 8% 的普通股，也是公司最大的个人股东。1995 年到 2007 年的《福布斯》全球亿万富翁排行榜中，比尔·盖茨连续 13 年蝉联世界首富。2008 年 6 月 27 日正式退出微软公司，并把 580 亿美元个人财产尽数捐到比尔与美琳达·盖茨基金会。《福布斯》杂志 2009 年 3 月 12 日公布全球富豪排名，比尔·盖茨以 400 亿美元资产重登榜首。

哈佛
大学

斯坦福
大 学

牛津
大学

耶鲁
大学

杜兰
大学

杜克
大学

威斯康
辛大学

清华
大学

北京
大学

亚利桑
那州立
大 学

加利福
尼 亚
大 学

Thank you! President Bok, former President Rudenstine, incoming President Faust, members of the Harvard Corporation and the Board of Overseers, members of the faculty, parents, and especially the graduates:

I've been waiting more than 30 years to say this: "Dad, I always told you I'd come back and get my degree."

I want to thank Harvard for this honor. I'll be changing my job next year ... and it will be nice to finally have a college degree on my resume.

I applaud the graduates for taking a much more direct route to your degrees. For my part, I'm just happy that the Crimson has called me "Harvard's most successful dropout." I guess that makes me valedictorian of my own special class ... I did the best of everyone who failed.

But I also want to be recognized as the guy who got Steve Ballmer to drop out of business school. I'm a bad influence. That's why I was invited to speak at your graduation. If I had spoken at your orientation, fewer of you might be here today.

Harvard was a phenomenal experience for me. Academic life was fascinating. I used to sit in on lots of classes I hadn't even signed up for. And dorm life was terrific. I lived up at Radcliffe, in Currier House. There were always a lot of people in my dorm room late at night discussing things, because everyone knew I didn't worry about getting up in the morning. That's how I came to be the leader of the anti-social group. We clung to each other as a way of validating our rejection of all those social people.

Radcliffe was a great place to live. There were more women up there, and most of the guys were math-science types. That combination offered me the best odds, if you know what I mean. That's where I learned the sad lesson that improving your odds doesn't guarantee success.

One of my biggest memories of Harvard came in January 1975, when I made a call from Currier House to a company in Albuquerque in New Mexico that had begun

谢谢大家！尊敬的伯克校长，鲁登斯坦前校长，即将上任的福斯特校长，哈佛集团的各位成员，监管理事会的各位理事，各位老师，各位家长，尤其是毕业生们：

有一句话我等了三十多年，现在终于可以说了："老爸，我总是跟你说，我会回来拿到我的学位的！"

我要感谢哈佛大学给我这个荣誉。明年，我就要换工作了（注：指从微软公司退休）……我终于可以在简历上填上大学学位，这真是不错。

我为今天在座的毕业生喝彩，你们拿到学位可比我简单多了。哈佛的校报称我是"哈佛大学历史上最成功的辍学者"。我想这大概使我有资格代表我这一类学生发表毕业演讲——在所有的辍学者中，我做得最好。

但是，我还要提醒大家，我使得史蒂夫·鲍尔默（微软首席执行官）也从哈佛商学院退学了。因此，我是个有着不良影响的人。那就是我被邀请来在你们的毕业典礼上演讲的原因。如果我在你们的入学欢迎仪式上演讲，那么能够坚持到今天在这里毕业的人也许会少得多吧。

对我来说，哈佛的求学经历是一段非凡的经历。校园生活很有趣，我常去旁听许多我没选修的课。在哈佛的宿舍生活也很不错，我当时住在雷迪夫的柯里尔公寓。每天我的寝室里总有很多人一直待到半夜，讨论着各种事情。因为每个人都知道我从不考虑第二天早起。那使得我变成了校园里那些不安分学生的头头，我们互相粘在一起，做出一种拒绝所有正常学生的姿态。

雷迪夫是个生活的好地方。那里的女生比男生多，而且大多数男生都是理工科的。那种状况为我创造了最好的机会，如果你们明白我的意思。也正是在这里我学到了人生中令人悲伤的教训：机会大，并不等于你就会成功。

我在哈佛最深刻的回忆发生在 1975 年 1 月。那时，我从柯里尔公寓给位于美国新墨西哥州阿尔伯克基的一家公司打

热词空间

incoming ['in,kʌmiŋ] *adj.* 即将上任的

faculty ['fækəlti] *n.* 全体教员

resume [ri'zju:m] *n.* 履历；个人简历

dropout ['drɔpaut] *n.* 辍学学生

valedictorian [,vælidik'tɔ:riən] *n.* 告别演说者

orientation [,ɔ:rien'teiʃən] *n.* 入学欢迎仪式

phenomenal [fə'nɔminəl] *adj.* 不寻常的

clung [klʌŋ] *vi.* 粘着

validate ['vælideit] *vt.* 证实

rejection [ri'dʒekʃən] *n.* 抛弃；拒绝

odds [ɔdz] *n.* 几率；胜算

guarantee [,gærən'ti:] *vt.* 保证；担保

making the world's first personal computers. I offered to sell them software.

I worried that they would realize I was just a student in a dorm and hang up on me. Instead they said: "We're not quite ready, come see us in a month", which was a good thing, because we hadn't written the software yet. From that moment, I worked day and night on that extra credit project that marked the end of my college education and the beginning of a remarkable journey with Microsoft.

What I remember above all about Harvard was being in the midst of so much energy and intelligence. It could be exhilarating, intimidating, sometimes even discouraging, but always challenging. It was an amazing privilege — and though I left early, I was transformed by my years at Harvard, the friendships I made, and the ideas I worked on.

But taking a serious look back … I do have one big regret.

I left Harvard with no real awareness of the awful inequities in the world — the appalling disparities of health, and wealth, and opportunity that condemn millions of people to lives of despair.

I learned a lot here at Harvard about new ideas in economics and politics. I got great exposure to the advances being made in the sciences.

But humanity's greatest advances are not in its discoveries — but in how those discoveries are applied to reduce inequity. Whether through democracy, strong public education, quality health care, or broad economic opportunity — reducing inequity is the highest human achievement.

I left campus knowing little about the millions of young people cheated out of educational opportunities here in this country. And I knew nothing about the millions of people living in unspeakable poverty and disease in developing countries.

It took me decades to find out.

You graduates came to Harvard at a different time. You know more about the world's inequities than the classes that came before. In your years here, I hope you've

了一个电话，那家公司已经在着手制造世界上第一台个人电脑。我提出想向他们出售软件。

我很担心他们会发觉我只是一个住在宿舍的学生从而挂断电话。但是他们却说："我们还没准备好，一个月后你再来找我们吧。"那是个好消息，因为那时我们根本没有写出软件。从那一刻起，我日以继夜致力于这个课外项目，这标志着我大学教育的结束，也标志着通往微软公司的非凡的旅程的开始。

我对哈佛的回忆全都与充沛的精力和丰富的智力活动有关。哈佛的生活令人振奋，也令人生畏，有时甚至会让人感到泄气，但永远充满了挑战性。生活在哈佛是一种吸引人的特殊待遇……虽然我离开得比较早，但是在这里生活学习的岁月，在这里结识的朋友，在这里发展起来的一些想法，改变了我。

但是，如果现在认真回顾一下，我确实有一个很大的遗憾。

我离开哈佛的时候，根本没有意识到这个世界是多么的不平等。人类在健康、财富和机遇上的差距令人震惊，这使得数百万人被迫生活在绝望之中。

我在哈佛学到了很多经济学和政治学方面的新思想。我也了解了很多科学上的新进展。

但是，人类最大的进步并不在于这些发现，而在于如何用这些发现来减少不平等现象。无论通过民主制度、健全的公共教育体系、高质量的医疗保健，还是通过广泛的经济机会，减少不平等才是人类最大的成就。

我离开校园的时候，根本不知道在这个国家有数百万年轻人无法获得接受教育的机会。我也不知道，在发展中国家有无数的人们生活在无法形容的贫穷和疾病中。

我花了几十年才明白了这些事情。

在座的各位同学，你们是在与我不同的时代来到哈佛的。你们比以前的学生更了解世界的不平等。你们在哈佛求学的

热词空间

in the midst of 在……之中

intelligence [in'telidʒəns] n.
智力

exhilarating [ig'ziləreitiŋ]
adj. 令人振奋的

intimidating [in'timideitiŋ]
adj. 吓人的

privilege ['privilidʒ] n. 特权；
优待

appalling [ə'pɔːliŋ] adj. 可怕
的；令人震惊的

disparity [dis'pærəti] n. 差异

condemn [kən'dem] vt. 使处
于……境地

哈佛
大学

斯坦福
大学

牛津
大学

耶鲁
大学

杜兰
大学

杜克
大学

威斯康
辛大学

清华
大学

北京
大学

亚利桑
那州立
大学

加利福
尼亚
大学

had a chance to think about how — in this age of accelerating technology — we can finally take on these inequities, and we can solve them.

Imagine, just for the sake of discussion, that you had a few hours a week and a few dollars a month to donate to a cause — and you wanted to spend that time and money where it would have the greatest impact in saving and improving lives. Where would you spend it?

For Melinda and I, the challenge is the same: how can we do the most good for the greatest number with the resources we have.

During our discussions on this question, Melinda and I read an article about the millions of children who were dying every year in poor countries from diseases that we had long ago made harmless in this country. Measles, malaria, pneumonia, hepatitis B, yellow fever. One disease I had never even heard of, rotavirus, was killing half a million children each year — none of them in the United States.

We were shocked. We had assumed that if millions of children were dying and they could be saved, the world would make it a priority to discover and deliver the medicines to save them. But it did not. For under a dollar, there were interventions that could save lives that just weren't being delivered.

If you believe that every life has equal value, it's revolting to learn that some lives are seen as worth saving and others are not. We said to ourselves: "This can't be true. But if it is true, it deserves to be the priority of our giving."

So we began our work in the same way anyone here would begin it. We asked: "How could the world let these children die?"

The answer is simple, and harsh. The market did not reward saving the lives of these children, and governments did not subsidize it. So the children died because their mothers and fathers had no power in the market and no voice in the system.

But you and I have both.

We can make market forces work better for the poor if we can develop a more

比尔·盖茨：如何解决这个世界最严重的不平等？
How to Tackle the World's Worst Inequities?

几年里，我希望你们已经思考过一个问题：在这个新技术快速发展的时代，我们如何最终应对这种不平等，如何解决这个问题。

为了便于讨论，假想你每个星期可以捐献一些时间，每个月可以捐献一些钱——你希望这些时间和金钱可以用到对拯救生命和改善人类生活有最大作用的地方。你会选择什么地方？

我和美琳达（注：盖茨的妻子）也面临着这样的问题：如何能将我们拥有的资源发挥最大的作用，为最多的人做有益的事情。

在讨论这个问题的过程中，我和美琳达读到了一篇文章，说在那些贫穷的国家，每年有数百万的儿童死于那些在美国早已不成问题的疾病。麻疹、疟疾、肺炎、乙型肝炎、黄热病，还有一种我以前甚至从未听说过的轮状病毒，这些疾病每年导致 50 万儿童死亡，但是在美国没有一例死亡。

我们震惊了。我们假设几百万儿童正在死亡线上挣扎，然而他们是可以挽救的，那么世界理应将运送药物来拯救他们作为头等大事。但事实并非如此。由于没有实施干预政策，那些价格还不到一美元的救命的药剂，并没有送到他们的手中。

如果你相信生命都是平等的，那么当你发现某些生命被认为值得挽救，而另一些生命则不然，你会感到无法接受。我们对自己说："事情不可能是这样的。如果这是真的，那么它理应是我们努力的头等大事。"

所以，我们用在座的任何人都会想到的方式开始工作。我们问："这个世界怎么可以眼睁睁看着这些孩子死去？"

答案很简单，也很无情。在市场经济中，拯救这些儿童是一项没有利润的工作，政府也不会提供补助。这些儿童之所以会死亡，是因为他们的父母在经济上没有实力，在这种政治体制中没有发言权。

热词空间

accelerating [æk'seləreitiŋ] adj. 加速的
malaria [mə'lɛəriə] n. 疟疾
pneumonia [nju:'məunjə] n. [医] 肺炎
hepatitis [ˌhepə'taitis] B 乙型肝炎
rotavirus ['rəutəˌvaiərəs] n. [微] 轮状病毒（一种致婴儿或新生畜胃肠炎的病毒）
priority [prai'ɔrəti] n. 优先；优先权；优先考虑的事
give priority to 优先考虑；给……以优先权
revolting [ri'vɔ:ltiŋ] adj. [口] 令人厌恶的，糟糕透顶的；反叛的
subsidize ['sʌbsidaiz] vt. 资助

creative capitalism — if we can stretch the reach of market forces so that more people can make a profit, or at least make a living, serving people who are suffering from the great inequities. We can also press governments around the world to spend taxpayer money in ways that better reflect the values of the people who pay the taxes.

If we can find approaches that meet the needs of the poor in ways that generate profits for business and votes for politicians, we will have found a sustainable way to reduce inequity in the world. This task is open-ended. It can never be finished. But a conscious effort to answer this challenge can change the world.

I am optimistic that we can do this, but I talk to skeptics who claim there is no hope. They say: "Inequity has been with us since the beginning, and will be with us until the end — because people just … don't … care." I completely disagree.

I believe we have more caring than we know what to do with.

All of us here in this Yard, at one time or another, have seen human tragedies that broke our hearts, and yet we did nothing — not because we didn't care, but because we didn't know what to do. If we had known how to help, we would have acted.

The barrier to change is not too little caring; it is too much complexity.

To turn caring into action, we need to see a problem, see a solution, and see the impact. But complexity blocks all three steps.

Even with the advent of the Internet and 24-hour news, it is still a complex enterprise to get people to truly see the problems. When an airplane crashes, officials immediately call a press conference. They promise to investigate, determine the cause, and prevent similar crashes in the future.

But if the officials were brutally honest, they would say: "Of all the people in the world who died today from preventable causes, one half of one percent were on this plane. We're determined to do everything possible to solve the problem that took the lives of the one half of one percent."

但是，你们和我在经济上有实力，在政治上也有发言权。

如果我们能够设计出一种更有创新性的资本主义制度——如果我们可以改变市场，让更多的人可以获得利润，或者至少可以维持生活，这就可以帮助那些正在极端不平等的状况中受苦的人们，那么，我们就可以让市场更好地为穷人服务。我们还可以向全世界的政府施压，要求他们将纳税人的钱花到更体现纳税人价值的地方。

如果我们能够找到这样的方法，既可以帮到穷人，又可以为商人带来利润，为政治家带来选票，那么我们就找到了一种可持续的减少世界上不平等现象的发展道路。这是一项永无止境的任务。它不可能完全完成，但是任何有意识地解决这一问题的尝试都可以改变这个世界。

我们可以做到这个，对于这一点我很乐观。但是，我与宣称没有希望的怀疑主义者谈论时，他们说："不平等从人类诞生的第一天就存在，到人类灭亡的最后一天也将存在——因为人类根本不在乎这个问题。"我完全不同意这种观点。

我相信，问题不是我们不在乎，而是不知道怎么做。

此刻在这个院子里的所有人，生命中总有这样或那样的时刻，目睹人类的悲剧，感到万分伤心。但是我们什么也没做，并非我们无动于衷，而是因为我们不知道做什么和怎么做。如果我们知道怎样做才会有所帮助，那么我们就会采取行动。

改变世界的阻碍，并非人类的冷漠，而是世界实在太复杂。

为了将关心转变为行动，我们需要发现问题，找到解决问题的方法，并评估其造成的影响。但是世界的复杂性使得所有这些步骤都难以做到。

即使有了互联网和 24 小时直播新闻，让人们真正发现问题所在，仍然十分困难。当一架飞机坠毁了，官员们会立刻召开新闻发布会，他们承诺进行调查，下定决心找到原因以防止将来再发生类似事故。

但是如果那些官员敢说真话，他们就会说："在今天，全

热词空间

capitalism ['kæpitəlizəm] n. 资本主义；资本主义制度

make a living 谋生，维持生活

approach [ə'prəutʃ] n. 方法；途径；接近

generate ['dʒenəreit] vt. 产生，造成，引起，导致

open-ended ['əupən'endid] adj. 无止境的；开放式的

conscious ['kɔnʃəs] adj. 自觉的，意识到的

skeptic ['skeptik] n.. 怀疑者，怀疑论者

tragedy ['trædʒidi] n. 悲剧

complexity [kəm'pleksiti] n. 复杂，复杂性

impact [im'pækt] n. 影响；效果

advent ['ædvənt] n. 到来；出现

with the advent of 随着……的出现

enterprise ['entəpraiz] n. 事业；企业；进取心；事业心

investigate [in'vestigeit] vi. 调查；研究

哈佛
大学

斯坦福
大 学

牛津
大学

耶鲁
大学

杜兰
大学

杜克
大学

威斯康
辛大学

清华
大学

北京
大学

亚利桑
那州立
大 学

加利福
尼 亚
大 学

The problem is not just the plane crash, but the millions of preventable deaths.

We don't read much about these deaths. The media covers what's new — and millions of people dying is nothing new. So it stays in the background, where it's easier to ignore. But even when we do see it or read about it, it's difficult to keep our eyes on the problem. It's difficult to look at suffering if the situation is so complex that we don't know how to help. And so we look away.

If we can really see a problem, which is the first step, we come to the second step: cutting through the complexity to find a solution.

Finding solutions is essential if we want to make the most of our caring. If we have clear and proven answers anytime an organization or individual asks "How can I help?", then we can get action — and we can make sure that none of the caring in the world is wasted. But complexity makes it hard to mark a path of action for everyone who cares — and makes it hard for their caring to matter.

Cutting through complexity to find solutions runs through four predictable stages: determine a goal, find the highest-leverage approach, deliver the technology ideal for that approach, and in the meantime, use the best application of the technology you already have — whether it's something sophisticated, like a new drug, or something simple, like a bednet.

The AIDS epidemic offers an example. The broad goal, of course, is to end the disease. The highest-leverage approach is prevention. The ideal technology would be a vaccine that gives lifetime immunity with a single dose. So governments, drug companies, and foundations are funding vaccine research. But their work is likely to take more than a decade, so in the meantime, we have to work with what we have in hand — and the best prevention approach we have now is getting people to avoid risky behavior.

Pursuing that goal starts the four-step cycle again. This is the pattern. The crucial thing is to never stop thinking and working — and never do what we did with malaria and tuberculosis

比尔·盖茨：如何解决这个世界最严重的不平等？
How to Tackle the World's Worst Inequities?

世界所有由于可以避免的原因而死亡的人之中，只有 0.5% 的死者来自于这次空难。我们下定决心尽一切努力，调查这个 0.5% 的死亡原因。"

显然，问题不是这次空难，而是其他几百万可以预防的死亡事件。

我们并没有很多机会了解这些死亡事件。媒体总是报道新闻，几百万人将要死去并非新闻。如果没有人报道，那么这些事件就很容易被忽视。另一方面，即使我们确实目睹了事件本身或者看到了相关报道，我们也很难持续关注这些事件。看着他人受苦是令人痛苦的，何况问题又如此复杂，我们根本不知道如何去提供援助。所以我们会转移视线。

就算我们真正发现了问题所在，也不过是迈出了第一步，接着还有第二步：那就是从复杂的世界中找到解决办法。

如果我们要让关心落到实处，我们就必须找到解决办法。如果我们有一个清晰可靠的答案，那么无论何时当组织和个人发出"我如何能提供帮助？"的疑问的时候，我们就可以采取行动。我们就能够保证不浪费一丁点全世界人类对他人的关心。但是，世界的复杂性使得我们很难找到对全世界每一个有爱心的人都有效的行动方法，因此人类对他人的关心往往很难产生实际效果。

从这个复杂的世界中找到解决办法，可以分为四个步骤：确定目标，找到最高效的方法，提供适用于那个方法的理想技术，最后利用现有的最佳技术，不管它是复杂的新药物，还是最简单的蚊帐。

艾滋病就是一个例子。毫无疑问，总的目标是彻底消灭这种疾病。最高效的方法是预防。最理想的技术是发明一种疫苗，只要注射一次，就可以终生免疫。所以，政府、制药公司、基金会都在资助疫苗研究。但是，这样的研究工作很可能十年之内都无法完成。因此，与此同时，我们必须使用现有的技术——目前最有效的预防方法就是设法让人们避免

热词空间

in the background 在幕后

proven ['pruːvən] *adj.* 被证实的

highest-leverage ['haiistlevəridʒ] *adj.* 高效的

sophisticated [sə'fistikeitid] *adj.* 复杂的

bednet ['bednet] *n.* 蚊帐

epidemic [,epi'demik] *n.* 〔病理学〕流行病，传染病；（流行病的）迅速传播

vaccine ['væksiːn] *n.* 疫苗

immunity [i'mjuːnəti] *n.* 免疫力

tuberculosis [tju:,bə:kju'ləusis] *n.* 肺结核

哈佛
大学

斯坦福
大学

牛津
大学

耶鲁
大学

杜兰
大学

杜克
大学

威斯康
辛大学

清华
大学

北京
大学

亚利桑
那州立
大学

加利福
尼亚
大学

in the 20th century — which is to surrender to complexity and quit.

The final step — after seeing the problem and finding an approach — is to measure the impact of the work and share that success and failure so that others can learn from your efforts.

You have to have the statistics, of course. You have to be able to show that a program is vaccinating millions more children. You have to be able to show, for example, a decline in the number of children dying from these diseases. This is essential not just to improve the program, but also to help draw more investment from business and government.

But if you want to inspire people to participate, you have to show more than numbers; you have to convey the human impact of the work — so people can feel what saving a life means to the families affected.

I remember going to Davos some years back and sitting on a global health panel that was discussing ways to save millions of lives. Millions! Think of the thrill of saving just one person's life — then multiply that by millions … Yet this was the most boring panel I've ever been on — ever. So boring even I couldn't stand it.

What made that experience especially striking was that I had just come from an event where we were introducing version 13 of some piece of software, and we had people jumping and shouting with excitement. I love getting people excited about software — but why can't we generate even more excitement for saving lives?

You can't get people excited unless you can help them see and feel the impact. Way to do that is another complex question.

Still, I'm optimistic. Yes, inequity has been with us forever, but the new tools we have to cut through complexity have not been with us forever. They are new — they can help us make the most of our caring — and that's why the future can be different from the past.

The defining and ongoing innovations of this age — biotechnology, the personal

比尔·盖茨：如何解决这个世界最严重的不平等？
How to Tackle the World's Worst Inequities?

那些危险的行为。

要实现那个新的目标，又可以采用新的四步循环。这是一种模式。关键是永远不要停止思考和行动。我们千万不能再犯上个世纪在疟疾和肺结核上犯过的错误，那时我们因为它们太复杂而放弃采取行动。

在发现问题和找到解决方法之后，就该进行最后一步了——评估工作结果，与其他人分享你的成功经验或者失败经验，这样他们就可以从你的努力中有所收获。

当然，你必须有一些统计数字。你必须让他人知道，你的项目为几百万儿童新接种了疫苗。你也必须让他人知道，死于这些疾病的儿童人数下降了多少。这些都是很关键的，不仅有利于改进项目，也有利于从商界和政府得到更多的帮助。

但是，这些还不够，如果你想激励其他人参加你的项目，你需要拿出的就远不止一些统计数字了；你必须展示你的项目的人性因素，这样其他人就会感到拯救一个生命对那些处在困境中的家庭到底意味着什么。

几年前，我去达沃斯（注：瑞士东部的一个城市）旁听一个关于全球健康问题的论坛，会议的内容是关于如何拯救几百万条生命。天哪，是几百万！想一想吧，拯救一个人的生命是何等让人激动，现在你要把这种激动再乘上几百万……但是，不幸的是，这是我参加过的最最乏味的论坛，乏味到连我都无法强迫自己听下去。

那次经历之所以让我难忘，是因为之前我们刚刚发布了一个软件的第 13 个版本，我们让观众激动得跳了起来，喊出了声。我喜欢人们因为软件而感到激动，那么我们为什么不能够让人们因为能够拯救生命而感到更加激动呢？

除非你能够让人们看到或者感受到行动的影响力，否则你无法让人们激动。如何做到这一点，并不是一件简单的事。

同前面一样，在这个问题上，我依然是乐观的。不错，人类的不平等有史以来一直存在，但是那些能够化繁为简的新工

热词空间

statistics [stə'tistiks] *n.* 统计资料；统计学；统计

vaccinate ['væksineit] *vt.* 给……注射疫苗

affect ['æfekt] *vt.* 侵袭；影响；感染

panel ['pænl] *n.* 座谈小组

thrill [θril] *n.* 激动

striking ['straikiŋ] *adj.* 给人印象深刻的，显著的

version ['və:ʃən] *n.* 版本

computer and the Internet — give us a chance we've never had before to end extreme poverty and end death from preventable disease.

Sixty years ago, George Marshall came to this commencement and announced a plan to assist the nations of post-war Europe. He said, I quote, "I think one difficulty is that the problem is one of such enormous complexity that the very mass of facts presented to the public by press and radio make it **exceedingly** difficult for the man in the street to reach a clear **appraisement** of the situation. It is virtually impossible at this distance to grasp at all the real significance of the situation."

Thirty years after Marshall made his address, which was thirty years ago, as my class graduated without me, technology was emerging that would make the world smaller, more open, more visible, less distant.

The emergence of low-cost personal computers **gave rise to** a powerful network that has transformed opportunities for learning and communicating.

The magical thing about this network is not just that it **collapses** distance and makes everyone your neighbor. It also dramatically increases the number of brilliant minds we can bring in and work together on the same problem — and that scales up the rate of potential innovation to a **staggering** degree.

At the same time, for every person who has access to this technology, five people don't. That means many creative minds are left out of this discussion — smart people with practical intelligence and relevant experience who don't have the technology to **hone** their talents or contribute their ideas to the world.

We need as many people as possible to gain access to this technology, because these advances are **triggering** a revolution in what human beings can do for one another. They are making it possible not just for national governments, but for universities, corporations, smaller organizations, and even individuals to see problems, see approaches, and measure the impact of their efforts to address the hunger, poverty, and **desperation** George Marshall spoke of 60 years ago.

比尔·盖茨：如何解决这个世界最严重的不平等？
How to Tackle the World's Worst Inequities?

具，却是最近才出现的。这些新工具可以帮助我们，将人类的同情心发挥最大的作用，那就是将来同过去不一样的原因。

这个时代无时无刻不在涌现出新的革新——生物技术、个人计算机、互联网——它们给了我们一个前所未有的机会，去终结那些极端的贫穷和非恶性疾病的死亡。

六十年前，乔治·马歇尔也是在这个地方的毕业典礼上，宣布了一个计划，帮助那些欧洲国家进行战后建设。他说："我认为，困难的一点是这个问题太复杂，报纸和电台源源不断地向公众提供各种事实，使得大街上的普通人极难清晰地判断形势。事实上，经过层层传播，想要真正地把握形势是根本不可能的。"

马歇尔发表这个演讲三十年后，也就是三十年前，我那一届学生毕业，当然我不在其中。那时，新技术刚刚开始萌芽，它们将使得这个世界变得更小、更开放、更容易看到、距离更近。

低成本的个人电脑的出现，使得一个强大的互联网诞生，它为学习和交流提供了巨大的机会。

互联网的神奇之处，不仅仅是它缩短了物理距离，使得天涯若比邻。它还极大地增加了怀有共同想法的人们聚集在一起的机会，我们可以为了解决同一个问题，一起共同工作。这就大大加快了潜在的革新的进程，发展速度简直让人震惊。

与此同时，世界上有条件上网的人只是全部人口的六分之一。这意味着，许多有创造性思想的人没有加入到我们的讨论中来。那些有着实际的智力水平和相关经验的英才，却没有技术来帮助他们，将他们的天赋或者想法与全世界分享。

我们需要尽可能地让更多的人有机会使用这项技术，因为这些新技术正在引发一场革命，人类将因此可以互相帮助。这些新技术正在创造一种可能，不仅是国家政府，还包括大学、公司、小机构，甚至个人，能够发现问题所在、能够找到解决办法、能够评估他们努力的效果，去改变乔治·马歇尔六十年前就说到过的那些问题——饥饿、贫穷和绝望。

热词空间

exceedingly [ik'si:diŋli] *adv.* 非常
appraisement [ə'preizmənt] *n.* 评价
give rise to 使发生，引起
collapse [kə'læps] *vt.* 瓦解
staggering ['stægəriŋ] *adj.* 令人震惊的
hone [həun] *vt.* 锤炼，使精通
trigger ['trigə] *vt.* 引发
desperation [despə'reiʃən] *n.* 失望，绝望

哈佛
大学

斯坦福
大 学

牛津
大学

耶鲁
大学

杜兰
大学

杜克
大学

威斯康
辛大学

清华
大学

北京
大学

亚利桑
那州立
大 学

加利福
尼 亚
大 学

Members of the Harvard Family: Here in the Yard is one of the great collections of **intellectual** talent in the world.

For what purpose?

There is no question that the faculty, the **alumni**, the students, and the **benefactors** of Harvard have used their power to improve the lives of people here and around the world. But can we do more? Can Harvard **dedicate** its intellect to improving the lives of people who will never even hear its name?

Let me make a request of the deans and the professors — the intellectual leaders here at Harvard: As you hire new faculty, award **tenure**, review **curriculum**, and determine degree requirements, please ask yourselves:

Should our best minds **be** more **dedicated** to solving our biggest problems?

Should Harvard encourage its faculty to take on the world's worst inequities? Should Harvard students know about the depth of global poverty … the **prevalence** of world hunger … the **scarcity** of clean water … the girls kept out of school … the children who die from diseases we can cure?

Should the world's most privileged learn about the lives of the world's least privileged?

These are not **rhetorical** questions — you will answer with your policies.

My mother, who was filled with pride the day I was admitted here — never stopped pressing me to do more for others. A few days before I was married, she hosted a bridal event, at which she read aloud a letter about marriage that she had written to Melinda. My mother was very ill with cancer at the time, but she saw one more opportunity to deliver her message, and at the close of the letter she said, "From those to whom much is given, much is expected."

When you consider what those of us here in this Yard have been given — in talent, privilege, and opportunity — there is almost no limit to what the world has a right to expect from us.

比尔·盖茨：如何解决这个世界最严重的不平等？
How to Tackle the World's Worst Inequities?

哈佛大家庭的成员们，这个院子里在场的人们，你们是全世界最有智力的人类群体之一。

我们可以做些什么？

毫无疑问，哈佛的老师、校友、学生以及哈佛的资助者，已经用他们的能力改善了全世界各地人们的生活。但是，我们还能够做更多吗？哈佛的人们能将他们的智慧用来帮助那些甚至从来没有听到过"哈佛"这个名字的人吗？

请允许我向各位院长和教授提出一个请求——你们是哈佛的智力领袖，当你们雇用新的老师、授予终身教职、评估课程、决定学位颁发标准的时候，请问你们自己如下的问题：

我们最优秀的人才是否更加应该致力于解决我们最大的问题？

哈佛是否应该鼓励它的老师去研究解决世界上最严重的不平等？哈佛的学生是否应了解全球那些极端的贫穷……世界性的饥荒……清洁水资源的缺乏……无法上学的女童……死于可治愈疾病的儿童？

世界上那些过着最优越的生活的人们，是否应该对那些最困难的人们的境况有所了解？

这些问题并非语言上的修辞。你必须用自己的行动来回答。

我的母亲在我被哈佛大学录取的那一天，曾经感到非常骄傲。她从没有停止督促我去为他人做更多的事情。在我结婚的前几天，她主持了一个新娘进我家的仪式。在这个仪式上，她高声读了一封关于婚姻的信，这是她写给美琳达的。那时，我的母亲已经因为癌症病入膏肓，但是她还是认为这是又一个传播她的信念的机会。在那封信的结尾，她写道："对于那些接受了许多帮助的人们，人们对他们的期望也很大。"

想一想吧，我们在这个院子里的这些人，被给予了什么——天赋、特权、机遇——那么可以这样说，全世界的人们几乎有无限的权利，期待我们做出贡献。

同这个时代的期望一样，我在这里也要向今天在座的毕业生

热词空间

intellectual [ˌintəˈlektʃuəl] *adj.* 智力的

alumni [əˈlʌmnai] *n.* 校友

benefactor [ˈbenifæktə] *n.* 捐助者

dedicate [ˈdedikit] *vt.* 奉献

tenure [ˈtenjuə] *n.* 任期

curriculum [kəˈrikjuləm] *n.* 课程

be dedicated to 致力于，献身于

prevalence [ˈprevələns] *n.* 普遍，流行

scarcity [ˈskɛəsəti] *n.* 不足；缺乏

rhetorical [riˈtɔrikəl] *adj.* 修辞的

哈佛
大学

斯坦福
大 学

牛津
大学

耶鲁
大学

杜兰
大学

杜克
大学

威斯康
辛大学

清华
大学

北京
大学

亚利桑
那州立
大 学

加利福
尼 亚
大 学

In line with the promise of this age, I want to **exhort** each of the graduates here to take on an issue — a complex problem, a deep inequity, and become a specialist on it. If you make it the focus of your career, that would be phenomenal. But you don't have to do that to make an impact. For a few hours every week, you can use the growing power of the Internet to get informed, find others with the same interests, see the barriers, and find ways to cut through them.

Don't let complexity stop you. Be activists. Take on big inequities. I feel sure it will be one of the great experiences of your lives.

You graduates are coming of age in an amazing time. As you leave Harvard, you have technology that members of my class never had. You have awareness of global inequity, which we did not have. And with that awareness, you likely also have an informed conscience that will **torment** you if you abandon these people whose lives you could change with small effort. You have more than we had; you must start sooner, and carry on longer.

And I hope you will come back here to Harvard 30 years from now and reflect on what you have done with your talent and your energy. I hope you will judge yourselves not on your professional accomplishments alone, but also on how well you have addressed the world's deepest inequities … on how well you treated people a world away who have nothing in common with you but their humanity.

Good luck.

比尔 · 盖茨：如何解决这个世界最严重的不平等？
How to Tackle the World's Worst Inequities?

提出一个忠告：你们要选择一个问题，一个复杂的问题，一个有关于人类深刻的不平等的问题，然后你们要变成关于这个问题的专家。如果你们能够使得这个问题成为你们职业的核心，那么你们就会非常杰出。但是，你们不一定要去做那些大事。每个星期只用几个小时，你就可以通过互联网日益增长的效力得到信息，找到志同道合的朋友，发现困难所在并找到解决它们的途径。

不要让这个世界的复杂性阻碍你前进。要成为一个行动主义者。将解决人类的不平等视为己任。它将成为你生命中最重要的经历之一。

在座的各位毕业生，你们所处的时代是一个神奇的时代。当你们离开哈佛的时候，你们拥有的技术是我们那一届学生所没有的。你们已经了解到了世界上的不平等，而我们那时还不知道这些。了解了这些之后，要是你再弃那些你可以帮助的人们于不顾，就将受到良心的谴责，只需一点小小的努力，你就可以改变那些人们的生活。你们比我们拥有更大的能力，你们必须尽早开始，尽可能长时期地坚持下去。

我希望，30 年后你们还会再回到哈佛，回顾你们用自己的天赋和能力所做出的一切。我希望，在那个时候，你们用来评价自己的标准，不仅仅是你们的专业成就，还包括你们为改变这个世界深刻的不平等所做出的努力，以及你们如何善待那些远隔千山万水、除了同为人类之外与你们毫无共同之处的人们。

最后，祝各位同学好运。

热词空间

exhort [ig'zɔːt] vt. 劝诫，忠告
torment [tɔ:'ment] vt. 折磨

哈佛
大学

斯坦福
大学

牛津
大学

耶鲁
大学

杜兰
大学

杜克
大学

威斯康
辛大学

清华
大学

北京
大学

亚利桑
那州立
大学

加利福
尼亚
大学

比尔·盖茨给我们的 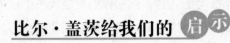 启示

That's where I learned the sad lesson that improving your odds doesn't guarantee success.

也正是在这里我学到了人生中令人悲伤的教训：机会大，并不等于你就会成功。

If you believe that every life has equal value, it's revolting to learn that some lives are seen as worth saving and others are not.

如果你相信生命都是平等的，那么当你发现某些生命被认为值得挽救，而另一些生命则不然，你会感到无法接受。

The barrier to change is not too little caring; it is too much complexity.

改变世界的阻碍，并非人类的冷漠，而是世界实在太复杂。

Cutting through complexity to find solutions runs through four predictable stages: determine a goal, find the highest-leverage approach, deliver the technology ideal for that approach, and in the meantime, use the best application of the technology you already have — whether it's something sophisticated, like a new drug, or something simple, like a bednet.

从这个复杂的世界中找到解决办法，可以分为四个步骤：确定目标，找到最高效的方法，提供适用于那个方法的理想技术，最后利用现有的最佳技术，不管它是复杂的新药物，还是最简单的蚊帐。

The crucial thing is to never stop thinking and working — and never do what we did with malaria and tuberculosis in the 20th century — which is to surrender to complexity and quit.

关键是永远不要停止思考和行动。我们千万不能再犯上个世纪在疟疾和肺结核上犯过的错误，那时我们因为它们太复杂而放弃了采取行动。

Don't let complexity stop you. Be activists. Take on big inequities. I feel sure it will be one of the great experiences of your lives.

不要让这个世界的复杂性阻碍你前进。要成为一个行动主义者。将解决人类的不平等视为己任。它将成为你生命中最重要的经历之一。

斯坦福大学

校训：Die Luft der Freiheit weht（德文，中文意思是"自由之风永远吹拂"）

总 括

　　美丽的斯坦福大学于1885年注册成立，1891正式招收学生。它位于加利福尼亚州的斯坦福市，临近旧金山，是当时的加州铁路大王、曾担任加州州长的利兰·斯坦福为纪念他在意大利游历时染病而死的儿子而捐钱成立的一所大学。斯坦福大学是美国一所私立大学，被公认为世界上最杰出的大学之一。斯坦福大学拥有的资产属于世界大学中最大的之一，是美国面积第二大的大学。如果说，哈佛与耶鲁大学代表着美国传统的人文精神，那么，斯坦福大学则是二十一世纪科技精神的象征。

　　斯坦福大学成就了硅谷。斯坦福大学的崛起为硅谷微电子工业创造了条件，同时，硅谷的发展也帮助了斯坦福大学，使它能有今天的成就。

Three Stories from My Life

我人生中的三个故事

Stanford University
Commencement Address
Steve Jobs
June 12, 2005

背景资料

　　毕业典礼上的演讲大都轻松愉快，但是容易被遗忘。然而，史蒂夫·乔布斯2005年6月在斯坦福大学的演讲在经过了一个夏天之后依然为人所提及。这位苹果电脑公司和皮克斯动画公司首席执行官在演讲中谈到了他人生中的三个故事，这三个故事不仅在斯坦福大学的毕业生，也在硅谷乃至其他地方的技术同行中引起了巨大反响。

Remembering that I'll be dead soon is the most important tool I've ever encountered to help me make the big choices in life. Because almost everything — all external expectations, all pride, all fear of embarrassment or failure — these things just fall away in the face of death, leaving only what is truly important. Remembering that you are going to die is the best way I know to avoid the trap of thinking you have something to lose. You are already naked. There is no reason not to follow your heart.

　　让我能够做出人生重大抉择的最主要办法是，记住生命随时都有可能结束。因为几乎所有的东西——所有外在的需求、所有的尊严、所有对困窘和失败的恐惧——在死亡来临时都将不复存在，只剩下真正重要的东西。记住自己随时都会死去，这是我所知道的防止患得患失的最好方法。你已经一无所有了，还有什么理由不听从自己的心声呢。

　　　　　　　　　　　　　　　　　　　　　——史蒂夫·乔布斯

姓　　名：	史蒂夫·保罗·乔布斯（Steve Paul Jobs）
性　　别：	男
职　　业：	IT 工程师 苹果电脑公司创始人及首席执行官 企业家
国　　籍：	美国
出生日期：	1955 年 2 月 24 日
成功点睛：	从对电脑的痴迷到挚爱。 25 岁就成为亿万富翁的背后是努力执着。 信息业永远的创新者。 我是天才，我一定会成功。 好学若饥，谦卑若愚。
荣　　誉：	创立苹果公司 被称为"天使与魔鬼结合体"的商业奇才，跻身于计算机、音乐和动画电影三大产业界 1977 年，他们成功开发出苹果二号电脑，这是有史以来第一台具有彩色图形显示功能、键盘、电源和造型的个人电脑产品，也是第一台在市场上进行销售的个人电脑

名人 简介

　　史蒂夫·保罗·乔布斯（Steve Paul Jobs），"苹果"电脑的创始人之一，同时也是前 Pixar 动画公司的董事长及首席执行官（Pixar 已在 2006 年被迪士尼收购）。乔布斯还是迪士尼公司的董事会成员和最大个人股东。乔布斯被认为是电脑业界与娱乐业界的标志性人物，同时人们也把他视作麦金塔电脑、iPod、iTunes 商店、iPhone 等知名数字产品的缔造者。1985 年获得了由里根总统授予的国家级技术勋章；1997 年成为《时代》周刊的封面人物；同年被评为最成功的管理者，是声名显赫的"计算机狂人"。2009 年被《财富》杂志评选为这十年美国最佳首席执行官，同年当选《时代》周刊年度风云人物之一。

哈佛
大学

斯坦福
大　学

牛津
大学

耶鲁
大学

杜兰
大学

杜克
大学

威斯康
辛大学

清华
大学

北京
大学

亚利桑
那州立
大　学

加利福
尼　亚
大　学

I am honored to be with you today for your commencement from one of the finest universities in the world. Truth be told, I never graduated from college, and this is the closest I've ever gotten to a college graduation. Today I want to tell you three stories from my life. That's it. No big deal. Just three stories.

The first story is about connecting the dots.

I dropped out of Reed College after the first 6 months, but then stayed around as a **drop-in** for another 18 months or so before I really quit. So why did I **drop out**?

It started before I was born. My **biological mother** was a young, **unwed** college graduate student, and she decided to put me up for adoption. She felt very strongly that I should be adopted by college graduates, so everything was all set for me to be adopted at birth by a lawyer and his wife. Except that when I **popped** out they decided at the last minute that they really wanted a girl. So my parents, who were on a waiting list, got a call in the middle of the night asking, "We've got an unexpected baby boy; do you want him?" They said, "Of course." My biological mother found out later that my mother had never graduated from college and that my father had never graduated from high school. She refused to sign the final adoption papers. She only **relented** a few months later when my parents promised that I would go to college. This was the start in my life.

And 17 years later I did go to college. But I **naively** chose a college that was almost as expensive as Stanford, and all of my working-class parents' savings were being spent on my college **tuition**. After six months, I couldn't see the value in it. I had no idea what I wanted to do with my life and no idea how college was going to help me **figure** it **out**. And here I was spending all of the money my parents had saved their entire life. So I decided to drop out and trust that it would all work out OK. It was pretty **scary** at the time, but looking back it was one of the best decisions I ever made. The minute I dropped out I could stop taking the required classes that didn't

很荣幸和你们一起参加世界上最好的一所大学的毕业典礼。说实话，我大学没毕业，这是我第一次离大学毕业典礼这么近。今天我想给大家讲我人生中的三个故事，不讲别的，也不讲大道理，就讲三个故事。

第一个故事讲的是把生命中的点滴串连起来。

我在里德学院只读了六个月就退学了，此后便在学校里旁听，又过了大约一年半，我彻底离开。那么，我为什么退学呢？

这得从我出生前讲起。我的生母是一名年轻的未婚在校研究生，她决定将我送给别人收养。她非常希望收养我的是有大学学历的人，所以把一切都安排好了，决定我一出生就将我交给一对律师夫妇收养。没想到我才刚刚出生，那对夫妇却决定收养一名女孩。就这样，我的养父母——他们的名字当时还在登记册上——半夜三更接到一个电话："我们这儿有一个没人要的男婴，你们要吗？""当然要。"他们回答。但是，我的生母后来发现我的养母不是大学毕业生，我的养父甚至高中都没有毕业，所以她拒绝在最后的收养文件上签字。不过，没过几个月她就心软了，因为我的养父母许诺日后一定送我上大学。这就是我生命的起点。

17 年后，我真的上了大学。但当时我幼稚地选了一所学费几乎和斯坦福大学一样昂贵的学校，而我的养父母只是工薪阶层，他们倾其积蓄为我支付了大学学费。过了六个月后，我却看不出上大学有什么意义。我既不知道自己这一生想干什么，也不知道大学是否能够帮我弄明白这一点。而且在那儿我会花光父母一辈子节省下来的钱。所以，我决定退学，并且坚信日后会证明我这样做是对的。当年做出这个决定时心里很害怕，但现在回想起来，这还真是我有生以来做出的最好的决定之一。

interest me, and begin dropping in on the ones that looked far more interesting.

It wasn't all romantic. I didn't have a dorm room, so I slept on the floor in friends' rooms, I returned coke bottles for the 5-cent **deposits** to buy food with, and I would walk the 7 miles across town every Sunday night to get one good meal a week at the Hare Krishna temple. I loved it. And much of what I **stumbled** into by following my curiosity and intuition turned out to be priceless later on. Let me give you one example:

Reed College at that time offered perhaps the best **calligraphy** instruction in the country. Throughout the campus every poster, every label on every drawer, was beautifully hand **calligraphed**. Because I had dropped out and didn't have to take the normal classes, I decided to take a calligraphy class to learn how to do this. I learned about **serif** and **san-serif typefaces**, about varying the amount of space between different letter combinations, about what makes great **typography** great. It was beautiful, historical, artistically **subtle** in a way that science can't **capture**, and I found it fascinating.

None of this had even a hope of any practical application in my life. But ten years later, when we were designing the first Macintosh computer, it all came back to me. And we designed it all into the Mac. It was the first computer with beautiful typography. If I had never dropped in on that single course in college, the Mac would have never had multiple typefaces or **proportionally** spaced **fonts**. And since Windows just copied the Mac, it's likely that no personal computer would have them. If I had never dropped out, I would have never dropped in on that calligraphy class, and personal computers might not have the wonderful typography that they do. Of course it was impossible to connect the dots looking forward when I was in college. But it was very, very clear looking backwards ten years later.

Again, you can't connect the dots looking forward; you can only connect them

一退学，我就可以不再选那些我一点都不感兴趣的必修课，开始旁听一些看上去有趣得多的课。

那种日子一点儿都不浪漫。我没有宿舍，只能睡在朋友房间的地板上。我去退还可乐瓶，用那五分钱的押金来买吃的。每个星期天晚上我都要步行七英里，走到城那头的黑尔·科里施纳礼拜堂去吃每周才能享用一次的美餐。我喜欢那里的饭菜。我凭着好奇心和直觉所做的许多事情后来都证明是无价的。我给大家举个例子：

当时，里德学院的书法课大概是全国最好的。校园里所有的公告栏和每个抽屉的标签上的字都写得非常漂亮。因为我已经退学，不用正常上课，所以我决定选修书法课，学学怎么写出漂亮的字。我学习写带短截线和不带短截线的字体，根据不同字母组合调整其间距，并学习怎样把版式调整得更好。这门课太棒了，既有历史价值，又有艺术造诣，这一点科学就做不到，我觉得它妙不可言。

当时我并不指望书法在我以后的生活中能有什么实用价值。但是，十年之后，我们在设计第一台 Macintosh 计算机时，它一下子浮现在我眼前。于是，我们把这些东西全都设计进了 Macintosh 计算机中。这是第一台有这么漂亮的文字版式的计算机。要不是我当初在大学里偶然选了这门课，Macintosh 计算机绝不会有那么多种印刷字体或间距安排合理的字号。要不是 Windows 照搬了 Macintosh，个人电脑可能不会有这些字体和字号。要是我当初没有退学，我绝不会碰巧选了这门书法课，个人电脑也可能不会有现在这些漂亮的版式了。当然，我在大学里不可能从这些点滴上看到它与将来的关系。十年之后再回头看，两者之间的关系就非常、非常清楚了。

你们同样不可能从现在这个点上看到将来；只有回头看

热词空间

deposit [diˈpɔzit] *n.* 存款；保证金

stumble [ˈstʌmbl] *vi.* 蹒跚

calligraphy [kəˈligrəfi] *n.* 书法

calligraph [ˈkæligrɑːf] *vt.* 用花体书写，用美术体书写

serif [ˈserif] *n.* [印] 衬线（指字母主线外起装饰作用的细线）

san-serif 无衬线

typeface [ˈtaipfeis] *n.* 印刷字体

typography [taiˈpɔgrəfi] *n.* 排印

subtle [ˈsʌtl] *adj.* 微妙的；精细的

capture [ˈkæptʃə] *vt.* 夺得

proportionally [prəuˈpɔːʃənəli] *adv.* 相称地，适当地

font [fɔnt] *n.* 字体；字形

哈佛
大学

斯坦福
大　学

牛津
大学

耶鲁
大学

杜兰
大学

杜克
大学

威斯康
辛大学

清华
大学

北京
大学

亚利桑
那州立
大　学

加利福
尼　亚
大　学

looking backwards. So you have to trust that the dots will somehow connect in your future. You have to trust in something — your **gut**, destiny, life, **karma**, whatever. Because believing that the dots will connect down the road, will give you the confidence to follow your heart, even will lead you off to one's own path, and then will make all the difference.

My second story is about love and loss.

I was lucky — I found what I loved to do early in life. Woz and I started Apple in my parents' garage when I was 20. We worked hard, and in 10 years Apple had grown from just the two of us in a garage into a $2 billion company with over 4000 employees. We had just **released** our finest creation — the Macintosh — a year earlier, and I had just turned 30. And then I got fired. How can you get fired from a company you started? Well, as Apple grew we hired someone who I thought was very talented to run the company with me, and for the first year or so things went well. But then our **visions** of the future began to **diverge** and eventually we **had a falling out**. When we did, our Board of Directors sided with him. So at 30 I was out. And very publicly out. What had been the focus of my entire adult life was gone, and it was **devastating**.

I really didn't know what to do for a few months. I felt that I had let the previous generation of **entrepreneurs** down — that I had dropped the **baton** as it was being passed to me. I met with David Packard and Bob Noyce and tried to apologize for **screwing up** so badly. I was a very public failure, and I even thought about running away from the valley. But something slowly began to **dawn** on me — I still loved what I did. The turn of events at Apple had not changed that one bit. I had been rejected, but I was still in love. And so I decided to start over.

I didn't see it then, but it turned out that getting fired from Apple was the best thing that could have ever happened to me. The heaviness of being successful was

时，才会发现它们之间的关系。所以，你们要相信这些点滴迟早会连接到一起。你们必须相信某些东西——勇气、命运、生命，以及因果报应，等等。要相信，这些点会为你铺平前进的道路，会给予你听从自己的心声的自信，会引导你走自己的路，然后取得成就。

我的第二个故事是关于好恶与得失。

幸运的是，我在很早的时候就发现自己喜欢做什么。我在 20 岁时和沃兹（注：苹果公司创始人之一）在我父母的车库里办起了苹果公司。我们干得很卖力，十年后，苹果公司从车库里只有我们两个人的小公司发展成为一个拥有 20 亿美元资产、4,000 余名员工的大企业。那时，我们刚刚推出了我们最好的产品——Macintosh 电脑——那是在第 9 年，我刚满 30 岁。可接下来，我被解雇了。你怎么会被自己办的公司解雇呢？是这样的，随着苹果公司越做越大，我们聘了一位我认为非常有才华的人和我一起管理公司。在开始的一年多时间里，一切都很顺利。可是，随后我们两个人对公司前景的看法开始出现分歧，最后我们反目了，而董事会站在了他那一边。所以在 30 岁那年，我离开了公司，而且这件事闹得满城风雨。我失去了成年后的整个生活重心，这使我心力交瘁。

一连几个月，我真的不知道该怎么办。我感到自己给老一代的创业者丢了脸——因为我扔掉了交到自己手里的接力棒。我去见了戴维·帕卡德（惠普公司创始人之一）和鲍勃·诺伊斯（英特尔公司创建者之一），想为把事情搞得这么糟糕说声道歉。这次失败弄得沸沸扬扬，我甚至想过逃离硅谷。但是，渐渐地，我开始有了一个想法——我仍然热爱我过去做的一切。在苹果公司发生的这些风波丝毫没有改变这一点。我虽然被拒之门外，但我仍然深爱我的事业。于是，我决定从头开始。

热词空间

gut [gʌt] n. 勇气，胆量
karma ['kɑ:mə] n. 因果报应
release [ri'li:s] vt. 发行；释放
vision ['viʒən] n. 洞察力；视野
diverge [dai'və:dʒ] vi. 分歧
have a falling out 吵翻，反目
devastating ['devəsteitiŋ] adj. 毁灭性的
entrepreneur [ˌɔntrəprə'nə:] n. 企业家
baton ['bætən] n. 指挥棒；接力棒
screw up 弄糟，搞乱，拧紧
dawn [dɔ:n] vt. 出现；被领悟

replaced by the lightness of being a beginner again, less sure about everything. It freed me to enter one of the most creative periods of my life.

During the next five years, I started a company named NeXT, another company named Pixar, and fell in love with an amazing woman who would become my wife. Pixar went on to create the world's first computer **animated** feature film, *Toy Story*, and is now the most successful **animation** studio in the world. In a remarkable turn of events, Apple bought NeXT, I **retuned** to Apple, and the technology we developed at NeXT is at the heart of Apple's current **renaissance**. And Laurene and I have a wonderful family together.

I'm pretty sure none of this would have happened if I hadn't been fired from Apple. It was awful tasting medicine, but I guess the patient needed it. Sometimes life hits you in the head with a brick. Don't lose faith. I'm convinced that the only thing that kept me going was that I loved what I did. You've got to find what you love. And that is as true for work as it is for your lovers. Your work is going to fill a large part of your life, and the only way to be truly satisfied is to do what you believe is great work. And the only way to do great work is to love what you do. If you haven't found it yet, keep looking, and don't settle. As with all matters of the heart, you'll know when you find it. And, like any great relationship, it just gets better and better as the years **roll on**. So keep looking. Don't settle.

My third story is about death.

When I was 17, I read a quote that went something like, "If you live each day as if it was your last, someday you'll most certainly be right." It made an impression on me, and since then, for the past 33 years, I have looked in the mirror every morning and asked myself, "If today were the last day of my life, would I want to do what I am about to do today?" And whenever the answer has been "No" for too many days in a row, I know I need to change something.

虽然当时我并没有意识到，但事实证明，被苹果公司炒鱿鱼是我一生中碰到的最好的事情。尽管前景未卜，但从头开始的轻松感取代了保持成功的沉重感。这使我轻松踏入了一生中最富有创造力的时期之一。

在此后的五年里，我开了一家名叫 NeXT 的公司和一家叫皮克斯的公司，我还爱上一位了不起的女人，后来娶了她。皮克斯公司推出了世界上第一部用电脑制作的动画片《玩具总动员》，它现在是全球最成功的动画制作室。世道轮回，苹果公司买下 NeXT 后，我又回到了苹果公司，我们在 NeXT 公司开发的技术成了苹果公司这次重新崛起的核心。我和劳伦娜也建立了美满的家庭。

我确信，如果不是被苹果公司解雇，这一切决不可能发生。这是一剂苦药，可我认为良药苦口利于病。有时生活会给你当头一棒，但不要灰心。我坚信让我不断前行的唯一力量就是我热爱我所做的一切。所以，你们一定得知道自己喜欢什么，选择爱人时如此，选择工作时同样如此。工作将是生活中的一大部分，让自己真正满意的唯一办法，是做自己认为有意义的工作；做有意义的工作的唯一办法，是热爱自己的工作。如果你们还没有发现自己喜欢什么，那就不断地去寻找，不要急于做出决定。就像一切要凭着感觉去做的事情一样，一旦找到了自己喜欢的事，感觉就会告诉你。就像任何一种美妙的东西，历久弥新。所以说，要不断地寻找，直到找到自己喜欢的东西。不要半途而废。

我的第三个故事与死亡有关。

17 岁那年，我读到过这样一段话："如果把每一天都当作生命的最后一天，总有一天你会如愿以偿。"我记住了这句话，从那时起，33 年过去了，我每天早晨都对着镜子问自己："假如今天是生命的最后一天，我还会去做今天要做的事吗？"如

热词空间

animated ['ænimeitid] *adj.* 动画片的

animation [,æni'meiʃən] *n.* 动画片

retune [ri:'tju:n] *vt.* 重新调整

renaissance ['renəsɒns] *n.* 复兴

roll on （时光）流逝

Remembering that I'll be dead soon is the most important tool I've ever encountered to help me make the big choices in life. Because almost everything — all **external** expectations, all pride, all fear of embarrassment or failure — these things just fall away in the face of death, leaving only what is truly important. Remembering that you are going to die is the best way I know to avoid the trap of thinking you have something to lose. You are already naked. There is no reason not to follow your heart.

About a year ago I was diagnosed with cancer. I had a scan at 7:30 in the morning, and it clearly showed a **tumor** on my **pancreas**. I didn't even know what a pancreas was. The doctors told me this was almost certainly a type of cancer that is incurable, and that I should expect to live no longer than three to six months. My doctor advised me to go home and get my affairs in order, which is doctor's code for prepare to die. It means to try to tell your kids everything you thought you'd have the next 10 years to tell them in just a few months. It means to make sure everything is **buttoned up** so that it will be as easy as possible for your family. It means to say your goodbyes.

I lived with that diagnosis all day. Later that evening I had a **biopsy**, where they stuck an **endoscope** down my throat, through my stomach and into my **intestines**, put a needle into my pancreas and got a few cells from the tumor. I was **sedated**, but my wife, who was there, told me that when they viewed the cells under a microscope the doctors started crying because it turned out to be a very rare form of **pancreatic** cancer that is curable with surgery. I had the surgery and thankfully I'm fine now.

This was the closest I've been to facing death, and I hope it's the closest I get for a few more decades. Having lived through it, I can now say this to you with a bit more certainty than when death was a useful but purely intellectual concept: No one wants to die. Even people who want to go to heaven don't want to die to get there. And yet death is the **destination** we all share. No one has ever escaped it. And that is as it should be, because Death is very likely the single best invention of Life. It is

果一连许多天我的回答都是"不"，我知道自己应该有所改变了。

让我能够做出人生重大抉择的最主要办法是，记住生命随时都有可能结束。因为几乎所有的东西——所有外在的需求、所有的尊严、所有对困窘和失败的恐惧——在死亡来临时都将不复存在，只剩下真正重要的东西。记住自己随时都会死去，这是我所知道的防止患得患失的最好方法。你已经一无所有了，还有什么理由不听从自己的心声呢。

大约一年前，我被诊断患了癌症。那天早上七点半，我做了一次扫描检查，结果清楚显示我的胰腺上长了一个瘤子，可那时我连胰腺是什么都还不知道呢！医生告诉我说，几乎可以确诊这是一种无法治愈的恶性肿瘤，我最多还能活 3 到 6 个月。医生建议我回去把一切都安排好，其实这是在暗示"准备后事"。也就是说，把今后十年要跟孩子们说的事情在这几个月内嘱咐完；也就是说，把一切都安排妥当，尽可能不给家人留麻烦；也就是说，去跟大家诀别。

我那一整天一直在想这个诊断。到了晚上，我做了一次组织切片检查，他们把一个内窥镜通过喉咙经由我的胃进入肠子，用针头在胰腺的瘤子上取了一些细胞组织。当时我服用了麻醉剂，陪在一旁的妻子后来告诉我，医生在显微镜里看了细胞之后叫了起来，原来这是一种少见的可以通过外科手术治愈的恶性肿瘤。我做了手术，谢天谢地，现在好了。

这是我和死神离得最近的一次，我希望这也是今后几十年里最近的一次。有了这次经历之后，现在我可以更加实在地和你们谈论死亡，而不是纯粹纸上谈兵：谁都不愿意死。就是那些想进天堂的人也不愿意为了去那里而死。但是，死亡是我们共同的归宿，没人能摆脱。我们注定会死，因为死亡很可能是生命最好的一项发明。它推进生命的变迁，旧的不去，新的不

热词空间

external [ik'stə:nəl] adj. 外部的；表面的

tumor ['tju:mə] n. 肿瘤

pancreas ['pænkriəs] n. 胰腺

button up 扣住；完成

biopsy ['baiˌɔpsi] n. 活组织切片检查

endoscope ['endəskəup] n. 内窥镜

intestine [in'testin] n. 肠

sedate [si'deit] vt. 给……服镇静剂

pancreatic [ˌpænkri'ætik] adj. 胰腺的

destination [ˌdesti'neiʃən] n. 目的地，终点

Life's change agent. It clears out the old to **make way for** the new. Right now the new is you, but someday not too long from now, you will gradually become the old and be cleared away. Sorry to be so dramatic, but it is quite true.

Your time is limited, so don't waste it living someone else's life. Don't be trapped by **dogma** — which is living with the results of other people's thinking. Don't let the noise of others' opinions drown out your own inner voice. And most important, have the courage to follow your heart and intuition. They somehow already know what you truly want to become. Everything else is **secondary**.

When I was young, there was an amazing publication called *The Whole Earth Catalog*, which was one of the bibles of my generation. It was created by a fellow named Stewart Brand not far from here in Menlo Park, and he brought it to life with his poetic touch. This was in the late 1960's, before personal computers and desktop publishing, so it was all made with typewriters, scissors, and **polaroid cameras**. It was sort of like Google in **paperback** form, 35 years before Google came along: it was idealistic, **overflowing** with neat tools and great notions.

Stewart and his team put out several issues of *The Whole Earth Catalog*, and then when it had **run its course**, they put out a final issue. It was the mid-1970s, and I was your age. On the back cover of their final issue was a photograph of an early morning country road, the kind you might find yourself hitchhiking on if you were so adventurous. Beneath it were the words: "Stay Hungry. Stay Foolish." It was their farewell message as they **signed off**. Stay Hungry. Stay Foolish. And I have always wished that for myself. And now, as you graduate to begin **anew**, I wish that for you.

Stay Hungry. Stay Foolish.

Thank you all very much.

来。现在，你们就是新的，但在不久的将来，你们也会逐渐成为旧的，也会被淘汰。很抱歉，话说得太过分了，不过这是千真万确的。

你们的时间都有限，所以不要将它们浪费在重复其他人的生活上。不要囿于成见，那是在按照别人设想的结果而活。不要让别人观点的聒噪声淹没自己的心声。最主要的是，要有跟着自己感觉和直觉走的勇气。无论如何，感觉和直觉早就知道你到底想成为什么样的人，其他都是次要的。

我年轻时有一本非常好的刊物，叫《全球概览》，这是我们那代人的宝书之一，创办人名叫斯图尔特·布兰德，就住在离这儿不远的门洛帕克市。他用诗一般的语言把刊物办得生动活泼。那是 20 世纪 60 年代末，那时候还没有个人电脑和桌面印刷系统，全靠打字机、剪刀和宝丽莱照相机。它就像一种纸质的谷歌（Google），却比谷歌（Google）早问世 35 年。这份刊物太完美了，查阅手段齐备、构思不凡。

斯图尔特和他的同事们出了好几期《全球概览》，到最后办不下去时，他们出了最后一期。那是 20 世纪 70 年代中期，我也就是你们现在的年纪。最后一期的封底上是一张清晨乡间小路的照片，就是那种爱冒险的人等在那儿搭便车的那种小路。照片下面写道：好学若饥、谦卑若愚。那是他们停刊前的告别辞。好学若饥，谦卑若愚。这也是我一直想做到的。眼下正值诸位大学毕业、开始新生活之际，我同样希望大家能做到：

好学若饥、谦卑若愚。

谢谢大家。

哈佛
大学

斯坦福
大 学

牛津
大学

耶鲁
大学

杜兰
大学

杜克
大学

威斯康
辛大学

清华
大学

北京
大学

亚利桑
那州立
大 学

加利福
尼 亚
大 学

史蒂夫·乔布斯给我们的 启示

Sometimes life hits you in the head with a brick. Don't lose faith. I'm convinced that the only thing that kept me going was that I loved what I did. You've got to find what you love. And that is as true for your work as it is for your lovers. Your work is going to fill a large part of your life, and the only way to be truly satisfied is to do what you believe is great work. And the only way to do great work is to love what you do. If you haven't found it yet, keep looking, and don't settle. As with all matters of the heart, you'll know when you find it. And, like any great relationship, it just gets better and better as the years roll on. So keep looking. Don't settle.

有时生活会给你当头一棒，但不要灰心。我坚信让我不断前行的唯一力量就是我热爱我所做的一切。所以，你们一定得知道自己喜欢什么，选择爱人时如此，选择工作时同样如此。工作将是生活中的一大部分，让自己真正满意的唯一办法，是做自己认为是有意义的工作;做有意义的工作的唯一办法，是热爱自己的工作。你们如果还没有发现自己喜欢什么，那就不断地去寻找，不要急于做出决定。就像一切要凭着感觉去做的事情一样，一旦找到了自己喜欢的事，感觉就会告诉你。就像任何一种美妙的东西，历久弥新。所以说，要不断地寻找，直到找到自己喜欢的东西。不要半途而废。

No one wants to die. Even people who want to go to heaven don't want to die to get there. And yet death is the destination we all share. No one has ever escaped it. And that is as it should be, because Death is very likely the single best invention of Life. It is Life's change agent. It clears out the old to make way for the new. Right now the new is you, but someday not too long from now, you will gradually become the old and be cleared away. Sorry to be so dramatic, but it is quite true.

谁都不愿意死。就是那些想进天堂的人也不愿意为了去那里而死。但是，死亡是我们共同的归宿，没人能摆脱。我们注定会死，因为死亡很可能是生命最好的一项发明。它推进生命的变迁，旧的不去，新的不来。现在，你们就是新的，但在不久的将来，你们也会逐渐成为旧的，也会被淘汰。很抱歉，话说得太过分了，不过这是千真万确的。

Stay hungry. Stay foolish.

好学若饥，谦卑若愚。

牛津大学

校训：Dominus illuminatio mea（拉丁文，意为"主照亮我"）

总　括

　　牛津大学位于英国牛津市，是英语世界中最古老的大学，是英国最负盛名的高等学府之一，是人类历史上最早出现的几所大学之一。牛津大学的确切建校日期尚不清楚，但其教学历史在 1096 年就以某种形式开始了，并于 1167 年开始快速发展。它不仅在英国社会和高等教育系统中占有极其重要的地位，而且有着世界性的影响。英国和世界很多的青年学子都把进牛津大学深造作为自己的理想。

Heal the Children, Heal the World

拯救儿童，拯救世界

Oxford University
Address
Michael Jackson
March, 2001

背景资料

2001 年 3 月，迈克尔·杰克逊拖着刚刚摔伤的右脚，架着双拐在久负盛名的英国牛津大学以"保障儿童权益"为主题发表了演讲，宣传由他捐资设立的儿童慈善机构。在演讲中，杰克逊强调父母的重要性、孩子心灵的成长，父母与孩子之间的相互谅解以及对孩子的爱等等，杰克逊建议所有父母都应做到每晚在床边给孩子讲故事，以使他们时刻都能感受到爱。在讲到自己的童年以及与父亲的关系时，杰克逊满含热泪，声音颤抖。同时也理解了父亲为什么对自己和兄弟姐妹那么严格要求。这篇演讲展示了迈克尔·杰克逊对儿童的观点及对全世界儿童真正的爱。

In a world filled with hate, we must still dare to hope. Keep hope alive. In a world filled with anger, we must still dare to comfort. In a world filled with despair, we must still dare to dream. And in a world filled with distrust, we must still dare to believe.

即使世界充满仇恨，我们也要勇于憧憬，让希望永存；即使世界充满愤怒，我们也要敢于安慰；即使世界充满绝望，我们也要勇于梦想；即使世界充满猜疑，我们仍然敢于信任。

——迈克尔·杰克逊

最名人档案

姓　　名：	迈克尔·杰克逊（Michael Jackson）
性　　别：	男
职　　业：	摇滚音乐之王
国　　籍：	美国
出生日期：	1958 年 8 月 29 日
毕业学校：	美国黑人联合大学
成功点睛：	音乐的灵感加上刻苦执着的努力成就了他在世界乐坛的巨大影响力。
个人成就：	《吉尼斯世界纪录》千禧版本中，迈克尔·杰克逊被评为支持慈善机构最多的流行歌星

名人简介

　　迈克尔·杰克逊，1958 年 8 月 29 日出生于美国中部印第安纳州的工业小城加里市的一个黑人家庭中，是一名在世界各地极具影响力的流行音乐歌手，被誉为流行音乐之王（King of Pop）。他是一个出色的音乐全才，在作词、作曲、场景制作、编曲、演唱、舞蹈、乐器演奏等方面都有着卓越的成就。他的音乐曲风完美地融合了黑人节奏蓝调与白人摇滚独特的 MJ 乐风。在 20 世纪 80 年代起的整个现代流行音乐史上缔造了一个时代。他魔幻般的舞步更是让无数的明星效仿。

　　他用音乐歌颂大爱、种族团结与世界和平，谱写了一首首慈善、公益名曲，他一生投身慈善事业，曾两次被提名诺贝尔和平奖。同时作为一名全面的艺术家，杰克逊不仅在音乐方面有着卓越成就，在舞蹈、舞台表演、时尚等方面都有着独特的贡献和非凡的影响力，他被公认为是有史以来最伟大的艺人。

哈佛
大学

斯坦福
大 学

牛津
大学

耶鲁
大学

杜兰
大学

杜克
大学

威斯康
辛大学

清华
大学

北京
大学

亚利桑
那州立
大 学

加利福
尼 亚
大 学

Thank you dear friends, from the bottom of my heart, for such a loving and spirited welcome, and thank you, Mr. President, for your kind invitation to me which I am so honored to accept. I also want to express a special thanks to you Shmuley, who for 11 years served as **Rabbi** here at Oxford. You and I have been working so hard to form Heal the Kids, as well as writing our book about childlike qualities, and in all of our efforts you have been such a supportive and loving friend. And I also want to thank Toba Friedman, our director of operations at Heal the Kids, who is returning tonight to the alma mater where she served as a Marshall scholar, as well as Marilyn Piels, another central member of our Heal the Kids team.

I am humbled to be lecturing in a place that has previously been filled by such **notable** figures as Mother Theresa, Albert Einstein, Ronald Reagan, Robert Kennedy and Malcolm X. I've even heard that Kermit the Frog has made an appearance here, and I've always felt a **kinship** with Kermit's message that it's not easy being green. I'm sure he didn't find it any easier being up here than I do!

As I looked around Oxford, I can't help but be aware of the majesty and **grandeur** of this great institution, not to mention the **brilliance** of the great and gifted minds that have **roamed** these streets for centuries. The walls of Oxford have not only housed the greatest **philosophical** and scientific **geniuses** — they also have ushered forth some of the most cherished creators of children's literature, from J.R.R. Tolkien to C.S. Lewis. Lewis Carroll's *Alice in wonderland* is immortalized in the **stained** glass windows in Christ Church. And even one of my own fellow Americans, the beloved Dr. Seuss, he graced these halls and then went on to leave his mark on the imaginations of millions of children throughout the world.

I suppose I should start by listing my qualifications to speak before you this evening. Friends, I do not have to claim the academic **expertise** of other speakers who have addressed this hall, just as they could lay little claim at being **adept** at the moonwalk — and you know, Einstein in particular was really terrible at that.

But I do have a claim to having experienced more places and cultures than most people will ever see. Human knowledge consists not only of libraries of **parchment**

热词空间

谢谢各位亲爱的朋友，对于大家如此热烈的欢迎，我由衷地表示感谢，谢谢校长，您的盛情邀请，我感到万分荣幸。同时，我特别地感谢犹太教律法师施慕礼，感谢您十一年来在牛津所做的工作。您和我一起努力建立"拯救儿童"组织，就如创作我们的那本关于儿童特质的书一样艰辛，但自始至终您都给予我极大的支持，是我最亲爱的朋友。我还要感谢"拯救儿童"的执行总监多巴·弗里德曼，她将于今晚返回母校，在此，她曾经作为一个 Marshall 学者工作过。当然还要感谢我们"拯救儿童"组织的另一位中心成员玛里琳·皮尔斯。

能来到这样一个曾经汇集过特蕾莎修女、阿尔伯特·爱因斯坦、罗纳德·里根、罗伯特·肯尼迪和马尔科姆艾克斯等著名人物的地方演讲，我感到受宠若惊。听说青蛙科密特曾经来过这里，我和他有同感的是，没有丰富阅历的人来这里可不容易，我相信他做到这点也不会比我容易多少。

参观牛津大学时，我情不自禁地被它的雄伟和壮观所折服，更不必说几个世纪以来那些伟大而有才华的精英所创造的卓越成就了。牛津不仅荟萃了最伟大的哲学英才和科学家——还蕴育了一些最出色的儿童文学创作家，从 J. R. R. 托尔金到 C. S. 刘易斯。刘易斯·卡罗尔的《爱丽斯梦游仙境》在基督教堂的彩色玻璃窗里被永久保存。同时，我还发现我的一位美国同胞，亲爱的苏斯博士也为此增色，在这项伟大的事业上留下了他的印记，启发了全世界上千万儿童的想象力。

今晚，我想先讲讲我为何有幸能在这里演讲。朋友们，我不具备那些来此地的演讲者所拥有的学术专业知识，正如他们不善于"太空步"一样——而且，大家都知道，爱因斯坦尤其不擅长。

但是我可以说，和大多数人相比，我游历了更多地方，也

rabbi ['ræbai] *n.* 法师；先生

notable ['nəutəbl] *adj.* 值得注意的，显著的；著名的

kinship ['kinʃip] *n.* 亲属关系，亲密关系

grandeur ['grændʒə] *n.* 壮丽；庄严；宏伟

brilliance ['briljəns] *n.* 光辉，才华，杰出

roam [rəum] *vt.* 在……漫步

philosophical [ˌfilə'sɔfikəl] *adj.* 哲学的

genius ['dʒi:njəs] *n.* 天才，天赋

stained [steind] *adj.* 染色的

expertise [ˌekspə:'ti:z] *n.* 专门知识

adept [ə'dept] *adj.* 熟练的；擅长……的

parchment ['pa:tʃmənt] *n.* 羊皮纸；羊皮纸文稿

哈佛
大学

斯坦福
大 学

牛津
大学

耶鲁
大学

杜兰
大学

杜克
大学

威斯康
辛大学

清华
大学

北京
大学

亚利桑
那州立
大 学

加利福
尼 亚
大 学

and ink — it is also **comprised** of the volumes of knowledge that are written on the human heart, **chiseled** on the human soul, and **engraved** on the human **psyche**. And friends, I have encountered so much in this short lifetime of mine that I still cannot believe that I am only 42. I often tell Shmuley that in soul years I'm sure that I'm at least 80 — and tonight I even walk like I'm 80! So please **harken** to my message, because what I have to tell you tonight can bring healing to humanity and healing to our planet.

Through the **grace** of God, I have been fortunate to have achieved many of my artistic and professional **aspirations** realized early in my lifetime. But these, friends, are accomplishments, and accomplishments alone are not who I am. Indeed, the cheery five-year-old who **belted out** *Rockin' Robin* and *Ben* to adoring crowds **was** not **indicative of** the boy behind the smile.

Tonight, I come before you less as an icon of pop (whatever that means anyway), and more as an icon of a generation, a generation that no longer knows what it means to be children. All of us are products of our childhood. But I am the product of a lack of a childhood, an absence of that precious and **wondrous** age when we **frolic** playfully without a care in the world, basking in the adoration of parents and relatives, where our biggest concern is studying for that big spelling test come Monday morning.

Those of you who are familiar with the Jackson Five know that I began performing at the **tender** age of five and that ever since then, I haven't stopped dancing or singing. But while performing and making music undoubtedly remain as many of my greatest joys, when I was young I wanted more than anything else to be a typical little boy. I wanted to build tree houses, have water balloon fights, and play hide and seek with my friends. But fate had it otherwise and all I could do was envy the laughter and playtime that seemed to be going on all around me. There was no **respite** from my professional lifetyle. For on Sundays I would go Pioneering, the term used for the **missionary** work that Jehovah's Witnesses do. And it was then that I was able to see the magic of other people's childhood.

Since I was already a **celebrity**, I would have to put on a **disguise** of fat suit,

体验了更多不同的文化。人类文明不仅仅是图书馆中纸墨所记载的——还包括那些书写在人们内心的，凿刻在人们灵魂里和精神中的知识。而且，朋友们，在我短暂的生命里，我经历了这么多，以至于现在我都难以相信自己只有42岁。我常对施慕礼说我的心理年龄肯定至少有80了——今晚，我走路的样子甚至像一个80岁的老人。那么就请大家认真听我说，因为今晚我要对大家讲的可以救赎人性，拯救地球！

多亏上帝的恩典，我有幸在我人生的早期就已实现了自己的大部分艺术和职业抱负。但，朋友们，这些只是我的成就，成就本身并不构成我这个人。事实上，在崇拜者面前活泼快乐地表演 Rockin's Robin 和 Ben 的五岁小男孩在舞台下不一定也同样快乐。

今晚，我不是以一个流行音乐偶像的身份出现在大家面前（不管那意味着什么），而是作为一代人的代表出现，这一代人不再了解作为孩子意味着什么。大家都有过童年，而我却缺少童年，缺少那些宝贵的美妙的可以无忧无虑嬉戏玩耍的时光，那些日子我们本该惬意地沉浸在父母及亲人的疼爱中，那时我们最担心的是为星期一早上重要的拼写考试做准备。

熟悉杰克逊五人组合的朋友都知道我5岁时就开始表演，而且从那以后，我就再也没有停止过跳舞唱歌。毫无疑问，表演和音乐创作是我最大的乐趣，但年少时我更想和其他的小男孩一样，和我的朋友搭树屋、打水仗、捉迷藏。但恰恰相反，命中注定我只能羡慕那些充斥在我周围的笑声和欢乐。我的职业生活方式不允许我停下来。不过每逢星期天，我都会去"先锋会"，这是一个指代耶和华见证会传教工作的术语。那时，我就会设想别人充满魔力的童年。

因为我已是名人，所以我不得不穿肥大的衣服、戴假发、

热词空间

comprise [kəm'praiz] *vt.* 包含；由…组成

chisel ['tʃizəl] *vt.* 欺骗；凿；刻

engrave [in'greiv] *vt.* 雕刻；铭记

psyche ['psaiki] *n.* 灵魂；心智

harken ['ha:kən] *vi.* 倾听；留心

grace [greis] *n.* 优雅；恩惠

aspiration [,æspə'reiʃən] *n.* 渴望；抱负

belt out *vi.* 引吭高歌

be indicative [in'dikətiv] **of** 暗示……；表示……

icon ['aikɔn] *n.* 偶像

wondrous ['wʌndrəs] *adj.* 奇妙的；令人惊奇的

frolic ['frɔlik] *vi.* 嬉戏

tender ['tendə] *adj.* 温柔的；幼稚的

respite [ri'spait] *n.* 缓解；暂缓

missionary ['miʃənəri] *adj.* 传教的

celebrity [si'lebrəti] *n.* 名人；名声

disguise [dis'gaiz] *n.* 伪装；用作伪装的东西

a wig, a beard and glasses and we would spend the day in the suburbs of Southern California, going door-to-door or making the rounds of shopping malls, distributing our *Watchtower* magazine. I loved to set foot in all those regular suburban houses and catch sight of the fireplaces and La-Z-Boy armchairs with kids playing Monopoly and grandmas baby-sitting and all those wonderful, ordinary and starry scenes of everyday life. Many, I know, would argue that these things seem like no big deal. But to me they were mesmerizing.

I used to think that I was unique in feeling that I was without a childhood. I believed that indeed there were only a handful of people with whom I could share those feelings. When I recently met with Shirley Temple Black, the great child star of the 1930s and 40s, we said nothing to each other at first, we simply cried together, for she could share a pain with me that only others like my close friends Elizabeth Taylor and McCauley Culkin could.

I do not tell you this to gain your sympathy but to impress upon you my important point: It is not just Hollywood child stars that have suffered from a non-existent childhood. Today, it's a universal calamity, a global catastrophe. Childhood has become the great casualty of modern-day living. All around us we are producing scores of kids who have not had the joy, who have not been accorded the right, who have not been allowed the freedom, or knowing what it's like to be a kid.

Today's children are constantly encouraged to grow up faster, as if this period known as childhood is a burdensome stage, to be endured and ushered through, as swiftly as possible. And on that subject, I am certainly one of the world's greatest experts.

Ours is a generation that has witnessed the abrogation of the parent-child covenant. Psychologists are publishing libraries of books detailing the destructive effects of denying one's children the unconditional love that is so necessary to the healthy development of their minds and character. And because of all the neglect, too many of our kids essentially have to raise themselves. They are growing more distant from their parents, grandparents and other family members, as all around us the

留胡须，戴眼镜，把自己伪装起来。我们会在加州南部的郊区度过一整天，挨家挨户串门，或在各个购物中心闲逛，发放我们的《望塔》杂志。我也喜欢到普通的郊区居民家里去，看壁炉旁和拉兹男孩扶手椅上，小孩子们在玩大富翁游戏、老奶奶在照看小孩，看所有那些普通却绚丽多彩的日常生活场景。我知道很多人会认为这些没什么大不了的，但它们对我来说却充满了诱惑。

　　我过去常常认为唯独自己没有这种童年的感觉，我想能和我分享这种感觉的人更是少之又少。近来，我有幸见到了三四十年代的一位很出名的童星秀兰·邓波儿·布莱克，一见面我们什么都不说，只是一起哭，因为她能分担我的痛苦，这种痛苦只有我的一些密友，像伊丽莎白·泰勒和麦考利·库尔金才能体会到。

　　我说这些并不是要博得大家的同情，只是想让你们牢记我的一个重点：遭遇这种没有童年的痛苦的不只是好莱坞的童星。如今，这个问题已经成为世界性的灾难、全球的灾难。童年已经成了现代生活的牺牲品。我们使很多孩子不曾享受童年的欢乐，不曾得到应有的权利，不曾获得自由，甚至不知道童年是什么样子的。

　　现在，人们常鼓励孩子要快点长大，好像这个叫做童年的时期是一个累赘的阶段，是一个折磨人的、需要被尽快度过的时期。在这个问题上，我无疑是世界上最专业的人士之一了。

　　我们这一代人见证了亲子盟约的废除。心理学家出版了大量的书籍详细表述了不给予孩子无条件的爱会导致的毁灭性影响，这种爱对孩子的思想和性格的健康发展极其重要。因为被忽视，很多孩子从根本上必须自己照顾自己。他们渐渐疏远自己的父母、祖父母以及其他家庭成员，曾经连接各代人的强有力的纽带已经瓦解。

　　这种违背常理的行为造就了一代新人，让我们称之为"0

热词空间

fireplace ['faiəpleis] n. 壁炉
mesmerize ['mezməraiz] vt. 施催眠术；迷住
calamity [kə'læməti] n. 灾难；不幸事件
catastrophe [kə'tæstrəfi] n. 大灾难；大祸
casualty ['kæʒjuəlti] n. 意外事故；伤亡人员
accord [ə'kɔ:d] vt. 使一致；给予
abrogation [,æbrəu'geiʃən] n. 废除；取消
covenant ['kʌvənənt] n. 契约，盟约

indestructible bond that once glued together the generations, unravels.

This violation has bred a new generation, Generation O, let us call it Generation O, that has now picked up the torch from Generation X. The O stands for a generation that has everything on the outside — wealth, success, fancy clothing and fancy cars, but an aching emptiness on the inside. That cavity in our chests, that barrenness at our core, that void in our centre is the place where the heart once beat and which love once occupied. It's not just the kids who are suffering. It's the parents as well. For the more we cultivate little-adults in kids'bodies, the more removed we ourselves become from our own child-like qualities, and there is so much about being a child that is worth retaining in adult life.

Love. Ladies and gentlemen, love is the human family's most precious legacy, its richest bequest, its golden inheritance. And it is a treasure that is handed down from one generation to the other. Previous ages may not have had the wealth we enjoy. Their houses may have lacked electricity, and they squeezed their many kids into small homes without central heating. But those homes had no darkness, nor were they cold. They were lit bright with the glow of love and they were warmed snugly by the very heat of the human heart. Parents, undistracted by the lust for luxury and status, accorded their children primacy in their lives.

As you all know, our two countries broke from each other over what Thomas Jefferson referred to as "certain inalienable rights". While we Americans and British might dispute the justice of his claims, what has never been in dispute is that children have certain obvious rights, and the gradual erosion of those rights has led to scores of children worldwide being denied the joys and security of childhood.

I would therefore like to propose tonight that we install in every home a Children's Universal Bill of Rights, the tenets of which are:

1. The right to be loved without having to earn it.

2. The right to be protected, without having to deserve it.

3. The right to feel valuable, even if you came into the world with nothing.

4. The right to be listened to without having to be interesting.

时代"的人，他们承接了"X时代"人传递下来的"火炬"。"O时代"的人拥有所有外在的东西——财富、成功、时尚漂亮的衣服以及名车，但他们的内心却很空虚很痛苦。那种胸口的空洞，心灵的荒芜以及内在的空虚也曾经是我们的心脏搏动的地方，那里也曾经被爱占据。其实，不仅孩子们遭受着这种痛苦，父母也备受煎熬。我们越是让孩子们早熟，我们就越来越远离了天真，而这种天真就算成年人也值得拥有。

女士们，先生们，爱是人类家庭最珍贵的遗产，是最贵重的馈赠，是最无价的传统，是我们应该世代相传的财富。前人可能没有我们现在所享有的财富，他们的房子里可能没有电，很多孩子挤在没有中央取暖设施的狭小房间里。但他们不会觉得黑暗，也不会觉得寒冷。爱的光芒照亮了他们的房间，炽热的心灵温暖了他们的身体。父母不会因贪求荣华富贵而分心，也不会因追求身份地位而心烦意乱，孩子才是他们生活中最重要的。

我们都知道，我们两国曾因托马斯·杰斐逊（注：美国第三任总统）提出的所谓"几个不可剥夺的权利"而决裂。美国人和英国人也许会争议杰斐逊的主张是否公正，但绝不会有人质疑儿童享有不可剥夺的权利，对这些权利的逐步剥夺已经导致世界上的很多儿童失去了童年的乐趣和安全保障。

因此，我建议今晚我们就为每个家庭设立一部"世界儿童人权法案"，其条款如下：

1. 不用去争取就可享受的被爱的权利。

2. 不必乞求就可享有的被保护的权利。

3. 即使来到这个世界时一无所有，也有被重视的权利。

4. 即使不引人注意也有被倾听的权利。

哈佛
大学

斯坦福
大　学

牛津
大学

耶鲁
大学

杜兰
大学

杜克
大学

威斯康
辛大学

清华
大学

北京
大学

亚利桑
那州立
大　学

加利福
尼　亚
大　学

5. The right to be read a bedtime story, without having to compete with the evening news or Eastenders.

6. The right to an education without having to **dodge** bullets at schools.

7. The right to be thought of as **adorable** — even if you have a face that only a mother could love.

Friends, the foundation of all human knowledge, the beginning of human **consciousness**, must be that each and every one of us is an object of love. Before you know if you have red hair or brown, before you know if you are black or white, before you know of what religion you are a part of, you have to know that you are loved.

About twelve years ago, when I was just about to start my *Bad* tour, a little boy came with his parents to visit me at my California home. He was dying of cancer and he told me how much he loved me and my music. His parents told me that he wasn't going to live, that any day he could just go, and I said to him: "Look, I am going to be coming to your hometown in Kansas to start my tour in three months. I want you to come to the show. I am going to give you this jacket that I wore in one of my videos." His eyes **lit up** and he said, "You are gonna give me the jacket?" I said, "Yeah, I'm going to give you the jacket, but you have to promise me that you will wear it to the show." I was trying to make him **hold on**. I said, "When you come to the show I want to see you in this jacket and in this glove", and I gave him one of my **rhinestone** gloves, which I never give to anyone. And he was just in heaven. But maybe he was too close to heaven, because when I came to his town, he had already died, and they had buried him in the glove and jacket.

He was just 10 years old. God knows, and I know, that he tried his best to hold on. But at least when he died, he knew that he was loved, not only by his parents, but even by me. As a near stranger, I also loved him. And with all of that love he knew that he didn't come into this world alone, and he certainly didn't leave it alone.

If you enter this world knowing you are loved and you leave this world knowing the same, then everything that happens in between can he dealt with. A professor may degrade you, but you will not feel degraded; a boss may crush you, but you will not be

5. 不需要与晚间新闻或《东区居民》抗争，就有在睡觉前听一段故事的权利。

6. 不需要躲避子弹，就可以在学校受教育的权利。

7. 哪怕你只有妈妈才会爱的脸蛋，也有被人尊重的权利。

朋友们，所有人类知识的基本原则、人类意识的起点必然是我们每一个人都成为被爱的对象。哪怕你还不知道自己的头发是红色还是棕色，还不知道自己是白人还是黑人，还不知道自己信仰哪种宗教，你也必须知道自己是被爱着的。

大约在 12 年前，我即将开始我的 *Bad* 专辑巡演，这时一个小男孩和他的父母来加州我的家里看望我。癌症正在威胁着他的生命，他告诉我他非常喜欢我和我的音乐。他的父母告诉我他生命将尽，说不上哪一天就会离开，我就对他说："你瞧，三个月之后我就要到堪萨斯城你的家乡去开演唱会，我希望你来看我的演出，我还要送给你一件我在录制一部录影带时穿过的夹克。"他眼睛一亮，说："你要把夹克送给我？"我说："是的，我要把夹克送给你，不过你必须答应我穿着它来看我的演出。"我只想尽力让他坚持住，就对他说："我希望在我的演唱会上看见你穿着这件夹克戴着这只手套。"于是，我又送了一只镶着莱茵石的手套给他。一般我决不送镶着莱茵石的手套给别人。但他就要去天堂了。不过，也许他离天堂实在太近了，我来到他的城市时，他已经走了，他们埋葬他时给他穿了那件夹克戴了那只手套。

他只有 10 岁。上帝知道，我知道，他曾经多么努力地坚持过。但至少，在他离开时，他知道自己是被深爱着的，不仅被父母爱着，也被我爱着。虽然几乎是个陌生人，我也爱着他。拥有了这些爱，他知道他不是独自来到这个世界的，当然也不会孤独地离开。

如果你降临或离开这个世界时都感到被爱着，那么其间发生的一切事情你都可以应付。教授可能给你降级，可你自己不会感到被降级；老板可能排挤你，可你不会被排挤掉；一个辩论对手可能会击败你，可你却仍能胜利。他们怎么能

crushed; a corporate **gladiator** might **vanquish** you, but you will still triumph. How could any of them truly **prevail** in pulling you down? For you know that you are an object worthy of love. The rest is just packaging.

But if you don't have that memory of being loved, you are condemned to search the world for something to fill you up. But no matter how much money you make or how famous you become, you will still feel empty. What you are really searching for is unconditional love, unqualified acceptance. And that was the one thing that was denied to you at birth.

Friends, let me paint a picture for you. Here is a typical day in America — six youths under the age of 20 will commit suicide, 12 children under the age of 20 will die from firearms — remember this is a DAY, not a year — 399 kids will be arrested for drug **abuse** , 1,352 babies will be born to teen mothers. This is happening in one of the richest, most developed countries in the history of the world.

Yes, in my country there is an epidemic of violence that parallels no other industrialized nation. These are the ways young people in America express their hurt and their anger. But don't think that there is not the same pain and **anguish** among their counterparts in the United Kingdom. Studies in this country show that every single hour, three teenagers in the UK **inflict** harm upon themselves, often by cutting or burning themselves — burning their bodies — or taking an **overdose**. This is how they have chosen to cope with the pain of neglect and emotional agony.

In Britain, as many as 20% of families will only sit down and have dinner together once a year. Once a year! And what about the time-honored tradition of reading your kid a bedtime story? Research from the 1980s showed that children who are read to, had far greater **literacy** and significantly **outperformed** their peers at school. And yet, less than 33% of British children ages two to eight have a regular bedtime story read to them. You may not think much of that until you take into account that 75% of their parents DID have that bedtime story when they were that age.

Clearly, we do not have to ask ourselves where all of this pain, anger and

真正战胜你击倒你呢？因为你知道你值得被爱，其余的只是一层包装罢了。

但是，如果你没有被爱的记忆，你就无法发现世界上有什么东西能够让你充实。无论你挣了多少钱，无论你有多出名，你仍会觉得空虚。你真正寻找的只是无条件的爱和完全的包容。而那些在你诞生时就已把你拒之门外。

朋友们，让我给大家描述一幅这样的情景，这是美国典型的一天——每一天将有 6 个不满 20 岁的青年自杀，12 个 20 岁以下的孩子死于枪击——记住这只是一天，不是一年——另外还有 399 个少年因为服用毒品而被逮捕，1352 个婴儿被十几岁的妈妈生下来，这些都发生在世界上最富有最发达的国家。

是的，我国所充斥的暴力，其他的工业化国家无法与之相比。这只是美国年轻人宣泄他们的伤痛和愤怒的方式，但是，不要认为英国就不存在有这样痛苦和烦恼的人。种种调查表明英国每小时都会有 3 个青少年自残，他们通常会割伤或烫伤自己的身体或者服用过量药剂。这是他们所选择的用来发泄被忽视的痛苦和烦恼的方法。

在大不列颠，多达 20% 的家庭一年只能聚在一起吃一次晚饭，一年才一次！那么给孩子们讲睡前故事的悠久传统又处于一种什么状况呢？20 世纪 80 年代以来的研究表明，听睡前故事的孩子在读写方面远远胜过学校的同龄孩子。然而，英国只有不到 33% 的 2 至 8 岁的孩子能固定地在晚上睡觉前听段故事。如果大家想想 75% 的家长在那个年龄的时候都能在睡前听到故事，那么你们可能就会深思。

显然，我们没必要问自己所有这些痛苦、愤怒和暴力行为从何而来。显然，孩子们正在对这种忽视发出怒吼，以对

violent behavior comes from. It is self-evident that children are thundering against the neglect, quaking against the indifference and crying out just to be noticed. The various child protection agencies in the US say that millions of children are victims of **maltreatment** in the form of neglect, in the average year. Yes, neglect. In rich homes, privileged homes, wired **to the hilt** with every electronic **gadget**. Homes where parents come home, but they're not really home, because their heads are still at the office.

And their kids? Well, their kids just make do with whatever emotional **crumbs** they get. And you don't get much from endless TV, computer games and videos.

These hard, cold numbers which for me, **wrench** the soul and shake the spirit, should indicate to you why I have devoted so much of my time and resources into making our new Heal the Kids initiative a **colossal** success.

Our goal is simple — to recreate the parent-child bond, to renew its promise and light the way forward for all the beautiful children who are destined one day to walk this earth. But since this is my first public lecture, and you have so warmly welcomed me into your hearts, I feel that I want to tell you more. We each have our own story, and in that sense statistics can become personal.

They say that parenting is like dancing. You take one step, your child takes another. I have discovered that getting parents to re-dedicate themselves to their children is only half the story. The other half is preparing the children to re-accept their parents.

When I was very young I remember that we had this crazy **mutt** ... I remember we had this crazy dog, it was a mutt dog named "Black Girl," she was a mix of wolf and **retriever**. Not only wasn't she much of a guard dog, she was such a scared and nervous thing that it is a wonder she did not pass out every time a truck **rumbled** by, or a thunderstorm swept through Indiana. My sister Janet and I gave that dog so much love, but we never really won back the sense of trust that had been stolen by her previous owner. We knew he used to beat her. We didn't know with what. But whatever it was, it was enough to suck the spirit right out of that dog.

抗来自长辈的漠视，他们大声疾呼只是为了引起注意。在美国，各种儿童保护机构表示，平均每年有数百万儿童成为被忽视的受害者。没错，是被忽视的受害者！富有的家庭，享有特权的家庭，完全被电子器件束缚了。父母回到了家里，可是他们的心并不在家里，他们还想着工作上的事情。

那孩子们呢？啊，他们只好以所能得到的破碎的爱勉强生活。在无休止的电视节目、电脑游戏和录像带上又能得到多少感情呢！

我觉得，这些扭曲灵魂震撼心灵的冷酷无情的数字正好可以让大家明白，我为什么要花费这么多的时间和资源来使我们新成立的拯救儿童组织一开始就能获得巨大成功。

我们的目标很简单——重建父母与子女之间的融洽关系，重新许下承诺，为终究会在这个世界上留下脚印的孩子们照亮前行的道路。因为这是我第一次公开演讲，而你们又从心底里如此热情地欢迎我，我觉得应该告诉你们更多。我们每个人都有自己的故事，从那个意义上来说，统计资料就属于私人信息了。

有人说抚养孩子就像跳舞。你走一步，你的孩子跟一步。我发现让父母全心全意养育孩子只是故事的一半，另一半是父母还需要让孩子重新接受他们。

我记得在我小的时候，我们养了一条名叫"黑妞"的又疯又笨的狗，这种狗是狼和猎狗的杂交品种。她不仅不能看家，而且很胆小并且有点神经质，甚至对卡车的声音和印地安那的雷雨也恐惧不已。我和妹妹珍妮特对她非常怜爱，但是我们从没真正赢得过她的信任，这种信任感已经被她的前主人剥夺了。我们知道她以前的主人总是打她。虽然不知道用什么方式虐待她，但不管怎样，那已足以让这条狗精神崩溃。

如今许多儿童就像受过伤害的小狗一样，放弃对爱的追

热词空间

maltreatment
[ˌmælˈtriːtmənt] *n.* 虐待

to the hilt [hilt] 最大限度地；完全地

gadget [ˈgædʒit] *n.* 小玩意；小配件

crumb [krʌm] *n.* 面包屑，碎屑；少许

wrench [rentʃ] *vt.* 扭伤；扭曲；折磨

colossal [kəˈlɔsəl] *adj.* 巨大的；异常的，非常的

mutt [mʌt] *n.* [美俚] 杂种狗

retriever [riˈtriːvə] *n.* 猎犬

rumble [ˈrʌmbl] *vt.* 使隆隆响

A lot of kids today are hurt puppies who have **weaned** themselves off the need for love. They couldn't care less about their parents. Left to their own devices, they cherish their independence. They have moved on their life and have left their parents behind. Then there are the far worse cases of children who **harbor animosity** and **resentment** toward their parents, so that any **overture** that their parents might undertake would be thrown forcefully back in their face.

Tonight, I don't want any of us to make this mistake. That's why I'm calling upon all the world's children — beginning with all of us here tonight — to forgive our parents, if we felt neglected, FORGIVE. Forgive them and teach them how to love again.

You probably weren't surprised to hear that I did not have an **idyllic** childhood. The strain and tension that exists in my relationship with my own father is well documented. My father is a tough man and he pushed my brothers and me hard, really hard from the earliest age, for the best ... he wanted us to be the best performers we could possibly be.

He had great difficulty showing affection. He never really told me he loved me. And he never really complimented me either. If I did a great show, he would tell me it was a good show. And if I did an OK show, he would say nothing. He seemed intent, above all else, (I need a tissue, I'm sorry ...) He seemed intent ... (excuse me) He seemed intent, above all else, on making us a commercial success. At that he was more than adept.

My father was a **managerial** genius and my brothers and I owe our professional success, in no small measure, to the forceful way that he pushed us. He trained me as a showman and under his guidance I couldn't miss a step. But what I really wanted was a Dad. I wanted a father who showed me love. And my father never did that. He never said I love you while looking me straight in the eye. He never played a game with me. He never gave me a **piggyback** ride, he never threw a pillow at me, or a water balloon. But I remember once when I was about four years old, there was a little **carnival** and he picked me up and put me on a **pony**. It was a tiny gesture, probably

求。他们一点也不关心他们的父母。他们独来独往，捍卫自己的独立。他们不停地向前，而把父母抛在了后面。还有更糟的孩子，他们对父母充满敌意和怨恨，父母可能采取的任何提议都会被激烈地驳回。

今晚，我不希望我们之中的任何一个人犯这样的错误，这就是我为什么呼吁全世界的孩子——和我们今晚在场的人一起开始——宽恕我们的父母，如果我们觉得被忽略，那么宽恕他们并且教他们怎样爱。

听到我没有拥有幸福的童年时你们可能并不吃惊，因为许多资料表明我和我父亲的关系不好。我父亲是个严厉的人，我和我的哥哥们在很小的时候，他对我们非常严格，要求我们尽可能地成为好演员。

他不善于表达爱，他从未对我说过他爱我，也从未真正夸过我。如果我的表演很棒，他会说不错，如果我表演得还行，他就一言不发。他是如此地迫切，（抱歉我需要一张纸巾）他是如此迫切地让我们取得商业上的成功，而且他在这方面很内行。

我的父亲是个天才管理者，我和我的兄弟们事业上的每一步成功都源自于他对我们采取的强迫方式。他训练我当演员，在他的指导下，我一步都不允许出错。但我真正想要的只是一个名副其实的父亲，一个能向我展示爱的父亲。然而我的父亲却从未那样做过，在他直视着我时从不说爱我，他从未和我一起玩过游戏，也从来没有让我骑在他的背上玩耍。他不会亲昵地朝我扔枕头或水球。但我记得大约在我四岁那年的一个小的狂欢节，他把我抱起来放在小马上。那只是一个很小的举动，或许他五分钟就忘记了，但因为那一刻，他在我心里有了一个特别的位置。这就是孩子，很小的事情对他们意味着很多。对我来说，那一刻意味着一切。我仅仅经历过一次，但那一次让我对他和对世界的感觉都特别好！

热词空间

wean [wi:n] *vt.* 使放弃

harbor ['hɑ:bə] *vt.* 庇护;怀有

animosity [ˌæni'mɔsəti] *n.* 憎恶，仇恨，敌意

resentment [ri'zentmənt] *n.* 愤恨，怨恨

overture ['əuvəˌtjuə] *n.* 提议;序幕

idyllic [i'dilik] *adj.* 质朴宜人的，田园诗的

managerial [ˌmæni'dʒiəriəl] *adj.* 管理的;经理的

piggyback ['pigibæk] *adj.* 背着的;在背肩上的

carnival ['kɑ:nivəl] *n.* 狂欢节

pony ['pəuni] *n.* 矮种马;小型马

something he forgot five minutes later. But because of that one moment I have this special place in my heart for him. Because that's how kids are, the little things mean so much. They mean so much. For me, that one moment meant everything. I only experienced it one time, but that one time made me feel really good, about him and about the world.

But now I am a father myself, and one day I was thinking about my own children, Prince and Paris and how I wanted them to think of me when they grow up. To be sure, I would like them to remember how I always wanted them with me wherever I went, how I always tried to put them before everything else. But there are also challenges in their lives. Because my kids are **stalked** by **paparazzi**, they can't always go to a park or to a movie with me.

So what if they resent me when they grow older, and what if they resent how my choices impacted their youth? Why weren't we given an average childhood like all the other kids, they might ask? And at that moment I pray that my children will give me the benefit of the doubt. That they will say to themselves: "Our daddy did the best he could, given the unique circumstances that he faced. He may not have been perfect, but he was a warm and **decent** man, who tried to give us all the love in the world."

I hope that they will always focus on the positive things, on the sacrifices I willingly made for them, and not criticise the things they had to give up, or the errors I've made, and will certainly continue to make, in raising them. For we have all been someone's child, and we know that despite the very best of plans and efforts, mistakes will always occur. That's just being human.

And when I think about this, of how I hope that my children will not judge me unkindly, and will forgive me, forgive my shortcomings, I am forced to think of my own father and despite my earlier **denials**, I am forced to admit that he must have loved me. He did love me, and I know that. There were little things that showed it. When I was a kid I had a real sweet tooth — we all did. My father ... he did try. But my favorite food to satisfy my sweet tooth was **glazed doughnuts** and my father knew that. So every few weeks I would come downstairs in the morning and there on

现在我自己也当爸爸了，有一天我正在想着我自己的孩子普林斯和派瑞斯，想着我希望他们长大后怎样看我。我敢肯定，我希望他们能记得，不管我去哪儿，总想把他们带在身边，能记得我把他们看得比一切都重要。但他们的生活中也会有挑战。因为我的孩子们总是被狗仔队跟踪，他们不能经常和我去公园或去看电影。

所以如果他们长大了之后怨恨我怎么办呢？如果他们怨恨我的选择给他们的童年带来影响我该怎么办呢？他们也许会问，为什么我们没有和其他孩子一样的童年呢？在那一刻，我祈祷，我的孩子能够理解我。他们会对自己说："在那种特殊的环境下，我们的爸爸已经尽了他最大的努力。或许不完美，但他却是个温和而正派的人，他想把这世上所有的爱都给我们"。

我希望他们能总是把焦点放在那些积极的方面，放在我心甘情愿为他们做出的牺牲上，而不是抱怨他们不得不放弃一些事情，或批判我在抚养他们的过程中犯过的或将来不免要犯的错误。因为我们都是父母的孩子，而且我们都清楚，尽管有最好的计划和努力，错误也在所难免。人，孰能无过？

当我想到这个，想到我是多么希望我的孩子不会觉得我不够好，而且会原谅我，原谅我的缺点时，我不得不想起我自己的父亲，不管我之前怎样否定他，我必须承认他一定是爱我的。他的确爱我，我是知道的。这从一些小事就可以看出来，我小时候非常喜欢吃甜食——孩子们都这样。我父亲知道我最喜欢吃甜面包圈。于是每隔几个星期，当我早上从楼上下来时，我都会在橱柜上发现一袋面包圈——没有字条、没有说明——只有面包圈，就像是圣诞老人送来的礼物。

有时我想待到深夜，希望能看到他把甜面包圈放在那儿。但就像对待圣诞老人一样，我不想破坏那种奇迹，唯恐他不

热词空间

stalk [stɔːk] vt. 追踪，偷偷接近
paparazzi [ˌpɑːpəˈrɑːtsiː] n. 狗仔队
decent [ˈdiːsənt] adj. 正派的
denial [diˈnaiəl] n. 否定，拒绝
glazed [gleizd] adj. 光滑的
doughnut [ˈdəunʌt] n. 甜甜圈面包

the kitchen counter was a bag of glazed doughnuts — no note, no explanation — just the doughnuts. It was like Santa Claus.

Sometimes I would think about staying up late at night, so I could see him leave them there, but just like with Santa Claus, I didn't want to ruin the magic for fear that he would never do it again. My father had to leave them secretly at night, so as no one might catch him with his guard down. He was scared of human emotion, he didn't understand it or know how to deal with it. But he did know doughnuts.

And when I allow the **floodgates** to open up, there are other memories that come rushing back, memories of other tiny gestures, however imperfect, that showed that he did what he could. So tonight, rather than focusing on what my father did not do, I want to focus on all the things he did do and on his own personal challenges. I want to stop judging him.

I have started reflecting on the fact that my father grew up in the South, in a very poor family. He came of age during the Depression and his own father, who struggled to feed his children, showed little affection towards his family and raised him. He raised my father and his **siblings** with an iron fist. Who could have imagined what it was like to grow up a poor black man in the South, robbed of dignity, **bereft** of hope, struggling to become a man in a world that saw my father as **subordinate**. I ... I was the first black artist to be played on MTV and I remember how big a deal it was even then. And that was in the 1980s!

My father moved to Indiana and had a large family of his own, working long hours in the **steel mills**, work that kills the lungs and humbles the spirit, all to support his family. Is it any wonder that he found it difficult to expose his feelings? Is it any mystery that he hardened his heart, that he raised the emotional **ramparts**? And most of all, is it any wonder why he pushed his sons so hard to succeed as performers, so that they could be saved from what he knew to be a life of indignity and poverty? I have begun to see that even my father's **harshness** was a kind of love, an imperfect love, to be sure, but love nonetheless. He pushed me because he loved me. Because he wanted no man ever to look down at his **offspring**.

再那样做。我父亲得在晚上悄悄地把它们留在那里，不想让任何人知道。他害怕提及人类的情感，他不懂也不知道怎么处理感情，但他懂得甜面包圈对我的意义。

当我打开记忆的闸门时，更多的回忆涌现出来，那些关于一些微妙举动的记忆，尽管已经不太清晰，但也足以表明他在尽力而为。所以今晚，我不想专注于我父亲所没有做到的，我想专注于所有他历尽艰难尽力做到的事情。我想停止对他的判断。

我回想我的父亲是在南方一个非常贫穷的家庭长大的。他来自大萧条时期，而他自己的父亲艰难地养育着孩子，也没有对家人表现出多少慈爱，我父亲和他的兄弟姐妹是在我爷爷的铁拳下长大的。谁能想到一个在南方长大的贫穷的黑人的处境是怎样的？被剥夺了尊严，失去希望，想拼力在这个视我父亲为下等人的世界里争得立足之地。我是第一个登上音乐电视台的黑人艺人。我还记得那有多艰难，那还是在20 世纪80 年代！

后来我父亲搬到印地安那州并且有了自己的大家庭。他在炼钢厂长时间地工作，那种工作很低下，而且对肺有损害，这一切都是为了养家。难怪，他很难表露自己的感情。于是，他的心肠变硬了，他树起了感情壁垒，这一切都不足为怪，不是吗？于是，他逼他的儿子们成为成功的演员，就是为了让他们不再过他所知道的那种没有尊严只有贫困的生活，这一切还奇怪吗？我开始明白，就连父亲的咆哮也是一种爱，尽管肯定是一种不完美的爱。他逼我是因为他爱我，他不希望有人会鄙视他的后代。

现在，我不再感到痛苦，我感觉很幸福。在愤怒中，我

热词空间

floodgate ['flʌdgeit] *n.* 水闸

sibling ['sibliŋ] *n.* 兄弟姊妹

bereave [bi'ri:v] *vt.* 使……失去；使……孤寂

bereft [bi'rɛft] *vt.* 失去……（bereave 的过去式）

subordinate [sə'bɔ:dinət] *n.* 附属，下级

steel mill 钢厂

rampart ['ræmpɑ:t] *n.* 壁垒

harshness ['hɑ:ʃnis] *n.* 严肃

offspring ['ɔfspriŋ] *n.* 后代，子孙

哈佛
大学

斯坦福
大　学

牛津
大学

耶鲁
大学

杜兰
大学

杜克
大学

威斯康
辛大学

清华
大学

北京
大学

亚利桑
那州立
大　学

加利福
尼　亚
大　学

And now with time, rather than bitterness, I feel blessing. In the place of anger, I have found **absolution**. And in the place of **revenge** I have found **reconciliation**. And my initial **fury** has slowly given way to forgiveness.

Almost a decade ago, I founded a children's charity called Heal the World. The title was something I felt inside me. Little did I know, as Shmuley later pointed out, that those two words form the **cornerstone** of *Old Testament* **prophecy**. Do I really believe that we can heal this world, that is riddled with war and **genocide**, even today? And do I really think that we can heal our children, the same children who as the papers reported this morning, can walk into a high school in San Diego and shoot down two beautiful students, just at the beginning of their lives? A horrifying reminder of the guns and hatred that shot through *Columbine* almost two years ago. Or children can beat a defenseless **toddler** to death, like the tragic story of Jamie Bulger? Of course I do. Of course I do, or I wouldn't be here tonight. But it all begins with forgiveness, because to heal the world, we first have to heal ourselves. And to heal the kids, we first have to heal the child within, each and every one of us. As an adult, and as a parent, I realize that I cannot be a whole human being, nor a parent capable of unconditional love, until I put to rest the ghosts of my own childhood.

And that's what I'm asking all of us to do tonight. Live up to the fifth of the Ten Commandments, "Honor your parents by not judging them. Give them the benefit of the doubt."

That is why I want to forgive my father and to stop judging him. I want to forgive my father, because I want a father, and this is the only one that I've got. I want the weight of my past lifted from my shoulders and I want to be free to step into a new relationship with my father, for the rest of my life, **unhindered** by the **goblins** of the past.

In a world filled with hate, we must still dare to hope. Keep hope alive. In a world filled with anger, we must still dare to comfort. In a world filled with despair, we must still dare to dream. And in a world filled with distrust, we must still dare to believe.

发现了宽恕，在报复中，我发现了和解，就连最初的愤怒也慢慢变成了宽恕。

差不多在十年前，我成立了一个叫作"拯救世界"的儿童慈善机构，这个机构的名字本身只是我内心的感觉。直到施慕礼告诉我，我才知道这两个词构成了《圣经》旧约预言的基石。我真的能相信我们能拯救这个因战争和种族灭绝屠杀而变得千疮百孔的世界吗？我真的相信我们能够拯救孩子吗？正如今早报纸报导的那样，正是这些孩子走进圣地亚哥的一所高中向两位漂亮的同学开枪，结束了他们年轻的生命。这些孩子能被拯救吗？这让人想起了大约两年前《科伦拜恩》里演的枪支和愤怒的可怕场面。或者说我们能拯救那些像杰米·巴尔格的悲剧故事一样，把毫无防御能力的蹒跚学步的小孩打死的孩子吗？当然可以。当然可以，否则我今晚就不会站在这里。但是这一切都要从宽恕开始，因为要拯救世界我们必须先拯救自己。而要拯救儿童，我们首先要拯救孩子的内心，我们每一个人都有责任这样做。作为一个成年人，作为一名父亲，我知道我并不完美，也不能给予孩子无条件的爱，直到我把自己对童年的怨恨完全释放出来。

这也是今晚我希望你们所有人能做到的事情。做到《圣经》十诫（犹太教、基督教的戒条；是上帝对以色列所讲的戒律，在西奈山上启示给摩西）中的第五戒：当孝敬父母。尊敬你们的父母而不要给予评判。要想着你们的父母是好的。

这就是我要宽恕我的父亲并且不再评论他的原因。我想要原谅他，因为我只想要一个"父亲"，而这也是我唯一得到的。在我的余生，我想卸掉一切包袱和我父亲和好，我想摆脱过去的阴影。

即使世界充满仇恨，我们也要勇于憧憬，让希望永存；即使世界充满愤怒，我们也要敢于安慰；即使世界充满绝望，我们也要勇于梦想；即使世界充满猜疑，我们仍然敢于信任。

今晚，你们当中因父母而失望的人，我希望你们不再失望；

热词空间

absolution [,æbsə'lju:ʃən] *n.* 宽恕

revenge [ri'vendʒ] *n.* 报复；复仇

reconciliation [,rekənsili'eiʃən] *n.* 和解；和谐

fury ['fjuəri] *n.* 狂怒；暴怒

cornerstone ['kɔːnə,stəun] *n.* 基础；柱石

prophecy ['prɔfisi] *n.* 预言

genocide ['dʒenəusaid] *n.* 种族灭绝；灭绝整个种族的大屠杀

toddler ['tɔdlə] *n.* 学步的小孩

unhindered [ʌn'hindəd] *adj.* 不受阻碍的

goblin ['gɔblin] *n.* 小妖精

To all of you tonight who feel let down by your parents, I ask you to let down your disappointment. To all of you tonight who feel cheated by your fathers or mothers, I ask you not to cheat yourself further. And to all of you who wish to push your parents away, I ask you to extend your hand to them instead. I am asking you, I am asking myself, to give our parents the gift of unconditional love, so that they too may learn how to love from us, their children. So that love will finally be restored to a **desolate** and lonely world.

Shmuley once mentioned to me an ancient Biblical prophecy which says that a new world and a new time would come, when "the hearts of the parents would be restored through the hearts of their children". My friends, we are that world, we are those children.

Mahatma Gandhi said, "The weak can never forgive. Forgiveness is the attribute of the strong." Tonight, be strong. Beyond being strong, rise to the greatest challenge of all — to restore that broken **covenant**. We must all overcome whatever **crippling** effects our childhoods may have had on our lives and in the words of Jesse Jackson, forgive each other, **redeem** each other and move on.

This call for forgiveness may not result in Oprah moments the world over, with thousands of children **making up with** their parents, but it will at least be a start, We'll all be so much happier as a result.

And so ladies and gentlemen, I conclude my remarks tonight with faith, with joy and excitement.

From this day forward, let a new song be heard.

Let that new song be the sound of children laughing.

Let that new song be the sound of children playing.

Let that new song be the sound of children singing.

And let that new song be the sound of parents listening.

今晚，你们所有曾感觉被父母亲欺骗的人，我希望你们不要再欺骗自己；你们当中希望远离父母的人，我希望你们向他们伸出爱的双手。我在要求你，也在要求我自己，无条件地去爱我们的父母，这样他们会从自己的孩子这里学会如何去爱。这样，爱最终会改变这个冷漠的世界。

施慕礼有一次曾向我提到《圣经》中的一段预言，"当父母的心能被他们的孩子拯救时"，一个新的世界、一个新的时代就会到来。朋友们，我们就是那个新的世界，我们就是那些拯救父母心灵的孩子。

圣雄甘地曾说："弱者从不原谅，宽恕是强者的特质。"今晚，让我们做一个强者，去迎接最大的挑战——去修复那已经被破坏了的亲子盟约。我们必须克服一切我们的童年对我们的生活所造成的严重影响。用杰西·杰克逊（美国黑人民权领袖和演说家）的话来说，就是彼此宽恕，互相救赎，继续生活下去。

呼吁宽恕或许不会带来奥普拉时代的重现，不会让成千上万的孩子与他们的父母重归于好，但这至少是一个开始，最终我们会为这个开始感到更加幸福。

好了，女士们，先生们，我满怀信念、愉悦和激动来总结我今晚的讲话。

从今往后，可以听到一首新歌。

让这首新歌成为孩子们欢笑的声音。

让这首新歌成为孩子们玩耍的声音。

让这首新歌成为孩子们歌唱的声音。

让这首新歌成为父母们聆听的声音。

热词空间

desolate ['desəleit] *adj.* 荒凉的

covenant ['kʌvənənt] *n.* 契约，盟约

crippling ['kripliŋ] *adj.* 造成严重后果的

redeem [ri'di:m] *vt.* 补偿

make up with sb. 与某人重修于好

迈克尔·杰克逊给我们的 启示

Human knowledge consists not only of libraries of parchment and ink — it is also comprised of the volumes of knowledge that are written on the human heart, chiseled on the human soul, and engraved on the human psyche.

人类文明不仅仅是图书馆中纸墨所记载的——还包括那些书写在人们内心的，凿刻在人们灵魂里和精神中的知识。

Love is the human family's most precious legacy, its richest bequest, its golden inheritance. And it is a treasure that is handed down from one generation to another.

爱是人类家庭最珍贵的遗产，是最贵重的馈赠，是最无价的传统，是我们应该世代相传的财富。

They were lit bright with the glow of love and they were warmed snugly by the very heat of the human heart.

但他们不会觉得黑暗，也不会觉得寒冷。爱的光芒照亮了他们的房间，炽热的心灵温暖了他们的身体。

Friends, the foundation of all human knowledge, the beginning of human consciousness, must be that each and every one of us is an object of love.

朋友们，所有人类知识的基本原则，人类意识的起点必然是我们每一个人都成为被爱的对象。

If you enter this world knowing you are loved and you leave this world knowing the same, then everything that happens in between can he dealt with.

如果你降临或离开这个世界时都感到被爱着，那么其间发生的一切事情你都可以应付。

Our goal is simple — to recreate the parent-child bond, renew its promise and light the way forward for all the beautiful children who are destined one day to walk this earth.

我们的目标很简单——重建父母与子女之间的融洽关系，重新许下承诺，为终究会在这个世界上留下脚印的孩子们照亮前行的道路。

耶鲁大学

校训：Lux et Veritas（拉丁文，意为"光明和真理"）

总　括

耶鲁大学是一所坐落于美国康涅狄格州纽黑文市的私立大学，始创于1701年，初名"大学学院"，于1718年为感谢捐助者伊利胡·耶鲁而更名为"耶鲁大学"。它和哈佛大学、普林斯顿大学齐名，历年来共同角逐美国大学和研究生院前三名的位置。耶鲁大学是美国历史上建立的第三所大学，今为常春藤联盟的成员之一。在美国历史上，有5位总统毕业于耶鲁：威廉·霍华德·塔夫脱、杰拉尔德·鲁道夫·福特、乔治·布什、比尔·克林顿、乔治·沃克·布什。耶鲁凭借其优秀的学子创造了一个政坛的奇迹。所以，耶鲁素有"总统摇篮"之称。教员之间经常开的玩笑就是："一不小心，你就会教出一个总统来。"

Cherishing What You Have Now, and Striving for the Future

珍惜现在，把握未来

Yale University
Commencement Address
Tony Blair
May, 2008

背景资料

英国前首相布莱尔2008年5月在美国耶鲁大学演讲，他在演讲中呼吁与中印两国建立合作伙伴关系。布莱尔还表示，台下毕业生将面对气候转变、粮食短缺、人口增长和涉及宗教的恐怖主义等国际议题，呼吁他们要追求有意义的人生。他还号召毕业生要做一个实干家而不是评论家，要勇于承担责任，要时刻准备迎接新的生活、不断思考、积极行动。

Be prepared to fail as well as to succeed, because it is failure not success that defines character.

不仅要接受成功，也要准备经历失败。因为是失败而非成功塑造了性格。

—— 托尼·布莱尔

姓　　名：	托尼·布莱尔（Tony Blair）
性　　别：	男
职　　业：	英国前首相
国　　籍：	英国
出生日期：	1953 年 5 月 6 日
毕业学校：	牛津大学圣约翰学院法律系
成功点睛：	年轻的面孔、乐观的精神促成了他政治上的成功
个人成就：	工党历史上在任时间最长的英国首相

名人 简介

　　布莱尔 1953 年出生于苏格兰的爱丁堡，1983 年进入下议院，开始了他的政治生涯。他先后任财政、贸工、能源和就业事务副发言人，1992 年起任内政事务发言人。他 1994 年当选工党领袖。布莱尔是工党历史上最年轻的领袖。1997 年 5 月任首相，成为自 1812 年以来英国最年轻的首相，后兼任首席财政大臣和文官部大臣。他出任首相后，对工党大胆进行革新，对原保守党政府的内外政策进行了一系列调整。2001 年 6 月在大选中再次获胜，连任首相，成为英国历史上首位连任的工党首相。

　　布莱尔是 20 世纪英国第一个在唐宁街生子育儿的在职首相。1998 年 12 月 26 日布莱尔成为第一位在爱尔兰议会发表演说的英国首相。布莱尔是工党历史上在任时间最长的英国首相，也是该党唯一一位带领工党连续 3 次赢得大选的首相。

　　布莱尔对法律、工会、税收、贸易、能源、就业、犯罪等问题感兴趣；喜欢读书，爱好网球和音乐；著有《新英国，我眼中的年轻国家》等书。

Thank you very much to thee. Thank you. It's a... so: after over 100 years of Class Days, finally you get a British speaker.

What took you so long? Did that little disagreement of 1776 **rankle** so much? And why now? Is it because British election campaigns only last four weeks long? For whatever reason, it is an honour to be here and to say to the Yale College Class of 2008: you did it; you **came through**; from all of us to all of you: congratulations, well done.

The invitation to a former British Prime Minister to address a college which boasts five former Presidents, many former Vice Presidents, Senators too numerous to mention, is either to give me an **exaggerated** sense of my own importance or you a reduced sense of yours.

It was Churchill or Oscar Wilde — and there is a difference — who called us two nations divided by a common language as you maybe judge me by the show and so we are.

Here I am at Yale and set to come back for the fall semester. My old Oxford tutor was, I'm afraid, **horrified** to hear I had been taken on by Yale. His worries were all for Yale I may say. He said, "I only hope for their sake you are going there to learn rather than to teach."

Now I know you Yale guys are smart. So what can I tell you that you don't already think you know?

I can tell you something of the world as I see it. Three days ago, in my role as Middle East **envoy**, I stood in the heart of Bethlehem. On one side of me, lay the concrete barrier which now separates Israel and Palestine. On the other, the historic birthplace of Jesus and the land of Palestine beyond.

A few days before that, I was in Jericho. If you look up from the town centre, to the left is the Mount of Temptation, where Jesus spent 40 days and 40 nights. To the right, you can see Mount Nebo where Moses looked down on the Promised Land. And right in front of you is the Valley of Jordan.

热词空间

rankle ['ræŋkl] vi. 怨恨

come through 成功

exaggerated [ig'zædʒəreitid] adj. 夸大的

horrified ['hɔrifaid] adj. 惊骇的

envoy ['envɔi] n. 使者

谢谢你们，谢谢你们。这……100 多年过去了，你们终于迎来了一位英国演讲者。

是什么让你们等了这么长时间？难道是因为 1776 年那次小小分歧而耿耿于怀？那为什么又选择现在呢？难道是因为英国的大选仅仅持续了四个星期？无论出于何种原因，能来到这里让我倍感荣幸。耶鲁大学 2008 届的毕业生们，我想对你们说：你们顺利完成了学业，你们取得了成功，我们大家都要恭喜你们，你们干得非常好。

贵校培养出了 5 位美国总统、很多副总统和难以数计的参议员，却邀请一位英国前首相来发表演讲，这要么是夸大了我的重要性，要么就是减小了你们的重要性。

是丘吉尔还是奥斯卡·王尔德——这两人当然是有区别的——把英美两国说成是由一种相同的语言划分的两个不同的国家，你们可以从我今天的出场来判断这一点，事实确实如此。

现在我来到耶鲁，并打算今年秋天来这里任职。我恐怕，我在牛津的老导师听到我在耶鲁任职会感到惊骇。我可以说，他的担忧全是为了耶鲁。他说：“为了耶鲁，我只希望你是去那儿学习，而不是教书。”

我知道耶鲁学子充满智慧，所以我能说的有哪些是你们认为自己不知道的呢？

我可以给你们讲讲我眼中的世界。三天前，我作为中东特使去了伯利恒市中心。我的一侧矗立着混凝土筑成的隔离墙，隔开了以色列和巴勒斯坦。而另一侧则是历史上著名的耶稣降生地，和远处巴勒斯坦的土地。

那之前的几天，我在杰里科。从那个小镇中心仰望，在左侧你会看到诱惑山，耶稣在那儿整整度过 40 个日日夜夜。在右侧，则会看到尼泊山，摩西就是在那儿俯视着上帝许给犹太人的迦南地。而在正前方则是约旦河谷。

哈佛
大学

斯坦福
大学

牛津
大学

耶鲁
大学

杜兰
大学

杜克
大学

威斯康
辛大学

清华
大学

北京
大学

亚利桑
那州立
大学

加利福
尼亚
大学

My guide, a Muslim, turned to me and said, "Moses, Jesus, Mohammed — why in God's name did they all have to come here?"

But in God's name they came and for centuries their followers have waged war in the name of prophets whose life work was in pursuit of peace.

Today, though the land that encompasses Israel and Palestine which is small, has the conflict which symbolizes the wider prospects of the entire vast region of the Middle East and beyond. There, the forces of modernisation and moderation battle with those of reaction and extremism and the shadow of Iran looms large.

What is at stake is immense. Will those who believe in peaceful co-existence triumph, matching the growing economic power and wealth with a politics and culture at ease with the 21st Century? Or will the victors be those that seek to use that economic power to create a politics and culture more relevant to the feudal Middle Ages?

Thousands of miles from here, this struggle is being played out in the suburbs of Baghdad and Beirut and the Gaza strip. But the impact of its outcome on our security here and our way of life here will register in the core of our well-being.

In fact, if I had to sum up my view of the world, I would say to you: turn your thoughts to the East. Not just to the Middle East. But to the Far East.

For the first time in many centuries, power is moving East. China and India each have populations roughly double those of America and Europe combined.

In the next two decades, those two countries together will undergo induztrialisation four times the size of the USA's and at five times the speed.

We must be mindful that as these ancient civilizations become some how younger and more vibrant, our young civilization does not grow old. Most of all we should know that in this new world, we must clear a path to partnership, not stand off against each other, competing for power.

The world in which you, in time to come, will take the reins, cannot afford a return to the 20th century struggles for hegemony.

我的向导，一位穆斯林，问我，"摩西、耶稣、穆罕默德——为什么都要以上帝的名义来到这里呢？"

然而，以上帝的名义，他们确实来了，而且数世纪以来，他们的追随者以先知的名义发动战争，尽管先知用毕生追求和平。

如今，虽然以色列和巴勒斯坦的国土面积很小，但它们之间的冲突却象征了更广泛的、整个中东地区的局势。在那里，现代化和中庸派正与反动势力和极端主义对峙。伊朗的阴影正在扩大。

危机重重，信仰和平共存的人们会取得胜利吗？日益增长的经济与财富能够与 21 世纪的政治和文化融合吗？或者胜利者会是那些企图用经济力量创造类似中世纪的封建政治和文化的人吗？

离这儿千里之外的地方，在巴格达、贝鲁特的郊区和加沙地带，这种斗争正在上演。但这种斗争的结果会对我们的安全、生活方式及我们的幸福产生影响。

事实上，如果必须要总结一下我对世界的看法，我要对你们说：把目光转向东方，不仅仅是中东，还有远东。

几个世纪以来，东方的势力第一次逐渐崛起。中国和印度的人口都几乎是美国和欧洲人口总和的两倍。

在未来的 20 年里，这两个国家的工业化进程在规模上将会是美国的四倍，在速度上将会是美国的五倍。

我们要注意到，这些文明古国正逐渐成为更年轻更有生机的国家，当然我们的文明并没有衰落。最重要的是，我们应该知道，在这个崭新的世界，我们必须开拓合作伙伴关系之路，而不应互相敌对、争权夺利。

即将到来的时代是你们掌控的时代，绝不能退回到 20 世纪的霸权争夺中去。

如今这个世界的特点是全球化的速度、范围和规模。全

热词空间

wage [weidʒ] vi. 进行；发动
prophet ['prɔfit] n. 先知
encompass [in'kʌmpəs] vt. 环绕；包含
loom [lu:m] vi. 可怕地出现
civilization [ˌsivilai'zeiʃən] n. 文明
vibrant ['vaibrənt] adj. 充满生机的
take the reins 支配；掌握
hegemony [hi'geməni] n. 霸权；领导权

The characteristic of this world is the pace, scope and scale of globalization. Globalization is driving this change and people are driving globalisation.

The consequence is that the world opens up; its boundaries diminish; we are pushed close together.

The conclusion is that we make it work together or not at all.

The issues you will **wrestle** with — the threat of climate change, food **scarcity**, population growth, worldwide terror based on religion, the **interdependence** of the world economy — my student generation would barely recognize. But the difference today is that they are all essentially global in nature.

You understand this. Yale has become a melting pot of culture, and language and civilization. You are the global generation. So be global citizens.

Each new generation finds the world they enter. But they **fashion** the world they leave. So what do you inherit and what do you pass on?

The history of humankind is marked by great events but it's written by great people. People like you.

Given Yale's record of achievement, perhaps by you.

So to you as individuals then, what wisdom, if any, have I learnt?

First, in fact, keep learning. Always **be alive to** the possibilities of the next experience, of thinking, doing and being.

When the Buddha was asked, near the end of his life, to describe his secret, he answered **bluntly**: "I'm awake."

So be awake. Understand conventional wisdom, but be prepared to change it.

Feel as well as analyse; use your **instinct** alongside your reason. Calculate too much and you will miscalculate.

Be prepared to fail as well as to succeed, because it is failure not success that **defines** character.

I spent years trying to be a politician failing at every attempt and nearly gave up.

球化正在推动着社会的变革，而人类正在推动着全球化进程。

全球化的结果是世界的开放，国界的削弱，我们彼此更将紧密相连。

结论就是，我们如果不同心协力争取成功，就会毫无所获。

如今你们面临着许多挑战——气候变化所造成的威胁、食品匮乏、人口增长、基于宗教信仰而引起的全球性恐怖袭击以及世界经济的相互依存等——而我们那一代人几乎没有意识到这些问题。如今这些问题在本质上都是全球性的，这也是与以往的不同之处。

你们对这一点了然于心。耶鲁已经成为文化、语言与文明的大熔炉。你们这一代人属于全世界，所以你们要成为世界的公民。

新的一代拥有它们所处的世界，并在离开时改变了这个世界。那么，你们继承了什么样的世界，又将给后人留下什么样的世界呢？

人类历史由重大事件标记，却由伟大的人类来谱写。由像你们一样优秀的人类谱写。

或许成就耶鲁的重大责任就落在你们肩上了。

那么，你们作为个人，又学到了什么样的智慧呢？

事实上，首先就是要不断学习。要时刻准备迎接新的生活、不断思考、积极行动。

佛陀临终前，人们要求他讲述成为圣人的秘诀，他坦率地说："因为我头脑清醒"。

所以，要保持头脑清醒。要了解传统的智慧，但要准备改变它。

不仅要学会分析，还要学着用心感受。直觉与推理并存，因为算计太多难免会出错。

不仅要接受成功，也要准备经历失败。因为是失败而非成功塑造了性格。

多年来我为了立足政坛一直在不断努力，但却屡遭失败，以致我几乎想要放弃。我知道你们一定在想：我本来就应该

热词空间

wrestle ['resl] *vi.* 摔跤；与……搏斗

scarcity ['skeəsəti] *n.* 不足；缺乏

interdependence [,intədi'pendəns] *n.* 互相依赖

fashion ['fæʃən] *vt.* 改变

be alive to 对……敏感；发觉，关心

bluntly ['blʌntli] *adv.* 坦率地，直率地

instinct ['instiŋkt] *n.* 本能，直觉

define [di'fain] *vt.* 定义；规定

I know you're thinking: I should have.

Sir **Paul McCartney** reminded me that the first record company the **Beatles** approached **rejected** them as a band no one would want to listen to.

Be good to people on your way up because you never know if you will meet them again on your way down.

Judge someone by how they treat those below them not those above them.

Be a firm friend not a **fair-weather** friend. It is your friendships, including those here at Yale, at this time, that will **sustain** and enrich the human spirit.

A good test of a person is who turns up at their funeral and with what **sincerity**. Try not to sit the test too early, of course.

Recently, I attended a **funeral** and the speaker said he would like to begin by reading a list of all those whose funerals he would rather have been attending, but the list was too long. It was a kind of sweet **compliment** to our friend.

Alternatively there was Spike Milligan, the **quintessential** English comic who when he was asked what he would like as the **epitaph** on his tombstone, replied, "They should write: I told you I was ill."

There was a colleague of mine in the British **Parliament** who once asked another: "Why do people take such an **instant** dislike to me?", and got the reply, "Because it saves time."

So, when others think of you, let them think not with their lips but their hearts of a good friend and a **gracious acquaintance**.

Above all, however, have a purpose in life. Life is not about living but about striving. When you get up, get up motivated. Live with a **perpetual** sense of urgency. And make at least part of that purpose about something bigger than you.

There are great careers. There are also great causes.

At least let some of them into your lives. Giving lifts the heart in a way that getting never can. Maybe it really was Oscar Wilde who said, "No one ever died,

放弃。

保罗·麦卡特尼先生提醒我，甲壳虫乐队联系的第一家唱片公司把他们拒之门外，理由是没人想听他们这样的音乐。

当你事业顺利的时候要善待他人，因为你永远不会知道，你遭遇挫折的时候是否会遇到他们。

评价一个人，要看他们怎样对待比自己地位低的人，而不是看他们怎样对待地位比自己高的人。

要做一个可靠的朋友，而不是靠不住的酒肉朋友。是友谊，包括现在你们在耶鲁大学结交的朋友之间的友谊，维持并丰富着人类精神。

考验一个人是否可靠的好方法是看他是否会参加你的葬礼，在葬礼上是否虔诚。当然不要太早就开始考验。

最近我参加了一个葬礼，主持人说在葬礼开始前他想先读一个名单，名单上这些人的葬礼他本该去参加的，结果却没去。这个名单很长。这对我的朋友来说也算是一种高度的赞美了。

还有一件事，当英国著名的喜剧演员斯派克·密歇根被问及希望在自己的墓碑上刻什么样的碑文时，他答道：他们应该写"我都说过我生病了。"

我在英国议会的一个同事问另一个同事："为什么人们这么快就不喜欢我了？"他得到的回答是："因为这样节省时间。"

所以你们要做到，当别人想起你的时候，让他们站在一个好朋友和一个亲切的相识的角度上去评价你，而不是随便说说。

然而，最重要的是，生活要有目标。生活不仅仅是活着，而是要不断追求。每天早晨起来时都要带着一种动机。生活要时刻有紧迫感。而且在制定个人目标时，至少有一部分要超出个人能力范围。

有伟大的事业，也要有伟大的理想。

至少要让其中的一部分理想融入你们的生活。给予可以

热词空间

Paul McCartney 保罗·麦卡特尼（大英帝国最高骑士勋章的拥有者）

Beatles ['bi:tlz] n. 甲壳虫乐队（摇滚乐队）

reject [ri'dʒekt] vt. 拒绝；抵制

fair-weather ['fɛə,weðə] adj. 只能同安乐不可共患难的

sustain [sə'stein] vt. 维持；支撑

sincerity [sin'siərəti] n. 真诚；诚挚

funeral ['fju:nərəl] n. 葬礼

compliment ['kɔmplimənt] n. 恭维；称赞

quintessential [,kwintə'senʃəl] adj. 精髓的，精萃的

epitaph ['epitɑ:f] n. 碑文，墓志铭

parliament ['pɑ:ləmənt] n. 议会，国会

instant ['instənt] adj. 立即的；紧急的；紧迫的

gracious ['greiʃəs] adj. 亲切的；高尚的；和蔼的

acquaintance [ə'kweintəns] n. 熟人；相识

perpetual [pə'petjuəl] adj. 永久的；不断的

哈佛
大学

斯坦福
大　学

牛津
大学

耶鲁
大学

杜兰
大学

杜克
大学

威斯康
辛大学

清华
大学

北京
大学

亚利桑
那州立
大　学

加利福
尼　亚
大　学

saying if only I had one more day at the office."

One small but shocking sentence: each year three million children die in Africa from preventable disease or conflict.

The key word? Preventable.

When all is said and done, there is usually more said than done.

So be a doer and not a **commentator**. **Seek** responsibility rather than shirk it. People often ask me about leadership, and I say, leadership is about wanting the responsibility to be on your shoulders, not ignoring its weight but knowing someone has to carry it and, reaching out for that person to be you. Leaders are heat-seekers not **heat-deflectors**.

And luck?

You have all the luck you need. You are here, at Yale, and what — apart from the hats — could be better?

You have something else: your parents.

You know when you are your age, you can never imagine being our age. But believe me, when you're our age we remember clearly being your age. That's why I am so careful about young men and my daughter, "Don't tell me what you're thinking. I know what you're thinking."

But as a parent, let me tell you something about parents. Despite all **rational impulses**, despite all evidence to the **contrary** , despite what we think you do to us and what you think we do to you — and yes, it is often hell on both sides — the plain, **unvarnished** truth is that we love you. Simply, **profoundly**, and **utterly**.

I remember, back in the mists of time, yes, the parents, you see. Yeah. And you love them too, Daniel. I remember, back in the mist of time, my Dad greeting me off the train at Durham railway station. I was a student at Oxford. Oxford and Cambridge are for Britain kind of like Yale and Harvard, only more so. So it was a big deal. I had been away for my first year and I was coming home.

提升心灵，而索取在某种程度上永远不可能做到。或许真的像奥斯卡·王尔德所说的那样："渴望再多工作一天的人就不会死去。"

有一句虽简短却很震撼的话：非洲每天有 300 万儿童死于可预防性疾病和暴力冲突。

关键词是什么呢？是"可预防的"。

当谈及言出必行时，人们通常都是说得多做得少。

要做一个实干家而不是评论家。要勇于承担责任，不要逃避退缩。人们经常问我关于领导力的事情，我说，领导力就是想要肩负责任，而不是忽视责任之重；领导力就是知道必须有人站出来承担责任，而且要努力成为那个人。领导者是勇于承担责任而非逃避责任的人。

那运气呢？

你们具备成功所需的一切运气。你们在耶鲁学习生活——还有什么比拥有耶鲁大学的桂冠更幸运的呢？

你们还拥有其他的，比如你们的父母。

你们在这个年龄的时候很难想象我们这个年龄的人的状况。但请相信我，当你们像我这么大时，我还能清楚记得我们在你们这个年龄所经历过的事情。这就是我如此关心年轻人和我的女儿的原因，"不要告诉我你们在想什么，我知道你们在想什么。"

但作为家长，让我告诉你们关于父母的一些事情。尽管父母会有一些合理的冲动行为，尽管所有的证据都证明父母的有些行为是不对的，尽管我们都认为对方的所作所为令自己不满意——而且有时候双方都觉得很伤心——但有一点是简单而朴实的，那就是我们爱你。这种爱朴实无华却又深刻而彻底。

回顾过去，我记得，是的，你知道的，我的父母，你也爱他们，丹尼尔。回顾过去，我记得有一次我父亲到达拉姆火车站接我。那时，我在牛津大学上学。牛津大学和剑桥大

热词空间

commentator ['kɔmenteitə] n. 评论员

seek [si:k] vt. 寻求；寻找；探索

heat-deflector 挡热板

rational ['ræʃənəl] adj. 合理的；理性的

impulse ['impʌls] n. 冲动

contrary ['kɔntrəri] n. 相反；反面

unvarnished [ˌʌn'vɑːniʃt] adj. 未加修饰的；朴实的

profoundly [prəu'faundli] adv. 深刻地

utterly ['ʌtəli] adv. 完全地；绝对地

哈佛
大学

斯坦福
大 学

牛津
大学

耶鲁
大学

杜兰
大学

杜克
大学

威斯康
辛大学

清华
大学

北京
大学

亚利桑
那州立
大 学

加利福
尼 亚
大 学

I stepped off the train. My hair was roughly the length of Rumpelstiltskin's and unwashed. I had no shoes and no shirt. My jeans were torn — and this was in the days before this became a fashion item. Worst of all, we just moved house. Mum had thrown out the sitting room drapes. I had retrieved them and made a sleeveless long coat with them.

My Dad greeted me. There were all his friends at the station. Beside me, their kids looked like paragons of respectability.

He saw the drapes, and visibly winced. They did kind of stand out. So I took pity on him.

"Dad", I said. "There is good news. I don't do drugs."

My father looked me in the eye and said: "Son, the bad news is if you're looking like this and you're not doing drugs we've got a real problem."

So your parents look at you today with love. They know how hard it is to make the grade and they respect you for making it.

And tomorrow as I know, as a parent of one of the graduates of this class, as you receive your graduation, their hearts will beat with the natural rhythm of pride. Pride in what you have achieved. Pride in who you are.

They will be nervous for you, as you stand on the threshold of a new adventure for they know the many obstacles that lie ahead.

But they will be confident that you can surmount those obstacles, for they know also the strength of character and of spirit that has taken you thus far.

So to my fellow parents: I say, let us rejoice and be glad together.

And to the Yale College Class of 2008, I say: well done. May blessings and good fortune be yours in all the years to come. Thank you very much indeed.

学对英国人就像耶鲁大学和哈佛大学对美国人一样重要，甚至更胜一筹。所以在牛津上学对我来说很重要。上完了第一个学年，我就要回家了。

下了火车，我披着脏兮兮的几乎和侏儒怪一样长的头发，光着脚丫子，而且还没有穿衬衫，牛仔裤也破烂不堪——这些在当时还没有成为一种时尚。更糟的是，我们刚换了房子，母亲把客厅的窗帘扔掉了，我把它们捡了回来做了一件无袖的大衣。

我的父亲跟我打招呼，车站到处是他的朋友。那里除了我之外，其他的小孩看上去都很体面。

当父亲看见我这用窗帘做的衣服时，皱了皱眉。这衣服确实太显眼了，我也为父亲感到尴尬。

"爸爸，"我说，"我要告诉你一个好消息，我不吸毒。"

他直视着我说："儿子，糟糕的是，你把自己打扮成这样却不吸毒，那我们就真有问题了。"

你们的父母用爱的眼光看着你们。他们知道要成功是多么困难，你们取得了成功，所以他们尊重你们。

我知道，明天你们就能顺利毕业。作为你们当中一个同学的父亲，我和你们的父母一样为你们骄傲，为你们所取得的成绩感到自豪，为你们而骄傲。

他们也为你们感到紧张，因为你们就要踏上新的征程，他们知道前方充满了挫折和坎坷。

但他们相信你们能够克服重重困难，因为他们知道，正因为拥有坚强的性格和精神你们才取得了今天的成就。

和我一样来到这里的家长们，我想对你们说，让我们一起庆祝吧！

耶鲁大学 2008 届的毕业生们，我想对你们说，你们做得很好，在今后的日子里，愿祝福和幸运常伴你们左右。非常感谢大家。

热词空间

Rumpelstiltskin
[,rʌmpəl'stiltskin] n. 侏儒怪（德国民间故事中的侏儒状妖怪）

drape [dreip] n. 窗帘

retrieved [ri'tri:vd] vt. 收回，找回

paragon ['pærəgən] n. 模范；优秀之人

respectability
[ri,spektə'biləti] n. 体面

wince [wins] vi. 畏缩，退避，面部肌肉抽搐

make the grade 成功；达到标准

rhythm ['riθəm] n. 节奏；韵律

obstacle ['ɔbstəkl] n. 障碍，干扰

surmount [sə:'maunt] vt. 克服，越过；战胜

rejoice [ri'dʒɔis] vi. 高兴；庆祝

哈佛
大学

斯坦福
大 学

牛津
大学

耶鲁
大学

杜兰
大学

杜克
大学

威斯康
辛大学

清华
大学

北京
大学

亚利桑
那州立
大 学

加利福
尼 亚
大 学

托尼·布莱尔给我们的

The history of humankind is marked by great events but written by great people.

人类历史由重大事件标记，却由伟大的人类来谱写。

Always be alive to the possibilities of the next experience, of thinking, doing and being.

要时刻准备迎接新的生活、不断思考、积极行动。

Judge someone by how they treat those below them not those above them.

评价一个人，要看他们怎样对待比自己地位低的人，而不是看他们怎样对待地位比自己高的人。

Above all, however, have a purpose in life. Life is not about living but about striving. When you get up, get up motivated. Live with a perpetual sense of urgency. And make at least part of that purpose about something bigger than you.

然而，最重要的是，生活要有目标。生活不仅仅是活着，而是要不断追求。每天早晨起来时都要带着一种动机。生活要时刻有紧迫感。而且在制定个人目标时，至少有一部分要超出个人能力范围。

Be a doer not a commentato. Seek responsibility rather than shirk it.

要做一个实干家而不是评论家。要勇于承担责任，不要逃避退缩。

Dare to Compete, Dare to Care

敢于竞争，勇于关爱

背景资料

　　这是希拉里 2001 年在母校耶鲁大学 300 周年纪念日发表的演讲。在演讲中，希拉里鼓励莘莘学子坚持自己的价值观和信仰，不仅要使自己的生活有所改观，也要改变别人的生活。希拉里号召耶鲁大学的学子们要敢于竞争，大胆关爱，勇往直前，不断创造奇迹。

Dare to compete. Dare to care. Dare to dream. Dare to love. Practice the art of making possible. And no matter what happens, even if you hear shouts behind, keep going.

　　要敢于竞争，敢于关爱，敢于憧憬，大胆去爱！要努力创造奇迹！无论发生什么，即使有人在你背后大声喊叫，也要勇往直前。

——希拉里·克林顿

姓　　名:	希拉里·黛安·罗德姆·克林顿 (Hillary Diane Rodham Clinton)
性　　别:	女
职　　业:	美国国务卿
国　　籍:	美国
党　　派:	民主党
出生日期:	1947 年 10 月 26 日
毕业学校:	耶鲁大学法学院、韦尔斯利学院
成功点睛:	博学、勤奋和勇气让她成为美国政坛上的一名成功女将。
个人成就:	当选总统奥巴马政府的国务卿 纽约州国会参议员

名人简介

　　希拉里 1947 年 10 月 26 日生于伊利诺伊州的芝加哥。1965 年，希拉里进入马萨诸塞州韦尔斯利学院主修政治学。1969 年，她又就读于耶鲁大学法学院，1973 年获法学博士学位，求学期间，她结识了后来成为美国总统的比尔·克林顿。

　　希拉里 1975 年 10 月与克林顿结婚后，进入美国著名的罗斯律师事务所工作，并曾两次当选全美百名杰出律师。随着克林顿 1993 年入住白宫，希拉里成为美国历史上学历最高的第一夫人。在 8 年白宫生涯中，希拉里积极参与政事，负责国家医疗保健改革，还推动国会通过国家儿童健康保险项目等。

　　2000 年 2 月，尚未离开白宫的希拉里宣布竞选纽约州参议员，成为美国历史上第一位谋求公职的第一夫人。同年 11 月 7 日，她当选为国会参议员。2006 年，她获得连任。2008 年 12 月 1 日，美国总统当选人奥巴马提名希拉里出任美国国务卿。

哈佛
大学

斯坦福
大学

牛津
大学

耶鲁
大学

杜兰
大学

杜克
大学

威斯康
辛大学

清华
大学

北京
大学

亚利桑
那州立
大 学

加利福
尼 亚
大 学

It is such an honor and pleasure for me to be back at Yale, especially on the occasion of the 300th **anniversary**. I have had so many memories of my time here, and as Nick was speaking I thought about how I ended up at Yale Law School. And it tells a little bit about how much progress we've made.

What I think most about when I think of Yale is not just the politically charged atmosphere and not even just the **superb** legal education that I received. It was at Yale that I began work that has been at the core of what I have cared about ever since. I began working with New Haven legal services representing children. And I studied child development, abuse and neglect at the Yale New Haven Hospital and the Child Study Center. I was lucky enough to receive a civil rights internship with Marian Wright Edelman at the Children's Defense Fund, where I went to work after I graduated. Those experiences fueled in me a passion to work for the benefit of children, particularly the most **vulnerable**.

Now, looking back, there is no way that I could have predicted what path my life would have taken. I didn't sit around the law school, saying, well, you know, I think I'll graduate and then I'll go to work at the Children's Defense Fund, and then the **impeachment inquiry**, and when Nixon retired or resigns, I'll go to Arkansas. I didn't think like that. I was taking each day at a time.

But, I've been very fortunate because I've always had an idea in my mind about what I thought was important and what gave my life meaning and purpose. A set of values and beliefs that have helped me **navigate** the **shoals**, the sometimes very **treacherous** sea, to **illuminate** my own true desires, despite that others say about what I should care about and believe in. A passion to succeed at what I thought was important and children have always provided that lone star, that guiding light. Because I have that absolute conviction that every child, especially in this, the most blessed of nations that has ever existed on the face of the earth, that every child deserves the opportunity to live up to his or her God-given potential.

But you know that belief and conviction — it may make for a personal mission statement, but standing alone, not translated into action, it means very little to anyone else, particularly to those for whom you have those concerns.

再回耶鲁，特别是在耶鲁大学 300 周年纪念日再回到这里，我感到非常高兴非常荣幸！耶鲁大学给我留下了许多美好的回忆，尼克发言时，我想起了当年从耶鲁法学院毕业的情景。这让我感受到了耶鲁大学所取得的巨大进步。

每当想起耶鲁时，我感触最深的不是这里浓郁的政治氛围，也不是我所接受的顶级的法律教育。正是在耶鲁，我开始做一些事情，这些事情从那时到现在都是我关注的核心。正是在耶鲁，我开始在纽黑文儿童法律机构工作。我还在耶鲁纽黑文医院和儿童研究中心研究儿童身心发展以及辱骂和忽视儿童的行为。之后，我很幸运地与玛丽安·莱特·埃德尔曼一起获得了在儿童保护基金委员会的民权实习机会，并在毕业后去了那里工作。所有这些经历激发了我为保护儿童权益而努力的激情，特别是保护那些最脆弱的儿童。

现在回想起来，当时我并不知道自己会走上什么样的人生道路。我没有坐在法学院里说，"恩，你知道，我想我毕业后要去儿童保护基金委员会工作，然后会遭到弹劾并接受调查，当尼克松退休或辞职后我会去阿肯色州。"事实上，我从未这样想过，只是顺其自然地过着每一天。

但是，我一直都很幸运，因为我始终知道什么对我来说才是最重要的、什么让我的人生更有意义和追求。尽管别人常常告诉我应该关注和信仰什么，但是我依然坚持自己的一套价值观和信仰，它们帮我度过了人生的浅海滩，让我在变幻莫测的大海自由航行，照亮了我内心深处的愿望。在我所认为的重要的事情上取得成功以及对儿童的关注像一颗启明星一样，指引着我前行的道路。因为我坚信，每一个孩子，特别是在美国这个地球上备受上帝恩惠的国度里的孩子，都应该有机会发挥他们天赐的潜能。

但是你们要知道，信仰和信念可以促进个人目标的实现。但如果仅仅挂在嘴上，而不付诸于行动的话，那这些对任何人来说都没有太大意义，特别是对于那些你所关注的人。

热词空间

anniversary [ˌænɪ'vɜ:sərɪ] n. 周年纪念日

superb [sju'pə:b] adj. 极好的

vulnerable ['vʌlnərəbl] adj. 脆弱的；易受伤害的

impeachment [im'pi:tʃmənt] n. 弹劾；控告

inquiry [in'kwaɪərɪ] n. 调查

navigate ['nævɪgeit] vt. 驾驶，操纵

shoal [ʃəul] n. 浅滩

treacherous ['tretʃərəs] adj. 暗藏危险的；不牢靠的

illuminate [i'lju:mineit] vt. 阐明，照亮

When I was thinking about running for the United States Senate — which was such an **enormous** decision to make, one I never could have dreamed that I would have been making when I was here on this campus — I visited a school in New York City and I met a young woman, who was a star athlete.

I was there because of Billy Jean King promoting an HBO special about women in sports called "Dare to Compete". It was about Title IX and how we finally, thanks to government action, provided opportunities to girls and women in sports.

And although I played not very well at **intramural** sports, I have always been a strong supporter of women in sports. And I was introduced to this young woman, and as I went to shake her hand she obviously had been reading the newspapers about people saying I should or shouldn't run for the Senate. And I was congratulating her on the speech she had just made and she held onto my hand and she said, "Dare to compete, Mrs. Clinton. Dare to compete."

I took that to heart because it is hard to compete sometimes, especially in public ways, when your failures are there for everyone to see and you don't know what is going to happen from one day to the next. And yet so much of life, whether we like to accept it or not, is competing with ourselves to be the best we can be, being involved in classes or professions or just life, where we know we are competing with others.

I took her advice and I did compete because I chose to do so. And the biggest choices that you'll face in your life will be yours alone to make. I'm sure you'll receive good advice. You've got a great education to go back and reflect about what is right for you, but you eventually will have to choose and I hope that you will dare to compete. And by that I don't mean the kind of **cutthroat** competition that is too often **characterized** by what is driving America today. I mean that small voice inside you that says to you, you can do it, you can **take this risk**, you can take this next step.

And it doesn't mean that once having made that choice you will always succeed. In fact, you won't. There are **setbacks** and you will experience difficult disappointments. You will be slowed down and sometimes the **breath** will just be **knocked out of** you. But if you carry with you the values and beliefs that you can **make a difference** in your own life, **first and foremost**, and then in the lives of

当我考虑要去参加美国参议院竞选活动时——这对我来说是一个非常艰难的决定，在耶鲁上大学时我从未梦想过的事情——我去参观了纽约的一所学校，在那里遇见了一个年轻女人，她是一名明星运动员。

我去那儿是因为比利·琼·金要在家庭影院频道宣传一个名为"敢于竞争"的体育节目。这个节目旨在宣传"第九项体育运动"，宣扬在政府的帮助下女性最终获得了参加体育比赛的机会。

尽管在学校时我并不擅长体育运动，但我非常支持女性参加体育运动。经过别人的介绍，我认识了这位年轻女士。我前去跟她握手，而她显然已经在报纸上看到了有关人们讨论我该不该参加竞选的报道。我在对她刚刚的成功演讲表示祝贺时，她紧紧握住我的手，对我说，"要敢于竞争，克林顿夫人。要敢于竞争。"

我牢牢地记住了她的话，因为有时候竞争真的很残酷，特别是通过公开方式进行竞争，因为在那种情况下你的失败人人可见，而且你不知道接下来的一天天会发生什么。然而，这就是生活，不管我们愿意接受与否，我们总是在不断挑战自我，力争做到做好。无论是在学校还是在职场甚至是在生活中，我们也都在和别人竞争。

我采纳了她的建议，参加了竞选，因为我已经做出了这样的决定。最重要的选择必须由自己来抉择。我相信你们会得到很好的建议。你们接受了良好的教育，这些教育能让你们明白什么最适合自己，但最终你们还是要做出选择，我希望你们敢于竞争。但是我指的并不是如今人们常说的推动美国发展的那种激烈的竞争，而是源于心底的那种微妙的声音，告诉你，你可以去做这件事情，你可以去冒这次险，你可以走这一步。

但这并不意味着一旦做了决定你就一定能取得成功。事实并非如此。成功路上难免挫折，也会有沮丧与失望。你们会放

热词空间

enormous [i'nɔ:məs] adj. 巨大的

intramural [,intrə'mjuərəl] adj. 校内的

cutthroat ['kʌt,θrəut] adj. 残酷的

characterize ['kærəktəraiz] vt. 描绘

take risk 冒险

setback ['setbæk] n. 挫折

knock breath out of sb 使某人窒息

make a difference 做出改观

first and foremost 首先

others. You can get back up, you can keep going.

But it is also important, as I have found, not to take yourself too seriously, because after all, every one of us here today, none of us is deserving of full credit. I think every day of the blessings my birth gave me without any doing of my own. I chose neither my family nor my country, but they as much as anything I've ever done, determined my course.

You compare my or your circumstances with those of the majority of people who've ever lived or who are living right now, they too often are born knowing too well what their futures will be. They lack the freedom to choose their life's path. They're imprisoned by circumstances of poverty and ignorance, bigotry, disease, hunger, oppression and war.

So, dare to compete, yes, but maybe even more difficult, dare to care. Dare to care about people who need our help to succeed and fulfill their own lives. There are so many out there and sometimes all it takes is the simplest of gestures or helping hands and many of you understand that already. I know that a number of graduates in the last 20 years have worked in community organizations, have tutored, have committed themselves to religious activities.

You have been there trying to serve because you have believed both that it was the right thing to do and because it gave something back to you. You have dared to care.

Well, dare to care to fight for equal justice for all, for equal pay for women, against hate crimes and bigotry. Dare to care about public schools without qualified teachers or adequate resources. Dare to care about protecting our environment. Dare to care about the ten million children in our country who lack health insurance. Dare to care about the one and a half million children who have a parent in jail. The seven million people who suffer from HIV/AIDS. And thank you for caring enough to demand that our nation do more to help those that are suffering throughout this world with HIV/AIDS, to prevent this pandemic from spreading even further.

And I'll also add, dare enough to care about our political process. You know, as I go and speak with students I'm impressed so much, not only in formal settings, on

慢脚步，甚至会感到窒息。但是，如果你们坚持自己的价值观和信仰，那么首先你们可以使自己的生活有所改观，同时也可以改变别人的生活。你们可以振作起来，也可以勇往直前。

但是我发现，同样重要的是，不要把自己太当一回事，因为毕竟我们今天在座的所有人中没有一个人是十全十美的。我在想每天生命赋予我多少祝福，我却没有主动去祝福别人。我既没有选择我的家庭也没有选择我的祖国，但是它们如同我所做过的事情一样决定着我的人生。

将我的或你们的生活境况与前人或现在的人的生活进行比较，你们会发现，这些人通常一出生就知道自己的未来会是怎样。他们没有选择人生道路的自由。他们被贫穷、无知、偏执、疾病、饥饿、压迫和战争困扰着。

因此，要敢于竞争。就要这样。但是，敢于关爱也许更艰难。我们要敢于关爱那些需要借助我们一臂之力获得成功或实现人生价值的人们。外面有很多人等待我们去帮助，你们中的许多人应该都已经明白，他们有时需要的不过就是一个最简单的手势或者仅仅是拉他们一把而已。我知道，过去 20 年许多从耶鲁毕业的大学生有的在社区组织工作，有的从事教育行业，有的把自己的一生奉献给了宗教事业。

你们竭尽全力服务社会，因为你们相信这正是你们要做的，而且会得到回报。这样，你们就做到了敢于关爱。

要敢于关爱，就意味着我们要敢于为全人类的平等正义而奋斗，敢于为妇女同工同酬而奋斗，敢于为打击犯罪和顽固势力而奋斗。我们要关注那些缺乏合格教师和教育资源的公立学校，要勇于承担保护环境的重任。我们要勇于关注我们国家 1000 万没有医疗保险的儿童、150 万父母有一方在监狱的儿童以及 700 万艾滋病患者。在此我要感谢那些呼吁我们国家给予全世界的艾滋病患者更多帮助、抑制艾滋病传播的人。

我还想再强调一点，那就是勇于去关注我们的政治进程。你们知道吗，每当我跟学生交谈时，不管是在正式场合还是在

热词空间

take oneself too seriously 把某人自己太当回事
bigotry ['bigətri] n. 偏执；盲从
oppression [ə'preʃən] n. 压迫
commit oneself to ... 致力于
health insurance 健康保险
pandemic [pæn'demik] n. 流行病

campuses, but with my daughter and her friends, about how much you care, about how willing you are to volunteer and serve. You may have missed the last wave of the dot com revolution, but you've understood that the dot community revolution is there for you every single day. And you've been willing to be part of remaking lives in our community.

And yet, there is a real resistance, a turning away from the political process. I hope that some of you will be public servants and will even **run for office** yourself, not to win a position to make an impression on your friends at your 20th reunion, but because you understand how important it is for each of us as citizens to make a commitment to our democracy.

Your generation, the first one born after the social **upheavals** of the 60's and 70's, in the midst of the technological advances of the 80's and 90's, are inheriting an economy, a society and a government that you have yet to understand fully, or even **come to grips with**, our rapidly changing world.

And so bring your values and experiences and insights into politics. Dare to help make, not just a difference in politics, but create a different politics. Some have called you the generation of choice. You've been raised with multiple choice tests, multiple channels, multiple websites and multiple lifestyles. You've grown up choosing among alternatives that were either not imagined, created or available to people in prior generations.

You've been invested with far more personal power to **customize** your life, to make more free choices about how to live than was ever thought possible. And I think as I look at all the surveys and research that is done, your choices reflect not only freedom, but personal responsibility.

The **social indicators**, not the **headlines**, the social indicators tell a positive story: drug use and cheating and arrests being down, teen **pregnancy** and suicides, **drunk driving deaths** being down. Community service and religious involvement being up. But if you look at the area of voting among 18 to 29 year olds, the numbers tell a far more troubling tale. Many of you I know believe that service and community **volunteerism** is a better way of solving the issues facing our country than political

校园里，或是在与我的女儿及她的朋友们交谈时，他们对社会的关注以及他们志愿为他人服务的精神都给我留下了深刻的印象。你们也许已经错过了互联网革命的最后一次革命浪潮，但是你们应该已经明白，互联网革命期待你们每一天都能参与。而且我相信你们一直都很乐意成为改造社会的一份子。

然而，很多人都对政治持有排斥心理，会对政治避而不谈。我希望你们中的一些人能成为人民的公仆，甚至能亲自参加竞选，而不是谋取高职只为能在 20 年同学聚会上炫耀。因为你们明白，我们每一个人作为公民都有义务为我们的民主事业做出贡献，这一点很重要。

你们这一代人生于 60 到 70 年代社会动荡的末期，成长于 80 到 90 年代技术革命期间，你们所面临的经济体制、社会体制和政府机构，已经清楚地意识到这是一个日新月异的世界，并开始认真对待这个瞬息万变的世界。

因此，把你们的价值观、阅历和洞察力都融于政治之中吧！你们不仅要敢于在政治上有所作为，而且还要敢于创造一个完全不同的政治体制。有人把你们这一代人称为有选择权利的一代人。你们是在多项选择测验、多渠道、多网站及多重生活方式中长大的，你们是在不停的选择中长大的，但这些选项既不为前人所致，也未为前人所用。

你们被赋予了很多力量，拥有规划自己人生的权利，能够比以往任何时候都更加自由地主宰自己的生活。当我看着你们完成的所有问卷调查和研究时，我认为你们的选择不仅反映了自由，也反映了你们的责任心。

是社会调查指标，而不是头版头条新闻，让我们感受到整个社会的进步：吸毒、诈骗以及在押人数均呈下降趋势；少女怀孕、自杀以及酒后驾车致死事件也在逐渐减少。同时，参加社区服务及宗教活动的人数呈上升趋势。但是，18 岁到 29 岁人群的投票选举情况则令人担忧。我知道，你们中的许多人都认为参加社会服务和志愿者活动比参与政治活动更能

热词空间

run for office 参加竞选
upheaval [ʌpˈhiːvəl] n. 剧变
come to grips with 认真对待；设法对付
customize [ˈkʌstəmaiz] vt. 定制
social indicator 社会调查
headline [ˈhedlain] n. 头版头条新闻
pregnancy [ˈpregnənsi] n. 怀孕
drunk driving death 酒后驾车致死事件
volunteerism [ˌvɒlənˈtiərizəm] n. 志愿服务

engagement, because you believe — choose one of the following multiples or choose them all — government either can't understand or won't make the right choices because of political pressures, inefficiency, incompetence or big money influence.

Well, I admit there is enough truth in that critique to justify feeling disconnected and alienated. But at bottom, that's a personal cop-out and a national peril. Political conditions maximize the conditions for individual opportunity and responsibility as well as community. Americorps and the Peace Corps exist because of political decisions. Our air, water, land and food will be clean and safe because of political choices. Our ability to cure disease or log onto the Internet have been advanced because of politically determined investments. Ethnic cleansing in Kosovo ended because of political leadership. Your parents and grandparents traveled here by means of government built and subsidized transportation systems. Many used GI Bills or government loans, as I did, to attend college.

Now, I could, as you might guess, go on and on, but the point is to remind us all that government is us and each generation has to stake its claim. And, as stakeholders, you will have to decide whether or not to make the choice to participate. It is hard and it is, bringing change in a democracy, particularly now. There's so much about our modern times that conspire to lower our sights, to weaken our vision — as individuals and communities and even nations.

It is not the vast conspiracy you may have heard about; rather it's a silent conspiracy of cynicism and indifference and alienation that we see every day, in our popular culture and in our prodigious consumerism.

But as many have said before and as Vaclav Havel has said so memorably, "It cannot suffice just to invent new machines, new regulations and new institutions. It is necessary to understand differently and more perfectly the true purpose of our existence on this Earth and of our deeds." And I think we are called on to reject, in this time of blessings that we enjoy, those who will tear us apart and tear us down and instead to liberate our God-given spirit, by being willing to dare to dream of a better world.

During my campaign, when times were tough and days were long I used to think

解决我们国家所面临的问题，因为你们认为，政府往往趋于政治压力，缺乏效率或无能，甚至是受金钱驱使而不能领会或作出正确选择。你们这样做可能是因为上述原因的一种，也可能因为所有这些原因。

我承认，人们批评的人类情感淡漠和疏远很多都是事实。但实际上，这只是个人托辞和国家危难。政局最大限度地扩大了个人机会和个人要承担的责任，同时也最大限度地扩大了社会机会和社会所要承担的责任。美国军团与美国和平部队因政治决策而存在。我们的空气、水、土地和食品因政治决策而安全卫生。以政治为导向的投资使医疗技术和网络技术取得了新的发展。政治领导结束了科索沃（南斯拉夫自治省名）的种族净化。你们的父母、祖父母能够到此旅游得益于政府资助修建的交通运输系统。和我一样，很多人在美国退伍军人权利法案和政府贷款条例的帮助下完成了大学教育。

现在，你们也许已经猜到，我会一直坚持下去。而且我要强调一点，政府是我们的，每一代人都要响应它的号召。作为其中的一份子，你们必须做出选择，决定要不要参与其中。这很艰难，却能给民主社会带来变革，尤其是现在。现代社会无形之中使我们个人、团体甚至国家放低眼光，缩小视野。

在一个大众文化和高消费的国度里，你们可能听说的不是巨大的阴谋，而是我们天天都能见到的无形的讽刺、冷漠和疏远。

很多人曾说过，瓦兹拉夫·哈维尔（曾任捷克斯洛伐克总统）也曾明确表示过，"仅仅发明新机器、制定新条例、设立新机构是不够的，对于我们存在于这个世界以及我们行为的真正目的有一个全新的、彻底的认识是非常重要的。"而且，我认为，生活在幸福中的我们要敢于去追求一个更加完美的世界，这种力量呼吁我们去反抗那些离间、诋毁我们而不是帮助我们发挥天赋的人。

在我参加竞选的过程中，当我遇到挫折，日子变得艰难时，

热词空间

critique [kri'ti:k] n. 批评

alienated ['eiljəneitid] adj. 疏远的

cop-out ['kɔpaut] n. 逃避；[俚] 借口

peril ['peril] n. 危险

maximize ['mæksimaiz] vt. 使增加（或扩大）到最大限度；极为重视

cleansing ['klenziŋ] n. 净化

subsidized ['sʌbsidaizd] adj. 补助的

stake [steik] vt. 支持

conspire [kən'spaiə] vi. 共谋；密谋

conspiracy [kən'spirəsi] n. 阴谋

prodigious [prəu'didʒəs] adj. 惊人的，巨大的

consumerism [kən'sju:mə,rizəm] n. 消费，消费主义

suffice [sə'fais] vi. 足够

about the example of Harriet Tubman, a heroic New Yorker, a 19th century Moses, who risked her life to bring hundreds of slaves to freedom. She would say to those who she gathered up in the South where she kept going back year after year from the safety of Auburn, New York, that no matter what happens, they had to keep going. If they heard shouts behind them, they had to keep going. If they heard gunfire or dogs, they had to keep going to freedom. Well, those aren't the risks we face. It is more the silence and apathy and indifference that dogs our heels.

Thirty-two years ago, I spoke at my own graduation from Wellesley, where I did call on my fellow classmates to reject the notion of limitations on our ability to effect change and instead to embrace the idea that the goal of education should be human liberation and the freedom to practice with all the skill of our being the art of making possible.

For after all, our fate is to be free. To choose competition over apathy, caring over indifference, vision over myopia, and love over hate.

Just as this is a special time in your lives, it is for me as well because my daughter will be graduating in four weeks, graduating also from a wonderful place with a great education and beginning a new life. And as I think about all the parents and grandparents who are out there, I have a sense of what their feeling. Their hearts are leaping with joy, but it's hard to keep the tears in check because the presence of our children at a time and place such as this is really a fulfillment of our own American dreams. Well, I applaud you and all of your love, commitment and hard work, just as I applaud your daughters and sons for theirs.

And I leave these graduates with the same message I hope to leave with my graduate. Dare to compete. Dare to care. Dare to dream. Dare to love. Practice the art of making possible. And no matter what happens, even if you hear shouts behind, keep going.

Thank you and God bless you all.

我常常把哈利特·塔布曼作为榜样。她是纽约的英雄，是19世纪的摩西，她冒着生命危险带领成百上千的奴隶走向了自由。每年她都会从安全的纽约奥本回到南方，将奴隶聚集到一起，告诉他们，无论发生什么都必须坚持往前走。如果听见背后有人大声喊叫，他们也必须坚持往前走。如果听见枪声或狗叫声，他们也必须向着自由继续前行。然而，这些并不是我们现在所面临的危险，我们此刻最主要的问题是沉默、无情和冷淡。

32年前，我在韦尔斯利学院自己的毕业典礼上演讲，号召我的同学反对我们改变世界的能力是有限的这样一种观念。并号召他们拥护这样的思想：教育的目标应该是解放人类，使人类获得行动的自由，用其所拥有的技能创造奇迹。

总之，自由是人类最终的归宿。我们要勇于竞争而非冷漠、勇于关爱而非漠不关心、高瞻远瞩而非鼠目寸光、大爱无私而非满目仇恨。

毕业典礼对你们来说是一个特殊的时刻，对我也是如此，因为我女儿再过四个星期也要毕业了，也要从一个颇具魅力而且拥有一流教育的大学毕业开始新的生活了。当我想起你们的父母和祖父母时，我想我们拥有同样的心情。他们的心中满是喜悦，情不自禁流下激动的泪水，因为当你们在这一时刻这一地点出席这样一个典礼的时候，你们已经实现了我们伟大的美国梦。我要为你们的父母们无私的爱、奉献和辛苦的工作而喝彩，也要为你们的儿女喝彩！

我希望在自己毕业的时候听到这样的话，同样我也要把这些话送给你们。要敢于竞争，敢于关爱，敢于憧憬，大胆去爱！要努力创造奇迹！无论发生什么，即使有人在你背后大声喊叫，也要勇往直前。

谢谢你们！愿上帝保佑你们！

热词空间

heroic [hi'rəuik] adj. 英雄的
apathy ['æpəθi] n. 冷漠，无情
dog [dɔg] vt. 跟踪；尾随
heel [hi:l] n. 脚后跟
notion ['nəuʃən] n. 观点，见解
indifference [in'difərəns] n. 冷漠
myopia [mai'əupiə] n. 目光短浅，缺乏远见
applaud [ə'plɔ:d] vt. 向……喝彩

希拉里·克林顿给我们的 启示

But you know that belief and conviction — it may make for a personal mission statement, but standing alone, not translated into action, it means very little to anyone else, particularly to those for whom you have those concerns.

但是你们要知道，信仰和信念可以促进个人目标的实现，但如果仅仅挂在嘴上，而不付诸于行动的话，那这些对任何人来说都没有太大意义，特别是对于那些你所关注的人。

Because I have that absolute conviction that every child, especially in this, the most blessed of nations that has ever existed on the face of the earth, that every child deserves the opportunity to live up to his or her God-given potential.

因为我坚信，每一个孩子，特别是在美国这个地球上备受上帝恩惠的国度里的孩子，都应该有机会发挥他们天赐的潜能。

And it doesn't mean that once having made that choice you will always succeed. In fact, you won't. There are setbacks and you will experience difficult disappointments. You will be slowed down and sometimes the breath will just be knocked out of you. But if you carry with you the values and beliefs that you can make a difference in your own life, first and foremost, and then in the lives of others. You can get back up, you can keep going.

但这并不意味着一旦做了决定你就一定能取得成功。事实并非如此。成功路上难免挫折，也会有沮丧与失望。你们会放慢脚步，甚至会感到窒息。但是，如果你们坚持自己的价值观和信仰，那么首先你们可以使自己的生活有所改观，同时也可以改变别人的生活。你们可以振作起来，也可以勇往直前。

But it is also important, as I have found, not to take yourself too seriously, because after all, every one of us here today, none of us is deserving of full credit.

但是我发现，同样重要的是，不要把自己太当一回事，因为毕竟我们今天在座的所有人中没有一个人是十全十美的。

希拉里·克林顿给我们的

Dare to care about people who need our help to succeed and fulfill their own lives. There are so many out there and sometimes all it takes is the simplest of gestures or helping hands and many of you understand that already.

我们要敢于关爱那些需要借助我们一臂之力获得成功或实现人生价值的人们。外面有很多人等待我们去帮助，你们中的许多人应该都已经明白，他们有时需要的不过就是一个最简单的手势或者仅仅是拉他们一把而已。

Everyone Can Be a President

人人都能成为总统

Yale University Commencement Address George Walker Bush May, 2001

背景资料

  在耶鲁大学的演讲中，布什用一种自嘲式的幽默，坦然地将自己归入 C 类学生，在赞扬那些获得各种奖励的优秀学生的同时，毫不掩饰地说，C 等生也能成功，也可以成为美国总统。整个演讲妙语连珠，耶鲁学子没有因为他的自嘲而看低了他，反而报以阵阵热烈的掌声。布什的演讲语句简短，用词平实，但出人意料。在演讲中，布什充分展示出谦逊的品格。尽管 Blum 教授曾在媒体上说对布什这个学生毫无印象，但布什仍然说，他能回忆起 Blum 教授是如何献身于教育事业和他治学是如何严谨的，由此向所有耶鲁的教师表示感谢。

To those of you who received honors, awards, and distinctions, I say, well done. And to the C students — I say, you, too, can be President of the United States.

  对于那些表现杰出、获得各种奖项和荣誉的同学，我要说，你们真棒！对于那些 C 等生，我要说，你们将来也可以当美国总统！

——乔治·布什

姓　　名：	乔治·沃克·布什（George Walker Bush）
性　　别：	男
职　　业：	美国第 43 任总统
国　　籍：	美国
党　　派：	共和党
出生日期：	1946 年 7 月 6 日
毕业学校：	1968 年获耶鲁大学历史学士学位，1975 年获哈佛大学工商管理硕士学位
成功点睛：	他的成功在于正视自己的不足，同时不放弃理想
个人成就：	美国第 46 任德州州长，第 43 任总统，并获得连任

名人 简介

　　乔治·沃克·布什 1946 年 7 月 6 日生于美国康涅狄格州，在德克萨斯州的米德兰和休斯敦长大，为美国第 43 任总统。布什在 2001 年 1 月 20 日就职，并且在 2004 年的选举中击败民主党参选人约翰·克里当选连任。在担任总统之前，布什于 1995 年至 2000 年间担任第 46 任德州州长。布什家族很早就开始投入共和党以及美国政治，布什的父亲是曾担任第 41 任总统的乔治·赫伯特·沃克·布什，他的弟弟杰布·布什也曾是佛罗里达州的州长，由于与父亲同样都是美国总统，因此又常被称为小布什以区别，而他父亲就被称为老布什。

哈佛
大学

斯坦福
大 学

牛津
大学

耶鲁
大学

杜兰
大学

杜克
大学

威斯康
辛大学

清华
大学

北京
大学

亚利桑
那州立
大 学

加利福
尼 亚
大 学

President Levin, thank you very much. **Dean** Brodhead, fellows of the Yale Corporation, fellow Yale parents, families, and graduates: It's a special **privilege** to receive this **honorary** degree. I was proud 33 years ago to receive my first Yale degree. I'm even prouder that in your eyes I've earned this one.

I congratulate my fellow **honorees**. I'm pleased to share this honor with such a distinguished group. I'm particularly pleased to be here with my friend, the former of Mexico.

I congratulate all the parents who are here. It's a **glorious** day when your child graduates from college. It's a great day for you; it's a great day for your wallet.

Most important, congratulations to the class of 2001. To those of you who received honors, awards, and **distinctions**, I say, well done. And to the C students — I say, you, too, can be President of the United States.

A Yale degree is worth a lot, as I often remind Dick Cheney — who studied here, but left a little early. So now we know — if you graduate from Yale, you become President. If you drop out, you get to be Vice President.

I appreciate so much the chance to say a few words on this occasion. I know Yale has a tradition of having no commencement speaker. I also know that you've **carved out** a single exception. Most people think that to speak at Yale's commencement, you have to be President. But over the years, the **specifications** have become far more demanding. Now you have to be a Yale graduate, you have to be President, and you have had to have lost the Yale vote to Ralph Nader.

This is my first time back here in quite a while. I'm sure that each of you will make your own journey back at least a few times in your life. If you're like me, you won't remember everything you did here. That can be a good thing. But there will be some people, and some moments, you will never forget.

Take, for example, my old classmate, Dick Brodhead, the accomplished dean of this great university. I remember him as a young scholar, a bright lad — a hard worker. We both put a lot of time in at the Sterling Library, in the reading room, where they have those big **leather** couches. We had a **mutual** understanding — Dick

非常感谢，莱文校长。布罗德黑德院长，耶鲁董事会的全体成员，耶鲁毕业生的家长们，各位毕业生们：获得这个荣誉学位让我感觉非常荣幸。我很自豪，在33年前获得了第一个耶鲁学位。而今天，在你们面前获得这一荣誉学位让我更加骄傲无比。

祝贺你们，与我同获殊荣的人们。我很高兴能和如此杰出的团体共享这一荣誉，尤其是能和我的朋友，墨西哥前总统在一起分享。

我要恭喜所有在座的家长们：恭喜你们的子女顺利地从耶鲁大学毕业，这是你们辛勤栽培后享受收获的日子，也是你们钱包解放的大好日子！

最重要的是，我要恭喜2001届的耶鲁毕业生们：对于那些表现杰出、获得各种奖项和荣誉的同学，我要说，你们真棒！对于那些C等生，我要说，你们将来也可以当美国总统！

耶鲁学位价值不菲。我时常这样提醒迪克·切尼（美国布什政府时期的副总统），他也曾在耶鲁就读，只是过早辍学了。所以，我想提醒正就读于耶鲁的莘莘学子，如果你们从耶鲁顺利毕业，你们也许可以当上总统；但如果你们中途辍学，那么你们就只能当副总统了。

我很荣幸能有机会在这个场合发表演讲。我知道，耶鲁向来不邀请毕业典礼演讲人，但也有例外。很多人认为，只有总统才能在耶鲁大学的毕业典礼上发表演讲。但近几年条件却更加严格。演讲人必须是美国总统，是耶鲁大学校友，而且他在总统选举中在耶鲁大学所在投票区里得到的票数要少于拉尔夫·纳德。

这是我毕业这么长时间以来第一次回到母校。我也相信你们每个人会在毕业以后至少回来几次。当你们像我这么老的时候，你们会不记得在这里做过的每一件事情。这或许是一件好事。不过，一些人，一些事你永远也不会忘记。

就拿我的老同学狄克·布罗德黑德来说，如今他是这所伟大的学校的杰出院长，他读书时的聪明、好学与刻苦至今让我记忆犹新。那时，我们经常泡在校图书馆那个有着大皮

热词空间

dean [di:n] *n.* 院长；系主任

privilege ['privilidʒ] *n.* 特权；优待

honorary ['ɔnərəri] *adj.* 荣誉的；名誉的

honoree [,ɔnə'ri:] *n.* 受勋者；领奖人

glorious ['glɔ:riəs] *adj.* 光荣的；辉煌的

distinction [dis'tiŋkʃən] *n.* 区别；荣誉、勋章

carve out 开辟；开拓

specification [,spesifi'keiʃən] *n.* 规格；详述；说明书

leather ['leðə] *n.* 皮革 *adj.* 皮的

mutual ['mju:tjuəl] *adj.* 共同的；相互的

wouldn't read aloud, and I wouldn't snore.

Our course selections were different, as we followed our own path to academic discovery. Dick was an English major, and loved the classics. I loved history, and pursued a diversified course of study. I like to think of it as the academic road less traveled. For example, I took a class that studied Japanese Haiku. Haiku, for the uninitiated, is a 15th century form of poetry, each poem having 17 syllables. Haiku is fully understood only by the Zen masters. As I recall, one of my academic advisers was worried about my selection of such a specialized course. He said I should focus on English. I still hear that quite often. But my critics don't realize I don't make verbal gaffes. I'm speaking in the perfect forms and rhythms of ancient Haiku.

I did take English here, and I took a class called "The History and Practice of American Oratory," taught by Rollin G. Osterweis. And, President Levin, I want to give credit where credit is due. I want the entire world to know this — everything I know about the spoken word, I learned right here at Yale.

As a student, I tried to keep a low profile. It worked. Last year the *New York Times* interviewed John Morton Blum because the record showed I had taken one of his courses. Casting his mind's eye over the parade of young faces down through the years, Professor Blum said, and I quote, "I don't have the foggiest recollection of him."

But I remember Professor Blum. And I still recall his dedication and high standards of learning. In my time there were many great professors at Yale. And there still are. They're the ones who keep Yale going after the commencements, after we have all gone our separate ways. I'm not sure I remembered to thank them the last time I was here, but now that I have a second chance, I thank the professors of Yale University.

That's how I've come to feel about the Yale experience — grateful. I studied hard, I played hard, and I made a lot of lifelong friends. What stays with you from college is the part of your education you hardly ever notice at the time. It's the expectations and examples around you, the ideals you believe in, and the friends you

沙发的阅读室里。我们俩之间有个默契：他不大声朗读课文，我睡觉不打呼噜。

后来，随着学术探索的领域不同，我们选修的课程也各不相同。狄克主修英语，酷爱古典文学，而我主修历史，喜欢多样化的学习过程。我喜欢把这种学习过程想成是少有人走过的学术之路。有趣的是，我选修过日本俳句，对门外汉来说，俳句是15世纪日本的一种诗歌形式，每首诗只有17个音节，我想其意义只有禅学大师才能明了。我记得一位学科顾问对我选修如此专精的课程表示担忧。他说我应该选修英语。现在，我仍然时常听到这类建议。我在其他场合演讲时，在语言表达上曾被人误解过，那些批评我的人不明白：我不是说错了字，我是在复诵古代俳句的完美格式与韵律呢。

在耶鲁大学我的确也学习了英语课程，我选修了罗琳·G.奥斯特维斯主讲的"美国演讲历史与实践"。莱文校长，我想在此给予他应有的赞许。我想让全世界的人都知道，我所知道的关于演讲的一切知识都是在耶鲁学会的。

作为一名学生，我努力保持低调，而这也十分奏效。去年，《纽约时报》采访了约翰·莫顿·布鲁姆教授，因为相关记录称我曾选修过他的课程。回顾多年来仍存留在脑海中的那些年轻的面孔之后，布鲁姆教授说，"我压根不记得有布什这个学生。"

但是我记得布鲁姆教授，我依然记得他无私奉献的精神和他的博学多才。我在耶鲁大学上学时，这里有很多优秀的教授任教，现在依然如此。在一届又一届的毕业典礼后，毕业生们各奔东西，是这些优秀的教授在推动着耶鲁大学不断向前发展。我已经不记得最后一次在这里的时候是否向他们表达过感激之情，但现在我还有机会，我要衷心感谢耶鲁大学的所有教授。

我很感激耶鲁大学给我们提供了这么好的读书环境。读书期间，我坚持"用功读书，努力玩乐"，结交了许多让我终生受益的朋友。大学期间，常陪伴你身边的那些东西是你学习生涯的一部分，但是那时你却从来没有注意过。那是大家对你的期望，是你身边值得你学习的榜样，是你坚持的理想，以及诸多你结交的朋友……

make.

In my time, they spoke of the "Yale man." I was really never sure what that was. But I do think that I'm a better man because of Yale. All universities, at their best, teach that degrees and honors are far from the full measure of life. Nor is that measure taken in wealth or in titles. What matters most are the standards you live by, the **consideration** you show others, and the way you use the gifts you are given.

Now you leave Yale behind, carrying the **written proof** of your success here, at a college older than America. When I left here, I didn't have much in the way of a life plan. I knew some people who thought they did. But it turned out that we were all in for **ups and downs**, most of them **unexpected**. Life takes its own turns, makes its own demands, writes its own story. And along the way, we start to realize we are not the author.

We begin to understand that life is ours to live, but not to waste, and that the greatest rewards are found in the **commitments** we make with our whole hearts — to the people we love and to the causes that earn our sacrifice. I hope that each of you will know these rewards. I hope you will find them in your own way and your own time.

For some, that might mean some time in public service. And if you hear that calling, I hope you answer. Each of you has unique gifts and you were given them for a reason. Use them and share them. Public service is one way — an honorable way — to mark your life with meaning.

Today I visit not only my **alma mater**, but the city of my birth. My life began just a few blocks from here, but I was raised in West Texas. From there, Yale always seemed a world away, maybe a part of my future. Now it's part of my past, and Yale for me is a source of great pride. I hope that there will come a time for you to return to Yale to say that, and feel as I do today. And I hope you won't wait as long.

Congratulations and God bless you.

我那个时代，常常听到大家说"耶鲁人"。我从不确定那是什么意思。但是因为耶鲁，因为有了在耶鲁深造的经历，我变成了一个更加优秀的人！许多大学都在尽力教导学生，学位和荣誉并非衡量人生的一切标准。财富和头衔也不能用来衡量人生。衡量人生的关键在于你的生活准则、你对他人的体恤以及你如何运用你的天赋。

现在你们即将带着从这所比美国历史还要悠久的大学获得的证明你们成功的证书离开耶鲁。我从这里毕业时，还没有仔细规划我的人生。我认识一些人，他们认为自己对人生做了规划。但结果表明，生活不可能一帆风顺，人生道路跌宕起伏，免不了会经历坎坷。生活自有轨迹，生活充满挑战，生活谱写着自己的故事，而历经漫漫人生路，我们才开始发现自己并不是这些故事的谱写者。

我们开始明白，生活需要用心经营而不是日日虚度。人生最大的意义在于对所爱的人的付出，以及对值得为之牺牲的事业的无私奉献。我希望你们能了解这些回报，并以自己的方式、自己的时间、自己的奋斗来实现这种意义。

对于有些人来说，这也许意味着在公共服务领域倾注心血，如果你们听到了这样的召唤，我希望你们能给予回应。你们每个人都有独特的天赋，上天赋予你们这些天赋是有其原因的。好好利用它们，与人分享它们。参与公共服务只是利用天赋的一种方式，一种值得人们尊敬的方式，这种方式赋予你更有意义的人生。

这次我不仅回到母校，也是回到我的出生地，我就是在离这里几条街之外的地方出生的，但我是在西德克萨斯长大的。在那里，耶鲁与我仿佛隔了一个世界之遥，可能只是未来的一个梦想。而现在，她是我过去的一部分。对我而言，耶鲁是令我极度骄傲的源泉。我希望，将来你们回到耶鲁时，能有与我一样的感受并说出相同的话。我希望你们不会等太久。

祝贺你们！上帝保佑你们。

哈佛
大学

斯坦福
大　学

牛津
大学

耶鲁
大学

杜兰
大学

杜克
大学

威斯康
辛大学

清华
大学

北京
大学

亚利桑
那州立
大　学

加利福
尼　亚
大　学

乔治·布什给我们的

A Yale degree is worth a lot, as I often remind Dick Cheney — who studied here, but left a little early. So now we know — if you graduate from Yale, you become President. If you drop out, you get to be Vice President.

耶鲁学位价值不菲。我时常这样提醒迪克·切尼（美国布什政府时期的副总统），他也曾在耶鲁就读，只是过早辍学了。所以，我想提醒正就读于耶鲁的莘莘学子，如果你们从耶鲁顺利毕业，你们也许可以当上总统；但如果你们中途辍学，那么你们就只能当副总统了。

What stays with you from college is the part of your education you hardly ever notice at the time. It's the expectations and examples around you, the ideals you believe in, and the friends you make.

大学期间，常陪伴你身边的那些东西是你学习生涯的一部分，但是那时你却从来没有注意过。那是大家对你的期望，是你身边值得你学习的榜样，是你坚持的理想，以及诸多你结交的朋友……

We begin to understand that life is ours to live, but not to waste, and that the greatest rewards are found in the commitments we make with our whole hearts — to the people we love and to the causes that earn our sacrifice.

我们开始明白，生活需要用心经营而不是日日虚度。人生最大的意义在于对所爱的人的付出，以及对值得为之牺牲的事业的无私奉献。

杜兰大学

校训：Not for oneself, but for one's own（不为自己，只为内心）

总 括

杜兰大学，成立于 1834 年，由最初的路易斯安那医学院发展而成，是一所历史悠久、享誉全球的综合性文理兼顾的四年制私立大学。学校素以教学、科研及学生的高素质而雄踞美国南部名校之首，在美国学界享有"南部的哈佛"之美誉。杜兰大学是一所教学严谨的优良学府，拥有包括诺贝尔奖得主及众多国际知名学者在内的 1000 余名教研人员。学校 99% 的教研人员拥有各自从事的研究领域里的最高学位。

Stay True to Yourself

做真正的自己

Tulane University
Commencement Address
Ellen DeGeneres
May, 2009

背景资料

　　艾伦风趣自然的风格似乎与生俱来，她在杜兰大学的演讲延续了自己的幽默风格，艾伦拆分了 commencement，在"笑果"十足的短短演说中透露自己艰辛的成长历程，让人从中受到很大鼓舞，她还给毕业学生们以诚恳的建议，让毕业生受益匪浅。

And really when I look back on it, I wouldn't change a thing. I mean, it was so important for me to lose everything because I found out what the most important thing is, is to be true to yourself. And ultimately, that's what's gotten me to this place. I don't live in fear. I'm free. I have no secrets. And I know I'll always be OK, because no matter what, I know who I am.

　　当我回首这些往事的时候，我一点也不会改变。因为我发现，即使失去一切，最重要的是做真正的自己。最终，我来到了这里。我不再恐惧，我感觉很自在，也不再有秘密，而且我知道一切都会好的，因为无论如何，我知道我是谁。

—— 艾伦·德詹尼丝

最名人档案

姓　　名：	艾伦·德詹尼丝（Ellen DeGeneres）
性　　别：	女
职　　业：	美国脱口秀节目主持人，演员
国　　籍：	美国
出生日期：	1958 年 1 月 26 日
成功点睛：	敢于听从自己的心声，做真正的自己，使得她在"脱口秀"领域取得了巨大的成功。
个人成就：	她在 CBS 主持的节目《艾伦秀》收视率一直居高不下。她还成功主持过第 38 和 39 届格莱美、第 46 届艾美等颁奖典礼。2007 年初的第 79 届奥斯卡颁奖典礼也是由她主持的。

名人简介

　　1958 年 1 月艾伦·德詹尼丝出生在路易斯安那的梅泰里。13 岁时父母离异，艾伦跟随母亲搬到新奥尔良定居。从事过女招待和售货员等多份工作后，她最终决定发挥自己的幽默感，成为一名喜剧演员。她在 Clyde's 喜剧俱乐部担任主持人期间，曾获得 Showtime1982 年度"全美最滑稽的人"称号。成名后的艾伦前往洛杉矶拍摄了 HBO 的"Young Comedians Reunion"、"One Night Stand"等专题片，后者为她赢得 Cable ACE 奖提名。1986 年她在约翰尼·卡森（Johnny Carson）的喜剧节目《今夜秀》担任常驻嘉宾，她充满机智的幽默为事业插上高飞的双翅。在福克斯的"Open House"中艾伦首次尝试表演，接下来她又出演了 ABC 的电视剧"Laurie Hill"，1994 年，ABC 邀她主演电视剧集《These Friends of Mine》（后更名为《艾伦》）。该剧从 1994 年一直播到 1998 年，高居收视榜首，德詹尼丝的喜剧才华得到观众认可，她也因此获得两项艾美提名。1993 年艾伦在《尖头外星族》中首度触电，之后又主演了《二见钟情之新好男人》、《再见爱人》、《当女人爱上女人的时候》等影片。

哈佛
大学

斯坦福
大学

牛津
大学

耶鲁
大学

杜兰
大学

杜克
大学

威斯康
辛大学

清华
大学

北京
大学

亚利桑
那州立
大 学

加利福
尼亚
大 学

Thank you, President Cowan, Mrs. President Cowen; distinguished guests, undistinguished guests — you know who you are, honored faculty and creepy Spanish teacher. And thank you to all the graduating class of 2009, I realize most of you are hungover and have splitting headaches and haven't slept since Fat Tuesday, but you can't graduate till I finish, so listen up.

When I was asked to make the commencement speech, I immediately said yes. Then I went to look up what commencement meant, which would have been easy if I had a dictionary, but most of the books in our house are Portia's, and they're all written in Australian. So I had to break the word down myself, to find out the meaning.

Commencement: common, and cement. Common cement. You commonly see cement on sidewalks. Sidewalks have cracks, and if you step on a crack, you break your mother's back. So there's that. But I'm honored that you've asked me here to speak at your common cement.

I thought that you had to be a famous alumnus — alumini — aluminum — alumis — you had to graduate from this school. And I didn't go to college here, and I don't know if President Cowan knows, I didn't go to college at all. Any college. And I'm not saying you wasted your time, or money, but look at me, I'm a huge celebrity.

Although I did graduate from the school of hard knocks, our mascot was the knockers. I spent a lot of time here growing up. My mom worked at Newcom and I would go there every time I needed to steal something out of her purse. But why am I here today? Clearly not to steal, you're too far away and I'd never get away with it.

I'm here because of you. Because I can't think of a more tenacious, more courageous graduating class. I mean, look at you all, wearing your robes. Usually when you're wearing a robe at 10 in the morning, it means you've given up. I'm here because I love New Orleans. I was born and raised here, I spent my formative years here, and like you, while I was living here I only did laundry six times. When I finished school, I was completely lost. And by school, I mean middle school, but

尊敬的考恩校长，校长夫人，尊贵的嘉宾——你们知道自己是谁，不用介绍了，尊敬的老师们，还有令人害怕的西班牙语老师，感谢你们！感谢所有杜兰大学2009届毕业生们！我知道你们绝大多数人还因为宿醉而头痛欲裂，狂欢到今天都还没有睡觉。但没听完我演讲不能毕业，所以要注意听了。

当我应邀来发表毕业演讲时，我毫不犹豫就答应了，然后我才去查毕业典礼是什么意思。如果我有字典的话就轻松多了，但我家大多数的书都是波西亚的，而且都是澳式英语，所以我得自己拆分单词，摸索它的意思。

Commencement 由 common 和 cement 构成，意思是"常见的水泥"。在人行道上你常看见水泥。人行道上有裂缝，你踩到了裂缝，撞伤了你妈妈的背。意思就是这样。但是我很荣幸应邀给你们做"常见的水泥"的演讲。

我本以为要够有名，必须要是校友才能来。我没在这儿上过大学，而且，不知道考恩校长知道不知道，我完全没念过大学。任何一所大学。我不是说你们在浪费时间和金钱，看看我，我可是超级成功的名人。

但是我确实从历经磨难的生活这所学校毕业了，我们的吉祥物就是磨难和挫折。我在此度过了许多成长岁月。我妈妈在纽科姆工作，每当我需要从她的钱包里偷偷拿些东西的时候，我都会去找她。但今天我为什么来这里呢？很明显我不是想要偷你们的钱，你们离我太远了，而且我也跑不了。

我来这儿是因为你们。没有比你们更坚韧更勇敢的毕业生了。我是说，看看你们每一个人都身着学士袍。通常在早上10点还穿着睡袍，说明你们已经放弃人生了。今天我来这里，因为我热爱纽奥良，我在这里出生，在这里长大，在这里度过年少岁月。和你们一样，我在这里生活时，只洗过6次衣服。

热词空间

distinguished [dis'tiŋgwiʃt] adj. 尊贵的

hungover ['hʌŋ'əuvə] adj. 因余醉未醒感到难受的

splitting ['splitiŋ] adj. 爆裂似的

cement [si'ment] n. 水泥

alumnus [ə'lʌmnəs] n. 男校友

mascot ['mæskət] n. 吉祥物

tenacious [tə'neiʃəs] adj. 顽强的，坚韧的

robe [rəub] n. 长袍

laundry ['lɑːndri] n. 衣服的洗熨

I went ahead and finished high school anyway. And I — I really, I had no ambition, I didn't know what I wanted to do. I did everything from — I shucked oysters, I was a hostess, I was a bartender, I was a waitress, I painted houses, I sold vacuum cleaners, I had no idea. And I thought I'd just finally settle in some job, and I would make enough money to pay my rent, maybe have basic cable, maybe not, I didn't really have a plan, my point is that, by the time I was your age, I really thought I knew who I was, but I had no idea.

Anyway, I had no idea what I wanted to do with my life, and the way I ended up on this path was from a very tragic event. I was maybe 19, and my girlfriend at the time was killed in a car accident. And I passed the accident, and I didn't know it was her and I kept going, and I found out shortly after that, it was her. And I was living in a basement apartment, I had no money, I had no heat, no air, I had a mattress on the floor and the apartment was infested with fleas. And I was soul-searching, I was like, why is she suddenly gone, and there are fleas here? I don't understand, there must be a purpose, and wouldn't it be so convenient if we could pick up the phone and call God, and ask these questions.

And I started writing and what poured out of me was an imaginary conversation with God, which was one-sided, and I finished writing it and I looked at it and I said to myself, and I hadn't even been doing stand-up, ever, there was no club in town. I said, "I'm gonna do this on the *Tonight Show* with Johnny Carson" — at the time he was the king — "and I'm gonna be the first woman in the history of the show to be called over to sit down." And several years later, I was the first woman in the history of the show, and only woman in the history of the show to sit down, because of that phone conversation with God that I wrote. And I started this path of stand-up and it was successful and it was great, but it was hard, because I was trying to please everybody and I had this secret that I was keeping, that I was gay. And I thought if people found out they wouldn't like me, they would laugh at me.

Then my career turned into — I got my own sitcom, and that was very

当我毕业后，我完全迷失了。我指的学校是初中，但是我接着上学，念完了高中。但我当时真的没有什么野心，不知道自己想做什么。我什么都做。我剥过牡蛎，当过迎宾员，做过酒保、服务员，粉刷过房子，卖过吸尘器。我完全不知道自己想做什么。我想随便找个工作稳定下来，只要有足够的钱付房租，可能有一台电视，也可能没有。我完全没有计划。我要说的重点是，我像你们这么大的时候，我真的以为我了解自己，但其实并不了解。

总之，当时我不知道自己的一生要干什么，最后因为一件十分悲惨的事情，我找到了自己的目标。可能是在 19 岁时，我的女朋友在一次车祸中身亡。我经过事故现场时不知道是她，就继续走，但不久我就发现，那就是她。当时我住在地下室的公寓里，我没有钱，没有暖气，没有新鲜空气，只是在地板上铺一个垫子，房间里到处都是跳蚤。我感到困惑不已，我在想，"为什么她突然走了？为什么我住在满是跳蚤的房子里？"我无法理解，但一定有理由的，要是能直接拿起电话问上帝不是太好了吗？

于是我开始写东西，脑海中涌现出一段与上帝的对话，那是只有我一个人的独白。写完之后，我看着我写的东西，对自己讲话。那时，我还没有开始做单人脱口秀节目，因为当时纽奥良没有俱乐部。我说，我将要在"今夜秀"上和约翰尼·卡森一起表演这一段。他在当时是主持界天王，我将成为该节目史上第一个和他一起坐下被访问的女性。数年之后，我成了该节目史上第一位、也是唯一一位和约翰尼一起坐下被访问的女性，全是因为我写的"与上帝打电话对话"的剧本。从此我开始做单人脱口秀节目，非常成功，非常棒，但也非常艰难，因为我想取悦每一个人，我守着自己是同志的秘密，我想人们要是发现我是个同性恋，就不会喜欢我了，还会嘲

热词空间

shuck [ʃʌk] v. 剥去
oyster ['ɔistə] n. 牡蛎
bartender ['bɑː,tendə] n. 酒保
vacuum cleaner 真空吸尘器
mattress ['mætris] n. 床垫
infest [in'fest] vt. 遍布于，大批滋生
flea [fliː] n. 跳蚤
soul-searching n. 自我反省
laugh at sb. 嘲笑某人
sitcom ['sitkɔm] n. 情景喜剧

successful, another level of success. And I thought, "what if they find out I'm gay, then they'll never watch," and this was a long time ago, this was when we just had white presidents — but anyway this was back, many years ago — and I finally decided that I was living with so much shame, and so much fear, that I just couldn't live that way anymore, and I decided to come out and make it creative. And my character would come out at the same time, and it wasn't to make a political statement, it wasn't to do anything other than to free myself up from this heaviness that I was carrying around, and I just wanted to be honest. And I thought, "What's the worst that could happen? I can lose my career." I did. I lost my career. The show was cancelled after six years, without even telling me, I read it in the paper. The phone didn't ring for three years. I had no offers. Nobody wanted to touch me at all. And yet, I was getting letters from kids that almost committed suicide, but didn't, because of what I did. And I realised that I had a purpose. And it wasn't just about me and it wasn't about celebrity, but I felt like I was being punished... it was a bad time, I was angry, I was sad, and then I was offered a talkshow. And the people that offered me the talkshow tried to sell it And most stations didn't want to pick it up. Most people didn't want to buy it because they thought nobody would watch me.

And really when I look back on it, I wouldn't change a thing. I mean, it was so important for me to lose everything because I found out what the most important thing is, is to be true to yourself. And ultimately, that's what's gotten me to this place. I don't live in fear. I'm free. I have no secrets. and I know I'll always be OK, because no matter what, I know who I am. So in conclusion, when I was younger I thought success was something different. I thought when I grow up, I want to be famous. I want to be a star. I want to be in movies. When I grow up I want to see the world, drive nice cars, I want to have groupies to quote the Pussycat Dolls. How many people thought it was "boobies", by the way? It's not, it's "groupies".

But my idea of success is different today. And as you grow, you'll realise the definition of success changes. For many of you, today, success is being able to hold

笑我。

接着，我有了自己的喜剧，也很成功，更进一步的成功。我又在想，要是人们发现我是同性恋了，该怎么办？他们再也不会看我的节目了。这是很早以前的事情，你们可能不知道，这是我们的总统都还是白人的时候，那是多年前的事了。我最后决定，我一直都是带着羞耻和恐惧而活，我不能再这么活着了。我最终决定将这个秘密公之于众，要有创造性，同时也要将我真实的个性展示出来，不是为了政治，也不是为了其他原因，只是要把我从背负已久的沉重的枷锁中解脱出来。我只是想要诚实。我想不会有更惨的事情了。失去演艺事业吗？结果我真的失去了我的演艺事业。我的节目在做了六年后，没有告诉我就停播了。我是看了报纸才知道的。家里的电话三年没有响过，没人想让我做节目。没人愿意碰我。然而，我接到了想要自杀的孩子的来信，他们因为我所做的而没有自杀。我才知道我活在世上是有目的的，不仅仅是因为我，不仅仅是因为我是名人，我感觉我是在受惩罚。那段时间很艰难，我很愤怒，也很难过，接着有人找我做脱口秀节目。制作单位努力想要卖出节目，但大多数的电视台都不想要。大多数人都不想要，因为他们认为没人想看我的节目。

当我回首这些往事的时候，我一点也不会改变。因为我发现，即使失去一切，最重要的是做真正的自己。最终，我来到了这里。我不再恐惧，我感觉很自在，也不再有秘密，而且我知道一切都会好的，因为无论如何，我知道我是谁。所以这还不是结论的结论，我年轻时，对成功有着不同的定义，我的志向是长大后，我要出名，我要成为明星，我想拍电影。我的愿望是长大后要周游世界、开名车、有一批流行乐团歌迷，引用"小野猫"这个组合。有多少人听成是"傻瓜"？并不是，是"流行乐团歌迷"。

down 20 shots of tequila. For me, the most important thing in your life is to live your life with integrity, and not to give into peer pressure; to try to be something that you're not. To live your life as an honest and compassionate person; to contribute in some way. So to conclude my conclusion: follow your passion, stay true to yourself. Never follow anyone else's path, unless you're in the woods and you're lost and you see a path, and by all means you should follow that. Don't give advice, it will come back and bite you in the ass. Don't take anyone's advice. So my advice to you is to be true to yourself and everything will be fine.

And I know that a lot of you are concerned about your future, but there's no need to worry. The economy is booming, the job market is wide open, the planet is just fine. It's gonna be great. You've already survived a hurricane. What else can happen to you? And as I mentioned before, some of the most devastating things that happen to you will teach you the most. And now you know the right questions to ask in your first job interview, like, "Is it above sea level?" So to conclude my conclusion that I've previously concluded, in the common cement speech, I guess what I'm trying to say is life is like one big Mardi Gras. But instead of showing your boobs, show people your brain, and if they like what they see, you'll have more beads than you know what to do with. And you'll be drunk, most of the time.

So the Tulane class of 2009, I say congratulations and if you don't remember a thing I said today, remember this: you're gonna be OK, dun-doom-doom-doom-doom, just dance.

但今天我对成功的定义变了。你们长大后就会明白，对成功的定义是会改变的。你们中的许多人对成功的定义就是灌完 20 杯龙舌兰烈酒。我认为，你们生活中最重要的事情就是要活得正直诚实，别屈从于同伴的压力，把自己变成本不是的那个人。要活得诚实，有同情心，要在某个方面有所贡献。这是结论的结论，追随热情，忠于自我。永远不要追随别人的脚步，除非你在森林里迷了路才能这么做，那时你真的该那样做。别给人忠告，它们会给你带来麻烦。也别接受任何人的忠告。那么我要给大家的忠告是，做真正的自己，一切都会顺利的。

我知道，在座的许多人都担心自己的前途，但不用担心。经济正在急速增长，就业市场极为广阔，地球也好得很。一切都会好的。你们经历了飓风，还有什么害怕的呢？我之前说过，从最惨痛的经历中可以吸取最多的教训。现在你们知道在你们的第一次面试中该问什么样的问题了吧？比如，公司高于海平面吗？（纽奥良地势低而淹水）总结我之前的结论，我的"常见的水泥"演讲，我想说的是，人生就像一场狂欢节嘉年华，但请展现你们的头脑，而非胸部，如果人家欣赏的话你就有更多的金银珠宝可以使用，而且在大多时间你都会醉。

因此，杜兰大学 2009 届的毕业生们，祝贺你们顺利毕业！如果你们不记得我说过的任何话，请记住这句，一切都会好的，尽管跳舞吧！

热词空间

tequila [tei'ki:la:] n. 龙舌兰酒
integrity [in'tegrəti] n. 诚实正直
compassionate [kəm'pæʃənit] adj. 有同情心的
ass [æs] n. 屁股
boom [bu:m] vi. 急速增长
hurricane ['hʌrikən] n. 飓风
Mardi gras [宗] 狂欢节

艾伦·德詹尼丝给我们的 启示

Usually when you're wearing a robe at 10 in the morning, it means you've given up.

通常在早上10点还穿着睡袍，说明你们已经放弃人生了。

For me, the most important thing in your life is to live your life with integrity, and not to give into peer pressure; to try to be something that you're not. To live your life as an honest and compassionate person; to contribute in some way.

我认为，你们生活中最重要的事情就是要活得诚实，别逼自己成为不是真正的你。要活得正直，有同情心，要在某个方面有所贡献。

…follow your passion, stay true to yourself. Never follow anyone else's path, unless you're in the woods and you're lost and you see a path, and by all means you should follow that. Don't give advice, it will come back and bite you in the ass. Don't take anyone's advice. So my advice to you is to be true to yourself and everything will be fine.

追随热情，忠于自我。永远不要追随别人的脚步，除非你在森林里迷了路才能这么做，那时你真的该那样做。别给人忠告，它们会给你带来麻烦。也别接受任何人的忠告。那么我要给大家的忠告是，做真正的自己，一切都会顺利的。

杜克大学

校训：Eruditio et Religio（拉丁文：知识和虔诚）

总 括

　　杜克大学由"三一大学"发展而来。1924年，北卡州的烟草大亨 James B. Duke 为纪念他的父亲 Washington Duke，利用慈善家 Julian S. Carr 所馈赠的 9000 英亩土地，无私无我地投入全部产业和资金，将"三一大学"扩建为"杜克大学"，至今已发展成为傲视全美的著名大学。

　　杜克大学历史上曾有过"南方哈佛"之称。其学费之昂贵与哈佛平分秋色，但杜克绝佳的设备、小班制、个别关照、城乡并重及文武合一的观念，是其他大学极为称羡的。

　　杜克大学是美国南部学术中心之一，当之无愧地成为美国最优秀的大学之一。其医学中心赢得了世界声誉，许多其他院系也持续位居美国最佳院系之列。杜克以其研究成果和学术革新引起社会各界的关注，其教授也常被邀请担任国内外许多学术和专业组织的负责人。

Follow Your Gut, and You Will Be a Huge Success

追随自己的心声，你们一定会成功

Duke University
Commencement Address
Oprah Winfrey
May, 2009

背景资料

2009 年 5 月，美国脱口秀女主奥普拉·温弗瑞在美国著名的杜克大学发表演讲，通过自己的采访经历，向毕业生提出忠告，希望毕业生能够追随自己的心声。同时她希望毕业生在走自己的道路的同时，要尽最大的努力帮助别人。

Trust your gut to help you stand proudly in your own shoes, as you help others stand in theirs, and I know you will be a huge success.

相信自己的心声，你才能自豪地穿上自己的鞋子走自己的路，如果你也能帮别人走他们自己的路，那你们一定会大有作为。

—— 奥普拉·温弗瑞

最名人档案

姓　　名：	奥普拉·温弗瑞（Oprah Winfrey）
性　　别：	女
职　　业：	脱口秀节目主持人
国　　籍：	美国
出生日期：	1954 年 1 月 29 日
毕业学校：	被普林斯顿大学授予荣誉博士学位
成功点睛：	她只是靠着"一个人可以非常清贫、困顿、低微，但是不可以没有梦想"的简单信念，实现了丑小鸭到黑天鹅的美丽蜕变。
个人成就：	美国第一位黑人亿万富翁

名人简介

　　奥普拉·温弗瑞 1954 年出生在密西西比的一个小镇。长相平平、肤色黝黑、身材欠佳，笑起来大嘴一咧，谈不上什么优雅。但就是这样一个女人，却占据着《福布斯》2005 年度"百位名人"排行榜的头把交椅，令麦当娜、安吉丽娜·朱莉等这一大串光彩照人的女明星望其项背。她就是美国的"传媒女皇"。

　　从 1986 年以她的名字命名的脱口秀节目在全美推出以来，她幽默机智的风格便迅速捕获了美国无数观众的心。如今，她以超过 14 亿美元的身价在美国黑人亿万富翁中名列第一；她在近 8 年里连续 5 次被评为全美最受欢迎主持人；她在电视读书会节目推荐过的新书转眼就会成为畅销书；美国伊利诺伊大学开设了一门课程专门研究这种以奥普拉为标志的"美国文化现象"；作为亿万富翁的她同样没忘记回馈社会，她通过自己设立的慈善机构向贫困妇女、儿童和家庭伸出援助之手。美国《名利场》杂志评价她说："在大众文化中，她的影响力，可能除了教皇以外，比任何大学教授、政治家或者宗教领袖都大。"

Oh, yes, I'm going to have everyone call me Doctor now. Thank you, President Brodhead. Ladies and gentlemen and graduates, and especially to all the mothers here — will all the mothers stand, so we can say Happy Mother's Day? Happy Mother's Day to you. What a great day to celebrate mothers. You love me still, even though I'm a doctor now?

Well, I wanted to just say, first of all, thank you for the doctorate degree, and I'm so happy to be here, and I'm here because someone I love is graduating today, my godson, William Bumpus, the son of Will Bumpus and my best friend, Gayle. You know, William never wants people to know that he knows me, and his sister, Kirby, never did either. I'm like the crazy aunt they keep in the attic, and they let me out to do commencements, so here I am. I just want to say I knew William before he was born. I saw the sonogram, and he was smiling even then. So those of you who know him know he has such a gorgeous smile.

I know you all have memories of graduates flooding through your minds today as we celebrate this milestone graduation, Class of 2009. One of my fondest memories of William, one time when he was a little boy, he was at my house, and I used to collect these antique museum quality Shaker boxes, and I walked into the room and William has my one of a kind Shaker boxes and he's stacking them up like Bric A Blocs and knocking them down and going, "Vroom." And I yelled, just — I just started — I said, "No, William, stop!" I think I stunned the boy, because he wasn't used to anybody yelling at him, and he stopped, he put the boxes back on the shelf and he found where he found them and he did not say a word to me. He didn't even cry. And a little later on, he goes up to his mom and he says, "Mom, Auntie O is mean. Can we go home?"

Well, William, Auntie O has some news for you. You're getting those scratched-up boxes for your graduation gift. You can knock them down all you want. But seriously, I don't know a better young man in the world than William Bumpus, and

哦，没错，现在你们每个人都会叫我博士了。非常感谢，布劳德海德校长。女士们，先生们，各位毕业生们，特别是所有在座的母亲——所有在座的母亲都站起来，让我们一起祝你们"母亲节快乐"，好吗？母亲节快乐！在这美好的日子庆祝母亲节真是太棒了。尽管我现在是博士了，但你们依然爱我，是吗？

首先，我想感谢贵校授予我博士学位。今天能来到这里，我感到非常高兴。来到这里还有一个原因，我爱的一个人，我的教子——威尔·彭勃斯和我最好的朋友盖尔的儿子——威廉·彭勃斯今天要毕业了。你们知道，威廉和他的姐姐科比从来都不想让人们知道他们认识我。我就像他们藏在阁楼里的疯狂的阿姨一样，他们让我出来做毕业演讲，所以我就来了。我要告诉你们，在威廉出生前我就认识他了。我看过超声波图，他那时就在微笑了。所以，认识他的人都应该知道他的笑容很灿烂。

2009届的毕业生们，当我们庆祝这一重要的毕业典礼时，我知道你们的脑海中都会浮现出对毕业生的印象。我对威廉最深刻的一次记忆是在他还是个小男孩的时候。他当时在我家做客，我过去常收集一些高级古董盒子，我走进房间，看见威廉拿着我的一个古董盒子，把它们像堆积木一样堆起来，然后再推倒，还发出"呜——呜——"的声音。看见这个，我就开始大声喊了起来，"威廉姆，停下来！"我想我肯定把这孩子给吓着了，因为他不习惯任何人对他大声喊叫，他停了下来，把盒子放回到架子上，一句话也没跟我说。他甚至没有哭。过了一会儿，他走到他妈妈那儿说，"妈妈，奥普拉阿姨太小气了，咱们回家好吗？"

威廉，奥普拉阿姨要告诉你一些消息。我将会把这些有抓痕的盒子作为毕业礼物送给你。你想怎么推倒它们都行。说实话，威廉·彭勃斯是我在这个世界上认识的最优秀的年轻人。

热词空间

godson ['gɔdsʌn] n. 教子

attic ['ætik] n. 阁楼

sonogram ['sɔnəgræm] n. 超声波图

milestone ['mailstəun] n. 里程碑，划时代意义的时间

antique [æn'tiːk] adj. 古老的，古董的

stack up 堆积起来

stun [stʌn] vt. 使震惊

yell at 对……吼叫

thank you, Duke, for making him an even greater young man. And I have to say that he is so kind and so generous of spirit. William, you're the son I wish I'd had, and so I'm thrilled to be here for you. Love you, Willzer.

I've been doing my show now for almost 25 years. Feels like 125, but almost 25 years. And my greatest lessons have come from my work; talking to murderers, doing makeovers, learning about flesh-eating diseases, have all been great growing tools for me, because I look at life every day from the experience of what can I grow from this. Actually, the show is why I never needed therapy. Well, I might have needed therapy, but I never went to therapy, because I have learned so many lessons from our show and the people I've met. And the miracle for me is that almost 25 years later, I get to go to work every day and I am still learning.

I just finished taping a show this week with so many powerful lessons that I wanted to weep, but I want to share some of those lessons with you today. As a matter of fact, there were so many lessons in the show that I taped just last week, that's going to air next week, you'll see it, I did weep. It was about some tough guys in prison for murder, for manslaughter, armed robbery, guys full of anger and violence. And they're involved in this program where dogs, little puppies, are taken from shelters and the eight-week-old puppies are given to the prisoners, eight-week-old puppies that would have otherwise been euthanized. The puppies live right in the prison cells with the prisoners 24 hours a day. And I forgot to ask them … how they housebreak them, because it's not like you can say, "I need to take the dog out."

But the prisoners train these puppies to then be service dogs to help our soldiers in Iraq who come back with traumatic brain injuries and post-traumatic stress, and then send them to the veterans from Iraq. Some of these inmates had never known love or responsibility. They'd never taken care of anybody, nor knew what it felt like to have somebody love you back when you take care of them.

But one of the things they teach the dogs is how to kiss the soldier's face. A lot of the soldiers come back with post-traumatic stress and have terrible experiences, and if the soldier is starting to go to a bad place in his mind, the dogs lick and kiss the

感谢杜克大学，让他变得更加优秀了。他真的很善良，很慷慨。威廉，我真希望有你这么一个儿子，所以因为你我来到这里，我感觉很激动。爱你，威廉！

　　我主持我的节目将近25年了。确切地说还不到25年，但感觉像过了125年似的。这些年来，我从工作中学到了很多东西；不管是跟凶手谈话也好，给嘉宾做大变身也好，对肉腐性疾病做调查也好，都丰富了我的人生，因为我每天都在借鉴别人的生活经验来使自己成长。事实上，有了这档节目我从不需要别的治疗。或者，也许我需要接受治疗，但是我从没有去过，因为我从自己主持的节目中和接触的人群中学到了很多。对我来说，在将近25年后，每天去工作发现自己仍然在学习，这简直就是个奇迹。

　　我这个星期刚刚录制完的一期节目让我学到了很多教训，让我想流泪，今天我想跟你们分享一些。实际上，那期节目真的可以让我们学到很多，这将会在下周播放，你们也都会看到，我真的哭了。节目是关于罪犯的，他们有的因为谋杀罪，有的因为过失杀人罪，有的因为持械抢劫罪被关进监狱。这群人满怀愤怒，极具暴力倾向。这群罪犯参与了一项计划，那就是驯养刚从避难所里抱出来的两个月大的小狗崽。如果不由他们来驯养，这些小狗崽就会被处以安乐死。就这样，小狗崽一天24小时都跟犯人们生活在监狱里。我忘了问，他们怎样驯养这些小狗崽呢？因为他们不能像常人那样说一句"我需要把狗带出去"就可以去遛狗。

　　这些犯人要把小狗崽训练成服务狗，让它们去帮助我们国家那些因为脑创伤或者脑创伤后遗症从伊拉克战场返回来的老兵。它们会被送到老兵那里。这些犯人们有的根本不知道什么是爱和责任。他们从来没照顾过别人，也不知道照顾别人时得到别人爱的回馈是什么样的感觉。

　　然而，犯人们教小狗做的一件事是让它们学会去亲吻老

热词空间

thrilled [θrild] *adj.* 极为激动的，非常兴奋的

makeover ['meikəuvə(r)] *n.* 大转变，化妆美容

therapy ['θerəpi] *n.* 治疗

tough [tʌf] *adj.* 粗暴的，不守秩序的

manslaughter ['mæn,slɔ:tə] *n.* 杀人，过失杀人

euthanize ['ju:θənaiz] *vt.* 使安乐死

housebreak ['hausbreik] *vt.* 驯养

traumatic [trau'mætik] *adj.* 外伤的，创伤的

veteran ['vetərən] *n.* 老兵

inmate ['inmeit] *n.* 同住者

lick [lik] *vt.* 舔

soldier's face to bring him back to reality. So this means that the prisoners themselves also had to get the kisses from the puppies they were training. It's clear the kisses were also bringing the prisoners back from a hard, cold place, and to see these criminals, who had never, many of them, experienced love themselves, cry on camera, in front of each other, cry in redemption, their voices quivering as they talk about the chance to do something good, to do something kind and unselfish, by helping the wounded soldiers in Iraq and teaching the dogs, was so moving.

And when the severely injured soldier — what we did was we went and found one of the soldiers who had received a dog and brought him back to the prison so that he could meet the prisoner who — who trained the dog. And when they met, I tell you, the audience and I were a puddle of tears. And what I learned from that I want to share with you, graduates. If you can find a way to give back just as these felons are giving from behind bars, you will be a huge success, because for sure one of the things I've learned is that the best way to enhance your own life is to contribute to somebody else's.

Now, last year we did a story on a woman named Monica George, and people often ask, you know, "Who's your favorite guest, who's your favorite guest," and they always expect me to name some movie star. Well, if it's a movie star, it would be Hugh Jackman. He's one of my favorite guests, and you can imagine why.

But my favorite guests are, for the most part, not celebrities and not people who've done famous or infamous things. My most favorite guests are ordinary people who've accomplished extraordinary triumphs in their life, and Monica George is one of those people I will never forget. She and her husband, Tony, were overjoyed at the C-section birth of a healthy baby girl that they named Sophie and Sophie was their second daughter. This was just last year.

But within hours, and while she was still in the hospital, Monica developed a

兵的脸。很多老兵从战场回来后有脑创后遗症和可怕的经历，每当老兵想起可怕的往事时，小狗就会舔舐并亲吻他的脸，把他带回现实中。这意味着犯人们训练小狗的时候也会得到小狗的亲吻。很显然，这些吻也会把犯人们带离那个无情而冰冷的地方。再看看这些犯人，他们中很多人没有经历过爱和被爱，他们在镜头前，在彼此面前痛哭流泪，因为忏悔而流泪。在讲述通过训练小狗去帮助受伤士兵的经历，使他们获得了改过自新、做些无私善举的机会时，他们的声音都在颤抖。这个场面实在是太感人了。

我们节目组要做的事是从中找到一个接受小狗的老兵，把他带到监狱去，这样他就能见到训练这只小狗的犯人了。最后我们找了一个严重受伤的老兵。他和犯人见面的那一瞬间，我告诉你们，我们这些旁观者的眼泪夺眶而出。毕业生们，我想与你们分享自己从那件事中学到的东西。如果你们能够找到一种回报的方式，就像这些重罪犯们在监狱里所做的回报一样，你们定会大有作为，因为我领悟到的一个真理就是：丰富人生的最好的方式就是为他人的生活做些贡献。

去年，我们播放了莫妮卡·乔治的故事。别人常常问我："你最喜欢的嘉宾是谁，你最喜欢的嘉宾是哪个？"你们知道他们总是期盼着我会说出某个影视明星的名字。如果一定要说某个明星的话，我会说是休·杰克曼。他确实是我最喜欢的嘉宾之一，你们可以想想为什么。

然而，我最喜欢的嘉宾中，大部分不是名人，不是那些名声显赫或者声名狼藉的人。我最喜欢的嘉宾往往是那些在生活中有着非凡事迹的普通人。莫妮卡·乔治就是这些我永远不会忘记的人中的一个。就在去年，她和丈夫托尼都还沉浸在剖腹产下第二个女儿所带来的欢乐中，他们给这个健康可爱的孩子取名叫索菲。

但是，在生下小索菲几个小时之后，莫妮卡还没离开产床，

热词空间

redemption [ri'dempʃən] n.
赎回，拯救

quiver ['kwivə] vi. 颤抖，发抖

puddle ['pʌdl] n. 水池，水坑

felon ['felən] n. 重罪犯

Hugh Jackman 休·杰克曼，
澳大利亚男演员，凭借电影
《X战警》成为影坛超级巨
星和帅酷型男，在美国畅销
杂志"People"中荣膺"全
球最性感男士"称号。

triumph ['traiəmf] n. 胜利，
成功

C-section ['si:,sekʃən] n. 剖
腹产

哈佛
大学

斯坦福
大学

牛津
大学

耶鲁
大学

杜兰
大学

杜克
大学

威斯康
辛大学

清华
大学

北京
大学

亚利桑
那州立
大学

加利福
尼亚
大学

fever and pain caused by a fast-moving, flesh-eating bacteria. She was dying, so they took some organs to save her, but the bacteria had spread, so the doctors came in and said to her, "We think, as a matter of fact, we know we're going to have to amputate. We're going to have to take both your arms and both your legs." And this woman said, "Get on with it. I want you to do it and do it as fast as you can, because I have to get home to take care of my girls."

So imagine going into the hospital to have a baby, you have the healthy baby and you expect to be coming home with this tiny little pink bundle of joy, with pink little arms and legs, and instead you go home without your arms and legs. The arms that were going to hold this child and legs that were going to walk with her in the park. Monica had 37 operations in two months, but she's now home with her girls, home without a trace of self-pity, home with a smile on her face and a peace in her heart. And when I talked to her, she said, sure, sometimes it hurts that she's not able to paint Sophie's nails and toenails and do the things that mothers and daughters do, but she also said, "What good are you to your children if you're miserable?"

There's so many lessons in this, because at some point, something in life is going to eat you inside. It could be anger; it could be guilt; it could be past hurts or some other strain of soul eating bacteria. But graduates, I want you to know that if you can summon the courage of Monica George in the face of your own life's hardships, and you will have them, and if you can remember what good are you to anyone if you're miserable, I know for sure you'll be a huge success, because you are responsible for your happiness and you are responsible for the energy you bring to everything.

One of my other favorite guests was a woman named Dr. Jill Bolte Taylor, who's a brain scientist, who had a stroke in the left hemisphere of her brain. She wrote a book called *My Stroke of Insight*. And so only the right hemisphere was working, and when she was in the hospital as a patient, she said she could sense through her right brain when a nurse would come into the room and meant her well, or when the nurse was thinking about what time she was going to be off that day. She could sense

就开始发高烧，浑身疼痛。医生诊断她感染了发展极快的肉腐性细菌。她奄奄一息了，为了挽救她，医生切除了她的部分器官，但是细菌扩散太快了，最后医生告诉她："照这个情况来看，我们只能实行切除术了。为控制病情，我们只能切除你的四肢。"这个女人坚定地回答："那就开始吧。我需要你们尽快施行手术，我还等着回家照顾我的两个女儿呢。"

你们想象一下，本来是去医院生孩子的，孩子健康地出生了，你本以为过后就可以高兴地带着这个粉嘟嘟的小生命回家了，但是结果自己却没了胳膊和腿。以后再没有双臂来拥抱这个孩子，再没有双腿来陪着这个孩子在公园散步了。莫妮卡在两个月中做了 37 次手术，现在她已经在家和女儿们生活在一起了，她丝毫不觉伤悲，总是面带微笑，心境坦然。我跟她谈话的时候，她说，当然，有时候她也会伤心，她不能够像个正常的母亲一样，给索菲涂涂指甲，也没法做其他母女可以做的事，但她又说："如果你整天都伤心欲绝，对孩子们能有什么好处呢？"

这件事中蕴含着很多哲理。有时候，生活中的某一件事就可以把你毁掉，或许因为愤怒，或许因为罪恶，或许因为过去受过的伤，或许因为精神疲惫。但是毕业生们，我希望你们明白，如果你们可以像莫妮卡·乔治一样鼓起勇气直面生活中的挫折；如果你们记得整天伤心对别人根本没什么好处的话，我敢肯定你们定会大有作为，因为做到这些你们就做到了对自己的幸福负责，对给他人所带来的影响负责。

我最喜欢的另一位嘉宾是吉尔·博尔特·泰勒博士，她是位脑体科学家，同时她自己的左脑也受过重创。吉尔写了一部书《我的重创观察记》。虽然只有右脑可以正常工作，但在住院期间，她说她能通过右脑很好地感知护士何时要来，对她做了什么，何时要下班。她能感知到带入病房的任何能量。不久，她就在病房里贴了个牌子，告诉进病房的所有人：你

热词空间

amputate ['æmpjuteit] *vt.* 截肢，切断

bundle ['bʌndl] *n.* 捆，束，包

strain [strein] *n.* 种，负担

stroke [strəuk] *n.* 中风，打击

summon ['sʌmən] *vt.* 鼓起

hemisphere ['hemi,sfiə] *n.* 半球

insight ['insait] *n.* 洞悉，理解

sense [sens] *vt.* 感觉到，意识到

the energy that was brought into the room. And after a while, she put up a sign in the room that said to everyone who came in the room, you are responsible for the energy that you bring. I love that moment, because we are responsible for the energy that we bring to everything we do in life.

One thing that gets a huge response on the show is makeover. You know, we did a makeover on Coretta Scott King, the late Coretta Scott King, wife of Dr. Martin Luther King, and this was like going to Mount Rushmore and giving George Washington a new do, because she hadn't changed her do since 1954. But we've done a lot of makeovers. One woman hadn't changed her hair in 37 years. She had this big old hair thing going on. Another young woman worked in a chicken house, and after we got all the feathers off, she was stunning. Another woman had worn her hair in a bun for 25 years and put on makeup to go to bed at night, because she said if she died in her sleep, she wanted to be ready.

People love makeovers, because the physical results are always so astonishing. But I like doing them because of the possibility of transforming more than the way people look. You want to change the way people feel about themselves. One man, a guy we'd just seen walking down the street, with a beard that was almost to the ground, it looked like he was hiding behind all of that beard. And after we got rid of all that hair and he could actually see himself, he said, "I feel alive again." The makeover allowed him to see himself in a way that he'd forgotten was there. You know, we all need makeovers from time to time in our lives, and graduates, I know this, that if you can see the possibility of changing your life, of seeing what you can become and not just what you are, you will be a huge success.

One of my life heroes is Nelson Mandela, and I had the great honor of spending some time with Nelson Mandela, 10 days and 29 meals at his house, and I was so worried about what I was going to talk about or what we would say at the dinner table. And Stedman said to me, "Why don't you try listening?" Thank you, Stedman. That worked.

们要对自己带进来的能量负责。我喜欢那一刻，因为我们要为生活中能够产生能量的所有行为负责。

在节目中，观众反应最强烈的是大变身。你们知道，我们对已步入晚年的科莱塔·司格特·金——马丁·路德·金博士的妻子，做了大变身。这就等于去罗斯摩尔山重塑乔治·华盛顿雕像。从1954年以来，她就没改变过。而我们已经做了很多大变身。有位老妇人，37年来一直坚持梳一种老式发型并决定以后也不会改变发型。另一位年轻女人在鸡棚工作，我们把粘在她身上的鸡毛都清理干净后，她简直惊呆了。还有一位妇女25年来一直梳好发髻，化好妆再睡觉，她说怕有一天在睡梦中死去，所以她必须每天都做好准备。

人们喜欢大变身，因为它们带来的结果总是让人吃惊。我喜欢做大变身不只因为它改变人们的形象，更因为转变的可能性。你想改变人们对自己的看法。举个例子来说，有一次我在街上遇见一个家伙，他的胡子都快长到地上了，好像他想把一切都挡在他那把长胡子后面。后来我们把他的胡子剃干净了，他才看清楚自己，然后他说："我觉得我又活过来了。"那次大变身让他再次找回了遗忘了很久的自己。你知道，在生活中我们都有需要变身的时候。毕业生们，我确定，如果能够发现改变自己生活的可能性，如果能抛开现在的自己，把眼光放远看到将来的自己，你们定会大有作为。

纳尔逊·曼德拉是我生命中的英雄之一，我很荣幸自己有机会同他一起生活了一段时间。在他的住所度过了10天，吃了29顿饭，每天吃晚饭的时候，我都担心我该和他说些什么，或者我们之间会谈点什么。斯特德曼对我说："为什么不试着倾听呢？"谢谢斯特德曼，这一招果然有效。

就这样，我从餐桌前的29顿晚饭中受益匪浅，我倾听了很多，听他讲述在南非监狱度过的27年艰难岁月，跟他讨论他是怎么能怀有一颗宽恕之心走出那段阴霾，抚平那场残酷

热词空间

Dr. Martin Luther King
马丁·路德·金博士(1927-1968)，美国民权运动领袖，曾发表著名的演讲《我有一个梦想》，是1964年度诺贝尔和平奖获得者。1968年被刺杀身亡。

bun [bʌn] *n.* 圆发髻

makeup ['meikʌp] *n.* 化妆品

astonishing [əs'tɔniʃiŋ] *adj.* 惊人的

get rid of 除去，摆脱

Nelson Mandela 纳尔逊·曼德拉(1918-)，于1994年至1999年间任南非总统。曼德拉曾在牢中服刑了27年，在其40年的政治生涯中获得了超过一百项奖项，其中最显著的便是1993年的诺贝尔和平奖。他是南非首位黑人总统，被尊称为"南非之父"。

So I had the benefit of sitting at his table for 29 meals and listened a lot, listened to the stories of how he spent 27 years in a South African prison, and talked to him about how he was able to come out of that with a sense of forgiveness, to bind the wounds of South Africa and saving it from a mean and violent civil war. So I asked him to come on our show, and I was — although I'd sat at his table and was very comfortable in his presence, I was really nervous having him come on the show, and I rarely, rarely, rarely get nervous. And for me, his warmth just filled our studio with a **glow**, and one of the things I will always remember him saying is how terrible it was to spend the best years of his life in that prison, but he said if he'd not been in prison, he would have not been able to achieve the most difficult task in his life, and that was to begin the change of himself.

But this is so — this tells the story of who he really is. He arrives at the studio and everybody's so excited and nervous and it's Nelson Mandela, and Nelson Mandela walks into the **green room** and says to the producer, "And what is the show about?" "Uh, you. The show's about you, sir." Nelson Mandela was so **humble** that being on the show for a whole hour was not something he expected. "How can such a great man be so humble," I thought. Graduates, if you can proceed through life with just a portion of Nelson Mandela's **humility**, you will be a huge success.

When I was eight years old, I was at church one day…. and a stranger came to me … and a man named John J. Hooker was running for governor at the time, and he had come to our church to campaign. And afterwards, outside as we were leaving the church, his wife, who was then a stranger, her name was Tish Hooker, a beautiful woman with **blonde** hair, classic **cheekbones**, **flawless** skin, saw me standing there. And you have to understand at the time I was a little black girl, but we didn't call ourselves black then. Actually, back then we were colored and Negro, but whatever. I was a little girl who didn't think much of herself, but Tish Hooker walked right up to me, as if she knew I needed to hear what she had to say. And she said it only as a Southern woman can. She said, "You know, you're just as pretty as a **speckled** pup."

170

猛烈的内战给南非所造成的创伤。所以，我邀请他来参加我们的节目，虽然我同他共进晚餐的时候处之泰然，但是请他来节目现场的时候，我还是非常紧张。我很少，很少，很少这么紧张过。对我来说，他的热情使得我们的演播室洋溢着温暖，我一直记得他说的那句话，他说在南非监狱里度过生命中最美好的时光真是太糟糕了，但是如果没有经历那段监狱生活的话，他也不可能完成他生命中最难的、开始改变他一生命运的任务。

确实是这样的——这告诉我们他到底是个怎么样的人物。他来到演播室，演播室里的每个人都很激动紧张，因为那是纳尔逊·曼德拉。纳尔逊·曼德拉则走进演员休息室，问制片人："这期节目是关于什么的？""唔，您啊。这期节目是关于您的啊，先生。"节目进行的整整一个小时期间，纳尔逊都表现得非常谦虚，完全不是制片人原来所料想的那样。我当时想，"这么伟大的人物怎么能如此谦虚呢？"毕业生们，如果你们能在接下来的生活中有纳尔逊·曼德拉的一点谦卑，你们定会大有作为。

我记得八岁的时候，有一天我去教堂，一个陌生人向我走来。那天恰逢一个名叫约翰·J·胡克的人为竞选执行长官在教堂举行活动。后来，我们走出教堂的时候，他妻子迪斯·胡克看见我站在那儿。她一头金发、颧骨完美、皮肤无瑕，当时对我们来说她还是个陌生人。你们要明白当时的我就是一个小小的黑人女孩，当然我们那时候不说自己是黑人。实际上，我们被叫做黑种人、黑鬼，但不管怎样，我就是个没把自己看得很重的小女孩，但是迪斯.胡克径直走向我，就好像知道我想听她说点什么一样。她对我说了只有南方女人才那样说的话，她说："你知道吗，你像小斑点狗一样漂亮可爱。"我并不知道什么是小斑点狗，她又说："你有着最漂亮的撅撅嘴。"

我只知道我长了两片厚嘴唇，我并不知道什么是撅撅嘴。

热词空间

glow [gləu] n. 热情，热烈
green room 演员休息室
humble ['hʌmbl] adj. 谦虚的，谦卑的
humility [hjuː'militi] n. 谦逊，谦虚
blonde [blɔnd] adj. 亚麻色的
cheekbone ['tʃiːkbəun] n. 颧骨
flawless ['flɔːlis] adj. 完美的，无瑕的
speckled ['spekld] adj. 有小斑点的

哈佛
大学

斯坦福
大学

牛津
大学

耶鲁
大学

杜兰
大学

杜克
大学

威斯康
辛大学

清华
大学

北京
大学

亚利桑
那州立
大学

加利福
尼亚
大学

Now, I didn't know what a speckled pup was, but she then said, "And you have the most beautiful **bee-stung** lips."

Well, I knew I had big lips. I didn't know what bee-stung lips were. But she said it with such warmth and such kindness that I remember going home from church and staring at myself in the mirror, because Tish Hooker had said that I was pretty, and she was the first person that ever looked at me and had the courage to speak the words, "You're pretty."

I'd never felt pretty. I knew I was smart, but this stranger, this woman who just came out of nowhere it seemed, was the first person to ever say it to me. And it made me see myself differently from that day forward, Tish Hooker saying, "You have such beautiful bee-stung lips," and I've remembered that my whole life. You never know what kindness you offer today to someone, how that might live with them forever. So, graduates, if you can be generous enough to say kind, **affirming** words to those who may **long** to hear them, you will be a huge success.

And finally, let me just tell you a story about my success. I had a **charity sale**, because I have clothes in every size, 8, 10, 12, 14, **elastic**. Sometimes it gets crowded in my closet. So I had a charity sale **awhile** back to get rid of all that stuff, and a woman named Joanie Jacks didn't have much money, because she didn't have a job at the time, and the least expensive thing she could find was a pair of black shoes.

Now, she wore a size seven and I'm a 10½ on a good day, 11 with **humidity**. So she bought a pair of my shoes and kept them in her bedroom, and she said that when she got depressed, when things weren't going well, she would take out the shoes and she would stand in my shoes. And she said she wanted to stand in the shoes until she'd be able to stand on her own, and she used the shoes as a sense of inspiration to herself. At age 50, she went back to college and got herself a degree, and today she's standing in her own shoes.

That is what makes me feel successful. Of all the wonderful things that have happened, including getting a doctorate, an honorary doctorate from Duke, what really

但是她说这些的时候语气是那么轻柔、和蔼，我就记着从教堂回家后，我一个劲地盯着镜子里的自己看，因为迪斯·胡克说我漂亮可爱，她是第一个看着我，有勇气对我说出"你很漂亮"这句话的人。

我以前从不觉得自己漂亮。我知道我很乖巧，但是这个陌生人，这个不知道从哪儿冒出来的女人，竟然成了第一个说我漂亮的人。从那天起这句话改变了我对自己的看法，迪斯·胡克说，"你长了这么漂亮的撅撅嘴"，这句话我一辈子都记得。你们不会知道无形之中会给别人带去怎样的善意，这样的善意或许会影响他们的一生。毕业生们，如果你们能做到慷慨大方，多向那些需要鼓励的人说些善意、赞扬的话，你们定会大有作为。

最后，让我给你们讲一个关于我成功的故事。我举行了一次义卖，因为我有不同型号的服装，8、10、12、14 以及有松紧带的。有时候，我的壁橱都有点放不下，所以我举行了义卖，处理那些衣物。有一个名叫乔安妮·杰克斯的女人没有太多钱，因为当时她没有工作，而她能从中找到的最便宜的东西是一双黑色的鞋。

那时，她的鞋码是 7，而我穿 10 码半的鞋，天气潮湿的话还会穿 11 码的。结果，她买了我的一双鞋，把它们放在自己的卧室里。她说，当她感到沮丧时，当事情不顺利时，她就会拿出这双鞋子，穿在自己脚上。她说，她想穿上这双鞋子，直到她能够穿上自己的鞋子，她把这双鞋子当作对自己的激励。在 50 岁时，她重返大学，获得了学位，如今，她穿着属于自己的鞋子。

这让我感觉自己很成功。把所有发生在我身上的好事都算上，包括获得杜克大学荣誉博士学位在内，真正让我有成就感的事情是用我的生命服务他人。当然，我得承认，有个漂亮的家真好，有个在圣巴巴拉市大火中幸免下来的漂亮的

热词空间

bee-stung ['bi:stʌn] *adj.* 撅起的
affirming [ə'fə:miŋ] *adj.* 肯定的，确定的
long [lɔŋ] *vi.* 渴望，热望
charity sale 义卖
elastic [i'læstik] *n.* 松紧带
awhile [ə'hwail] *adv.* 一会儿
humidity [hju:'miditi] *n.* 湿度，湿气

makes me feel successful is being able to use my life in service to someone else's. And I will have to say, it is a wonderful thing to have a beautiful home, or homes, a wonderful thing to have a beautiful home which just escaped the fire in Santa Barbara. And it is really fantastic to have your own jet, and anybody who says it isn't is lying to you. That jet thing is really good.

But you really haven't completed the circle of success unless you can help somebody else move forward. That's the truth. Move to higher ground. That's the real goal. How do you get someone else to move to higher ground.

So I spend my life doing that, thinking about how can I help somebody else move to higher ground. How can I help somebody else get to a stronger and better place, because that is success. That's it. That's why we're all alive, to use ourselves, our lives, for something bigger than ourselves.

So, graduates, in closing, each of us has to stand in our own shoes, and the real question is how will you stand in your own? Will you stand in them with humility and compassion and integrity and courage? Well, I'm here to tell you, every day and every experience of your life will give you a chance to make that choice. It still happens to me, every day, all the time.

Most recently, I was faced with a big decision as to whether or not — we had done this wonderful show, informative show, on Columbine, with an author of the book who had written this really fascinating, intriguing book on Columbine. And we finished taping the show, and I went upstairs and I said to the producers, who were all excited because he was doing his first interview with us, and they get really excited, "It's exclusive and it's wonderful, it's great." And I said, "Yes, but something about that bothered me. I'm not quite sure what it was, but something didn't feel right." I said, "But I have to — I have to take a look at it, I have to take some time to look at it, because in the moment, I really can't tell. I just have a feeling that something's off with that show."

So I said, "I want to take a chance to review the tape," and as my life would

家真好。拥有自己的喷气式飞机真好，如果有人认为这不好，他就是在撒谎。喷气式飞机真的是个好东西。

但是如果只是自己成功了，却没能帮助别人也走向成功，那不叫真正的成功。真正的成功是通向更高的地方，这是真理，但是你怎么做才能帮助别人也通往更高的地方呢？

因此我一生都在思考怎么做才能帮助别人通往更高的地方，我该怎样做才能帮助别人达到一个更好更牢固的地方，因为在我看来那才是真正的成功。那的确是真正的成功。我们活着的意义就是为了让我们的生命发光发热，去服务于更多的人。

毕业生们，最后，我们总要穿上自己的鞋子去走自己的路，真正的问题是你们会选择怎样走呢？你们会不会带着谦卑、同情、正直和勇气走呢？今天在这里我想告诉你们，生命中的每一天，每次经历都会给你选择的机会。我也是每一天每一刻都面临着选择。

刚刚过去的一些日子，我一直面临着一个重大的抉择——我们录制了一期很棒的节目，是关于科伦拜校园惨案的，我们的嘉宾是关于科伦拜校园惨案的一本很精彩的书的作者。当我们录制完节目，我上楼和制片人说话，他们都异常激动，因为这位作家是第一次做我们的嘉宾，他们兴奋地说，"这绝对是独家新闻，太棒了，太伟大了。"然而我说，"但是这期节目中有某种东西让我很困惑，我不确定是什么，但总感觉不对劲。我必须要看一下，我必须花些时间看一下，因为当时我确实说不清是哪里不对，我只是感觉这期节目会产生一些不好的影响。"

于是我说，"我要重新看一下这期节目，"然而我最终没有机会重新看。那是一个星期四，节目在接下来的周一播出。周六，我独自一人坐在圣巴巴拉市，坐了很长时间，突然我想起来这期节目哪里不对了。我所带给那期节目的精神出现了问题。

热词空间

jet [dʒet] n. 喷气式飞机

compassion [kəm'pæʃən] n. 同情，怜悯

integrity [in'tegriti] n. 正直，诚实

intriguing [in'tri:giŋ] adj. 有趣的，迷人的

exclusive [iks'klu:siv] adj. 独有的，独占的

have it, I didn't get a chance to review the tape. This was on a Thursday. The show was going to air on a Monday. Saturday, I'm sitting in Santa Barbara alone, quiet for a moment, and it occurred to me what's wrong with that show. There's something wrong with the energy that I brought to that show. And I called the producer and I said, "I know what's wrong with the show. I think the show focuses too much attention on the killers and it presents darkness, the energy of darkness, in a way that I really don't want to be responsible for."

And the producer said, "But the promos have gone out. It's already airing all over the country. We've told all the stations that it's airing and they have it in their lineup." And I said, "I am responsible for the energy that goes out over the air, so we're going to have to pull it, regardless of what we've told the stations, and they'll have to understand." So we pulled the show, because I felt that at the end of the day, if one person watching that show saw or heard something that made them feel inspired to go out and bring more darkness into the world, I didn't want that on me.

So it still happens every single day, decisions — decisions come my way that require me to decide who am I really, what am I really doing this for? Decisions that allow me to make a decision as to whether or not I will do the right thing or will I do the popular thing. So for every experience in life, you get a chance to know whether or not right or whether or not you'll follow the opinions of everyone else.

For me, it's all about following your gut. I am who I am because I trust my gut more than anyone else's opinion, and that is my best advice to you. You know what is right, and when everyone around you is telling you what you should do, what you shouldn't do, and when you … have to ask more than anybody other than yourself, you have to ask anyone other than yourself, it is your instinct, your higher self's way of saying, "Get still until you do know the answer, because your gut will never lead you wrong." Trust your gut to help you stand proudly in your own shoes, as you help others stand in theirs, and I know you will be a huge success. You have my warmest best wishes and my most heartfelt congratulations.

我给制片人打电话说，"我知道这期节目有什么问题。我认为这期节目更多关注杀人凶手，把一种精神的阴暗面展现给观众，在某种程度上说，我不想对那个所产生的影响负责。"

制片人说，"但是我们已经发布了预告片，而且已经在全国播放了。我们告诉所有的电视台将要播放这期节目，他们已经把这列入了节目单。"于是我又说，"我要对这期节目所展现的精神负责，所以我们必须取消节目，不管我们对电视台说了什么。他们必须理解这一点。"因此，我们取消了那期节目，因为我感觉，在那一天快要结束时，如果一个人在那期节目中看到的或听到的一些东西使他想要走出家门，从而给这个世界带来更多黑暗，这种后果我将无法承担。

每天我都要做出决定，而这需要我自己选择我真正想成为什么样的人，我做这些真正为了什么。这些决定允许我自己决定是去做正确的事情，还是去做流行的事情。所以对于生命中的每次经历来说，你都有机会明白这么做是否正确，还是仅仅为迎合或不迎合别人的观点。

对我来说，我会追随自己的心声。我之所以是我，就是因为与别人的观点相比，我更相信自己的心声，这也是我给你们的最好的建议。你们知道什么是正确的，所以当身边有人告诉你们什么该做，什么不该做的时候，当你们不得不征求别人的意见而不问自己想法的时候，你们的直觉、你们的自我就会告诉你："坚持做下去，直到自己弄清答案，因为你的心声不会带你走错路。"相信自己的心声，你才能自豪地穿上自己的鞋子走自己的路，如果你也能帮别人走他们自己的路，那你们定会大有作为。最后，将我最美好的祝愿送给你们，衷心祝贺你们。

热词空间

occur to 想到，意识到
promo ['prəuməu] n. 广告片，预告片
lineup ['lainʌp] n. 电视节目时间表
gut [gʌt] n. 本能的感觉，直觉

哈佛
大学

斯坦福
大　学

牛津
大学

耶鲁
大学

杜兰
大学

杜克
大学

威斯康
辛大学

清华
大学

北京
大学

亚利桑
那州立
大　学

加利福
尼　亚
大　学

奥普拉·温弗瑞给我们的 启示

…the best way to enhance your own life is to contribute to somebody else's.

……丰富人生的最好的方式就是为他人的生活做些贡献。

You know, we all need makeovers from time to time in our lives, and graduates, I know this, that if you can see the possibility of changing your life, of seeing what you can become and not just what you are, you will be a huge success.

你知道，在生活中每时我们都有需要变身的时候。毕业生们，我确定，如果能够发现改变自己生活的可能性，如果能抛开现在的自己，把眼光放远看到将来的自己，你们定会大有作为。

You never know what kindness you offer today to someone, how that might live with them forever. So, graduates, if you can be generous enough to say kind, affirming words to those who may long to hear them, you will be a huge success.

你们不会知道无形之中会给别人带去怎样的善意，这样的善意或许会影响他们的一生。毕业生们，如果你们能做到慷慨大方，多向那些需要鼓励的人说些善意、赞扬的话，你们定会大有作为。

But you really haven't completed the circle of success unless you can help somebody else move forward.

但是如果只是自己成功了，却没能帮助别人也走向成功，那不叫真正的成功。

You know what is right, and when everyone around you is telling you what you should do, what you shouldn't do, and when you … have to ask more than anybody other than yourself, you have to ask anyone other than yourself, it is your instinct, your higher self's way of saying, "Get still until you do know the answer, because your gut will never lead you wrong." Trust your gut to help you stand proudly in your own shoes, as you help others stand in theirs, and I know you will be a huge success.

你们知道什么是正确的，所以当身边有人告诉你们什么该做，什么不该做的时候，当你们不得不征求别人的意见而不问自己想法的时候，你们的直觉、你们的自我就会自己的方式说："坚持做下去，直到自己弄清答案，因为你的心声不会带你走错路。"相信自己的心声，你才能自豪地穿上自己的鞋子走自己的路，如果你也能帮别人走他们自己的路，那你们定会大有作为。

威斯康辛大学

校训：Numen Lumen（英文"God, our light"，中文"主，我们的光芒"）

总　括

  威斯康辛大学（麦迪逊分校），位于美国中部的威斯康辛州，建校于 1848 年，是一所著名的公立大学，教学严谨且学风优良。多年以来，学校以独具一格的教学和课程设置被评为全美优秀大学之一。

  威斯康辛大学设有 100 多个本科专业，一半以上可以授予硕士、博士学位。许多学科都具有相当雄厚的科研和教学实力，大部分在美国大学相应领域排名中居于前 10 位。威斯康辛大学已有 18 位教授或校友获得诺贝尔奖。

How to Make Your Dream Come True

如何实现你的梦想

University of
Wisconsin, Madison
Commencement Address
Jerry Zucker
May 2003

背景 资料

　　好莱坞的电影导演兼制片人杰里·朱克 2003 年在威斯康辛大学毕业典礼上发表了演讲。杰里·朱克通过自己的经历，规劝毕业生们不要等待，要走出去实现自己的梦想。他的这篇演讲被列入美国十大最有影响力的演讲。"如果你一生都在睡觉，你的梦想是否实现就无关紧要了。""问你自己一个问题：如果我不是必须做得完美，那我还努力什么呢？"他在演讲中提到的这两句话发人深省，让我们受益匪浅。

　　But it doesn't matter that your dream came true if you spent your whole life sleeping. So get out there and go for it, but don't be caught waiting. It's great to plan for your future. Just don't live there, because really nothing ever happens in the future. Whatever happens happens now, so live your life where the action is — now.

　　如果你一生都在睡觉，你的梦想是否实现就无关紧要了。所以，不要等待，要走出去，去实现你的梦想。规划未来是一件好事，但不要只活在未来，因为未来的事情实际上还没有发生。不管发生什么事情，都只是发生在现在，所以要活在现在。

—— 杰里·朱克

姓　名：	杰里·朱克（Jerry Zucker）
性　别：	男
职　业：	导演　制片人
国　籍：	美国
出生日期：	1950 年 3 月 11 日
毕业学校：	威斯康辛大学苏必略分校
成功点睛：	虽然历经多次失败，但总能勇敢面对，最终他找到了自己钟爱的事业并取得成功
个人成就：	《亡命夺宝》(2001) 《剑侠风流》(1995) 《人鬼情未了》(1990) 《笑破铁幕》(1984)

名人简介

　　杰里·朱克出生在威斯康辛州密尔沃基，他从肖尔伍德高中毕业，1972 年在威斯康辛大学获得了播音、电视以及电影的学士学位。他早期和兄弟大卫·朱克在亚伯拉军的肯德基剧院现场表演短剧，锻造了其表演戏剧的技能。杰里·朱克是著名的导演，曾执导《摇滚学校》(Rock 'n' Roll High School)；《笑破铁幕》(Top Secret!)；《人鬼情未了》(Ghost)；《亡命夺宝 / 疯狂世界》(Rat Race)，其中《人鬼情未了》被提名为奥斯卡最佳影片奖。

　　杰里·朱克也是著名的编剧和制片人，其代表作品有《笑破铁幕》(Top Secret!)、《空前绝后满天飞》(Airplane!) 等。

Thank you **Chancellor** Wiley, distinguished platform party, friends, guests and the very reason for our presence here today — the members of the class of 2003.

Before I start my remarks, I'd like everyone just to do something for me. Very simply — so everyone can kind of just get to know everyone else — on the count of three, I'd like everyone to turn around and shake the hand of the person sitting right behind you. One, two, three — right now, everybody, please do that.

So, I guess you still have a few things to learn.

My parents cried when I left for California. Not because I was leaving, (but) rather, I think, because they were afraid I'd be coming back. Not one teacher I ever had in grade school, high school or college would've believed that there was even the slightest chance that one day I would be asked to give the commencement address at a **major university**.

Many, given the opportunity, would've bet large sums of money against it, putting up their homes and children as **collateral**. Actually, I really like the idea of that, not because I'm **vindictive** — although in a few minutes I'm going to read the names of all the people in my life who never thought I would amount to anything — but because life should be **unpredictable**. And I'm very grateful that I never wasted any time trying to become somebody else's image of what I should be.

So, thirty-one years ago today, I drove from Madison, Wisconsin, to Los Angeles, California. On the way, I passed Camp Randall, where my college graduation ceremony was in progress. I thought about going to the ceremony, but it meant I would've arrived in Hollywood one day later, and at the time I just didn't see the point. I wanted to get there.

Gertrude Stein once said about Hollywood, "When you get there, there is no 'there' there." That's true. However, there will be a swimming pool and tennis court.

感谢威利校长，感谢在座的各位朋友、各位嘉宾以及我们今天最重要的主角——威斯康辛大学 2003 届的毕业生们。

在我正式开始讲话以前，我想让每个人先做一件小事，一件非常简单的事情，以便你们能认识其他一些人——当我数到三时，我希望每个人都转过身与坐在你后面的人握握手——一、二、三，现在，请按我说的做。

所以，我认为你们仍有一些东西需要学习。

当我动身前往加利福尼亚州的时候，我的父母哭了。我想，他们哭不是因为我要离开了，反而是怕我将会折回。从小学到高中再到大学的所有老师没有一个会想到我能有机会被一所重点大学邀请发表毕业演讲。

如果有机会的话，许多人都会下很大赌注，押大把的钱，甚至以自己的家庭和孩子为抵押。实际上，我很欣赏那种想法，不是因为我心怀仇恨——虽然在几分钟后我将会说出一些人名，这些人从不认为我会做成什么事——而是因为生活难以预测。我也非常欣慰，因为我没有浪费时间去变成别人认为我应该成为的样子。

31 年前的今天，我驾车从威斯康辛大学麦迪逊分校驶往加利福尼亚州的洛杉矶。途径兰德尔体育场，当时我们学院的毕业典礼正在那儿举行。我曾想过去参加毕业典礼，但那就意味着我会迟一天到达好莱坞。当时，我不知道什么是重点，我只是想到好莱坞去。

格特鲁德·斯坦因曾经这样形容好莱坞，"当你到了那儿的时候，在那里没有'那里'。"她的形容非常确切。但是，那里将会有游泳池和网球场。尽管这最后或许不足以证明生

热词空间

chancellor ['tʃænsələ] n. (美) 校长

major university 重点大学

collateral [kə'lætərəl] n. 抵押品

vindictive [vin'diktiv] adj. 怀恨的

unpredictable ['ʌnpri'diktəbl] adj. 不可预知的

Gertrude Stein(1874-1946) 格特鲁德·斯坦因，美国女作家，作品有《爱丽丝·托克拉斯的自传》（The Autobiography of Alice B. Toklas）及《温柔的纽扣》(Tender Button)

In the end, though, it's probably not enough to **justify** a life's journey. Getting there, particularly in **show business**, is tough enough. You need a **combination** of talent, ambition, luck and willingness to tell actors how beautiful they look today.

In retrospect, getting there was the easy part. Finding a "there" there is much harder. So today, before you get into your cars and race off to the rest of your lives, I want to give you some advice on how to get there. And I want to help make sure that when you get there, you find a "there" there.

To that end, I will give you my five rules to think about. Quickly forget, but years from now **kick** yourself for not having listened to.

Don't think about your future, especially right now. You'll miss my speech. There will be plenty of time to **contemplate** your future right after the ceremony, but then you'll miss all the celebrating and **adulation**. So just wait until you get home and have a good think about something that will happen in the future that will make you happy.

When I graduated from college, I spent a lot of time thinking about how cool it would be to be on the Johnny Carson show. A few years later, it happened. We appeared on the "Tonight" show, Joey Bishop was the guest host. We were **dreadful**. For years I ran into people who would stop me and say, "Hey, I saw you on the "Tonight" show. Huh... What's Joey Bishop like?" Eventually I got over the **embarrassment**, but I never got those years back — years I spent waiting for some future event to make me happy. I had **tricked** myself into thinking, "As soon as I get there, I'll be OK."

I work in a business where almost everyone is waiting for the next big thing. Sometimes it comes, and sometimes it doesn't. But it doesn't matter that your dream came true if you spent your whole life sleeping. So get out there and go for it, but don't be caught waiting. It's great to plan for your future. Just don't live there,

哈佛
大学

斯坦福
大 学

牛津
大学

耶鲁
大学

杜兰
大学

杜克
大学

威斯康
辛大学

清华
大学

北京
大学

亚利桑
那州立
大 学

加利福
尼 亚
大 学

命的旅程是否正当。在那里，特别是在娱乐行业闯荡是非常艰难的。你要有才华、野心以及运气，并且还要能心甘情愿地告诉演员们他们今天看上去是多么美丽。

回想过去，到达那里相对比较简单，而在那里寻找立足之地就比较困难了。因此，今天在你们坐在车里准备驶往未来时，我想给你们提几点建议，告诉你们如何实现自己的梦想。我想确保你们在到达那里的时候，可以找到自己的目标，实现自己的梦想。

为此，我想告诉你们我的 5 条规则，供你们思考，以便能尽快实现梦想。如果数年之后，你们懊悔没认真听我讲，那就只能怪你们自己了。

第一，不要思索你们的未来，特别是在现在这个时候。否则你就会错过我的演讲。毕业典礼之后，你们有大把的时间思考未来，但那时你们会怀念所有这些欢庆与喝彩。所以，等到回家后再好好去想未来将会发生的可以让你高兴的事情。

我大学毕业时，时常想如果能出现在约翰尼·卡尔森的脱口秀节目中该有多酷。几年以后，我的这个梦想实现了。我们参加了"今夜秀"，乔伊·毕夏普是嘉宾主持。我们的表演糟糕极了。数年之后，我还会撞见一些人，他们会问我，"嘿，我看你参加了'今夜秀'，乔伊·毕夏普怎么样？"最终我走出了这种窘境，但那过去的几年再也回不来了，那几年我只是在等待未来可能会发生某种事情让我感觉高兴。我曾欺骗自己，"只要能到那里，我就会过得很好。"

我在一个几乎每一个人都在等待一件大事发生的领域奋斗。而这种大事有时会发生，有时则不会发生。如果你一生都在睡觉，你的梦想是否实现就无关紧要了。所以，不要等待，要走出去，去实现你的梦想。规划未来是一件好事，但不要只活在未来，因为未来的事情实际上还没有发生。不管发生什么事情，都只是发生在现在，所以要活在现在。我还要告诉你们一件事情，如果你将要录制电视节目，在你看到这个

热词空间

justify ['dʒʌstifai] vt. 证明……是正当的

show business 娱乐业

combination [,kɔmbi'neiʃən] n. 结合；组合

in retrospect 回顾；回顾往事

kick [kik] vt. 踢

contemplate ['kɔntəm,pleit] vt. 沉思

adulation [,ædju'leiʃən] n. 奉承，过分赞扬

dreadful ['dredfəl] adj. 可怕的，糟糕的

embarrassment [im'bærəsmənt] n. 尴尬，窘境

trick [trik] vt. 欺骗，哄骗

哈佛
大学

斯坦福
大　学

牛津
大学

耶鲁
大学

杜兰
大学

杜克
大学

威斯康
辛大学

清华
大学

北京
大学

亚利桑
那州立
大　学

加利福
尼　亚
大　学

because really nothing ever happens in the future. Whatever happens happens now, so live your life where the action is — now. And one more thing: If you're going to be on television, don't call your friends and tell them to watch until after you've seen it.

Don't do anything that 30 years from now you'll look back at and say, "Oh, my God, why the hell did I do that?!" I wish I had a **nickel** for every time I heard someone start a sentence with, "If I only was younger, I would have... " So I did a little informal survey for you, and I found out that, amazingly, all of these people had the same regret. When they graduated from college, sadly, they bought furniture.

This probably needs a little explanation. Right at this moment in your life, you are in a **unique** position that you may never ever be in again. You have nothing to lose. Everything you have acquired of value is locked inside you. If you have a dream, now is the time to pursue it, before you buy furniture.

I was one of the lucky ones. I graduated from the University of Wisconsin with no employable skills, unless you count **jury duty**. It meant I had to **start from scratch** and figure out where I fit in. I didn't have money, but I could afford to fail, and there were many failures. But I found out what I was good at. I found something I loved. And now I have furniture — lots of furniture.

Mrs. Zubatsky's law. One day when I was a kid, our house caught on fire in Milwaukee. A large section of the wood **shingle** roof was burning as the fire trucks **pulled up**. The firemen ran into the back yard with a large **hose** and began **assembling** their metal ladders and positioning them against the house.

Mrs. Zubatsky was our next door neighbor and, at the time, she was standing on her upstairs **porch** taking in the **laundry**. She watched anxiously as the firemen struggled with their ladders. Suddenly she leaned over the balcony and shouted down to the professional firefighters, "Forget the ladders! Just point the hose at the fire!" The firemen, to their credit, responded immediately. They dropped their ladders,

电视节目前不要打电话告诉你的朋友。

第二，不要做任何会让你在 30 年后回顾时说："哦，我的天呐，我到底为什么会干出这样的事情？"的事情。每次有人以这样的句子开头："要是……多好，当我年轻的时候……，我应该……"，我都希望能有 5 美元可以赏给他们。所以我为你们做了一点非正式的调查，并且发现，所有的这些人都有着同样的遗憾。悲哀的是，当他们从大学毕业的时候，他们都买了家具。

这个可能需要稍作解释。在你人生的这个时刻，你处在一个对你来说也许是绝无仅有的独特位置。你没什么可以失去。你获得的所有有价值的东西都紧紧锁在你的内心。如果你拥有梦想，现在就是你去追随梦想的时刻，在买家具之前先去实现你的梦想。

我算是一个比较幸运的人。我从威斯康辛大学毕业却没有职业技能，除非你把做义务陪审员也算进去。那意味着我必须白手起家并且得弄清楚我适合什么行业。我没有钱，但我可以承受失败，而且失败过很多次。但我找到了我所擅长的领域。我找到了我钟爱的事业。并且现在我也有了家具，有很多的家具。

第三，Zubatsky 夫人的定律。当我还是小孩的时候，有一天，我们在密尔沃基的房子着火了。当消防车赶到的时候，一大片的木屋顶正在燃烧着。消防员拿着一个很大的水管跑进后院然后开始组装他们的金属梯子并且靠房子固定住。

Zubatsky 夫人是我们隔壁的一个邻居，当时她正站在她家楼上的走廊收衣服。她焦急地看着消防员们努力地组装梯子。突然间她在阳台上探出身并且向那些专业的消防员大声喊："不要用梯子了！把水管对准火焰喷！"值得称道的是，这些消防员立即响应了。他们扔掉了梯子，拿起消防水管对准火

热词空间

nickel ['nikəl] *n.* [美国俚语] 5 元钱

unique [ju:'ni:k] *adj.* 独一无二的，罕见的

jury duty 做义务陪审员

start from scratch 从头开始；白手起家

shingle ['ʃingl] *n.* 墙面板

pull up 停下来，开（车）到特定地点

hose [həuz] *n.* 软管

assemble [ə'sembl] *vt.* 装配

porch [pɔ:tʃ] *n.* 走廊

laundry ['lɔ:ndri] *n.* 洗好的衣服

pointed the hose at the fire and **extinguished** the **blaze** in about 40 seconds.

There are two **morals** to this story. One, never assume that just because it's someone's job, they know how to do it. And two, don't let yourself be **intimidated** by professionals or their uniforms.

Growing up in Wisconsin, I never knew anyone in the movie business. I never even knew anyone who knew anyone in the movie business. That world had a **mystique** that made it seem unattainable to me. But, like Mrs. Zubatsky, I sat on my porch and I watched someone else do it, and I said, "I have a better idea." And like her, I seized the moment.

If you have a better idea, if your plan makes more sense, if you have a vision, then put down your laundry and scream a little bit. **Throw your hat into the ring** and never let professionals or their uniforms prevent you from telling anyone where to point their hose.

If you're going to fail, fail big. If you don't, you're never going to make a difference. Creativity is allowing yourself to make mistakes. Art is knowing which ones to keep. Ask yourself one question: If I didn't have to do it perfectly, what would I try?

For many of you, the biggest **obstacle** to getting there will be a fear that you have carried with you since childhood — the fear of **humiliation**, of embarrassment, of **ridicule**. That is so stupid! Oh ... sorry. But really, you have to stop caring about that, which brings me to Travolta's law.

My brother David and Jim Abrahams and I were having pie at Rumpelmeyer's Coffee Shop in New York on the day after our third movie, "Top Secret" opened. The reviews were terrible and it was bombing at the box office. We were really getting into some serious **moping** and **self-flagellation** when **John Travolta** walked in. We knew him from the Paramount lot and he could see right away that we were in a **funk**.

焰喷洒，结果只用了大概 40 秒就把大火给熄灭了。

这个故事有两个寓意。第一，绝对不要认为是别人的工作，他们就肯定知道怎么做。第二，不要让自己被别人的职业和制服吓坏了。

在威斯康辛长大，我当时不认识任何在电影行业的人。我甚至都不认识一个在电影行业有熟人的人。电影世界当时对我来说似乎有一种不可企及的奥秘。但是，像 Zubatsky 夫人一样，我坐在走廊上并且观察着别人做这个事情，然后说："我有一个更好的想法。"并且，像她一样，我把握住了机会。

如果你有更好的想法，如果你的计划更有意义，如果你有一个设想，那就放下你手中的衣服并且喊出来，宣布加入，绝不要让他们的职业或者制服阻止你告诉任何人，他们应该把水管指向什么地方。

第四，如果你将要失败了，那就败得更厉害点。如果你不这样做，你将永远不能做出改变。创造力允许你自己犯错。艺术就是知道该留下哪些。问你自己一个问题：如果我不是必须做得完美，那我还努力什么呢？

对于你们当中的许多人来说，达到目标的最大障碍将是一种你们从孩童时期就有的恐惧，害怕遭到羞辱，害怕遭遇尴尬，害怕被人嘲笑。真是太愚蠢了！很抱歉这样说。但是，你真的必须停止这些担心，这就让我不得不说说特拉沃尔塔的定律。

在我们的第三部电影《笑破铁幕》上映的第二天，我和我的兄弟戴维还有吉姆·亚伯拉罕当时正在纽约 Rumpelmeyer 咖啡店里吃苹果派。人们对这部电影的评价很糟，售票处像被轰击过一样，空空如也。我们当时极其消沉，不断自责，这时约翰·特拉沃尔塔走了进来。我们在派拉蒙公司的时候就认识了他。他一眼就看出我们极度恐惧。于是我们立即向他倾诉心声，

热词空间

extinguish [ik'stiŋgwiʃ] *vt.* 熄灭

blaze [bleiz] *n.* 火焰

moral ['mɔrəl] *n.* 寓意

intimidate [in'timideit] *vt.* 恐吓，使畏惧

mystique [mi'sti:k] *n.* 奥秘，秘诀

throw one's hat into the ring 宣布参与某事

obstacle ['ɔbstəkl] *n.* 障碍

humiliation [hjuː.mili'eiʃən] *n.* 耻辱，羞辱

ridicule ['ridikju:l] *n.* 嘲笑

moping [məup] *n.* 消沉

self-flagellation ['self,flædʒə'leiʃən] *n.* 自责，自罚

John Travolta: 约翰·特拉沃尔塔，好莱坞男演员，1978 年获得奥斯卡最佳男演员提名。

funk [fʌŋk] *n.* 恐惧

We immediately poured out our heart to him, explaining the pain of our humiliating misfortune.

I'm not sure what we were expecting, but John just smiled and said, "Guys, the thing you have to remember is (that) nobody else is paying as much attention to your failures as you are. You're the only ones who **are obsessed with** the importance of your own life. To everyone else, it's just a **blip** on the **radar** screen, so just move on By the way, are you going to finish that pie?"

I found that advice very **liberating** — that the only one who my big failure was truly big for was me. So I thanked him and told him how beautiful he looked today, and now when I fail big, I just go out and have a piece of apple pie and I move on. And I always save a little piece for John Travolta. Amazingly, **more often than not** he **shows up** to eat it.

The next time you are in a restaurant, please don't look at the waitress and say, "Can I *get* some **ketchup**?" You're supposed to say, "May I please have some ketchup?" Sorry — that doesn't count. Just a personal **pet peeve** of mine.

Don't overuse the word "love". Everyone overuses the word "love". "I love your shoes." "I just love the new Justin Guarini CD." "I really love those little things they put on the chicken sandwiches at Subway." In Hollywood, they say "Love ya, babe!" So, OK, I get it. It's just the way people talk and it's probably harmless, but you shouldn't forget the real thing. The real thing is great. It's just not so easy with actual human beings, but if you work at it and you get it right, it will make you happier than anything else you do in your life.

Think of the world as a big glass of water with some salt in it. You have a choice. You can try to pick out all the salt or you can keep pouring in more water so eventually it gets less bitter. As you begin your new journey, you can try to remove everything that you find distasteful in the world, or you can just pour in more love. It's

告诉他遭遇了这样令人感觉羞辱的不幸我们有多痛苦。

我也不知道我们当时期盼得到什么样的安慰，但约翰只是笑了笑，然后说："伙计们，你们必须记住一点，没有人会像你自己那样对自己的失败那么在意。你是唯一沉湎于自己重要性的人。对于其他所有人来说，你只是雷达荧光屏上一个光点。所以，只管前行吧。顺便问一下，你们要吃完那个苹果派吗？"

那个建议让我释然，我的重大失败的严重性只是对我个人而言。因此，我非常感激他，并告诉他他那天看起来很英俊。现在，当我遭遇重大失败的时候，我就会走出去吃个苹果派，然后继续前行。每次我都会给约翰·特拉沃尔塔留一小块，令人惊讶的是，他通常都会出现并吃掉它。

下一次你去一个餐厅的时候，请不要盯着服务员说，"能给我点番茄酱吗？"你应该说，"请你帮我拿些番茄酱好吗？"不好意思，那个不算一个规则。这只是我个人的怪癖。

第五，不要过度使用"爱"这个字。每个人都过度使用"爱"这个字。"我爱你的鞋。""我只爱贾斯汀·古安瑞尼的新专辑。""我真的很爱地铁里他们放在鸡肉三明治上的东西。"在好莱坞，他们说"爱你，宝贝！"所以，我明白了，这只是人们聊天的方法并且也许并没有什么坏处，但你不应该忘记真正的爱。真正的爱是伟大的。做人不容易，但是如果能为人生不断奋斗，并且朝着正确的方向前进，你就会比做其他任何事情更感觉幸福。

把这个世界想象成一大杯放了盐的水。你可以做出选择，你可以把里面所有的盐都挑出来，你也可以往里面倒入更多的水使其不那么苦涩。就像你开始一段新的旅程一样，你可以费力去把所有令人不快的东西都清除掉，也可以倾注更多的爱。付出越多，得到的就越多，这是唯一的真理。

热词空间

be obsessed with 沉迷于

blip [blip] n. （在雷达屏幕显示出的）物体光点

radar ['reidə] n. 雷达

liberating ['libəreitiŋ] adj. 令人释然的

more often than not 多半，通常

show up 出现，露面

ketchup ['ketʃəp] n. 蕃茄酱

pet peeve 心病

the only thing that the more you give away, the more you have.

So take all that warm, **fuzzy stuff** you've been hiding and spread it around a little. And then judge yourself not by your accomplishments, but by the happiness of the people around you. If you do that, you can do anything, you can go anywhere, you can fail at anything, and wherever you are, you will find a "there" there, because you'll bring it with you.

I would like to conclude with a sad, but true, story from my childhood. When I was a young boy of only 7, it was decided that I should take piano lessons. This is a true story, by the way. I swear. I studied piano for three years and I learned to play one song poorly, which actually turned out to be an improvement over high school. Nobody was willing to tell me that I had no musical talent **whatsoever**. Finally, after three years, I was invited by my piano teacher, Mr. Dillman, to play in a **recital**. I was told recently that Mr. Dillman **twitched** visibly when my name was mentioned at his funeral.

I can't answer for others, but I was very excited that I was at last going to play my song in front of an audience. The day of the recital arrived. That morning, I got the **chicken pox** and, **tragically**, I never got to play my song. But today I've **taken the liberty of** bringing with me a small keyboard and, with your permission, I will finally get to play my song in front of an audience. I swear to you (that) this is the song that I learned to play after three years — the only song I know how to play on the piano. I think you will see that the lesson is patience. There comes a time for everything.

Congratulations! Welcome to real life! You graduated from the University of Wisconsin! You can do anything! Thank you.

所以，带着所有你一直深藏着的温暖而模糊的爱并把爱传播给周围的人。然后以你周围的人的快乐程度而不要用你所取得的成就来评价自己。如果你能做到这一点，你就可以做成任何事，你可以到任何地方，你能承受任何失败，无论你在哪里，你都能找到"目标"，因为你将把它带在身边。

我想以童年时一个悲伤但真实的故事结束我的演讲。当时我只有七岁，经过决定我应该去上钢琴课。我发誓，这是一个真实的故事。我学了三年钢琴，但只会弹一首曲子，而且弹得很糟，这种情况到高中结束后才有了改善。没人愿意告诉我我没有音乐天赋。结果，三年之后，我的钢琴老师迪尔曼先生邀请我在一个独奏会上演奏。最近我被告知，在迪尔曼先生的葬礼上，当提及我的名字的时候，他明显抽搐了。

我不能达到别人的标准，但当时我非常兴奋因为我终于有机会在观众面前弹奏我的歌曲了。独奏会的日子终于到来了，可是偏偏在那天早晨，我得了水痘，悲惨的是，我再未有机会演奏我的歌曲。但是今天我擅自带了一个小键盘，如果你们允许的话，我最终将能在观众面前演奏我的歌曲。我向你们发誓这是一首我学了三年的歌曲，是我唯一能弹奏的一首钢琴曲。我想你们将会明白这是关于耐心的课程。得到一切的时机就要来临了。

最后，再一次祝贺你们！欢迎来到真实的生活！你们从威斯康辛大学毕业了！你们能做任何事情！谢谢你们！

热词空间

fuzzy ['fʌzi] *adj.* 模糊的
stuff [stʌf] *n.* 东西
whatsoever [ˌhwɔtsəu'evə] *pron.* 无论什么
recital [ri'saitəl] *n.* 独奏会
twitch [twitʃ] *vi.* 抽搐
chicken pox [医] 水痘
tragically ['trædʒikəli] *adv.* 悲剧地
take the liberty of 擅自

杰里·朱克给我们的 启示

And I'm very grateful that I never wasted any time trying to become somebody else's image of what I should be.

我也非常欣慰，因为我没有浪费时间去变成别人认为我应该成为的样子。

- - - - - - - - - - - - - - - - - - - -

Right at this moment in your life, you are in a unique position that you may never ever be in again. You have nothing to lose. Everything you have acquired of value is locked inside you. If you have a dream, now is the time to pursue it, before you buy furniture.

在你人生的这个时刻，你处在一个对你来说也许是绝无仅有的独特位置。你没什么可以失去。你获得的所有有价值的东西都紧紧锁在你的内心。如果你拥有梦想，现在就是你去追随梦想的时刻，在买家具之前先去实现你的梦想。

- - - - - - - - - - - - - - - - - - - -

... nobody else is paying as much attention to your failures as you are. You're the only ones who are obsessed with the importance of your own life. To everyone else, it's just a blip on the radar screen, so just move on.

……没有人会像你自己那样对自己的失败那么在意。你是唯一沉湎于你自己重要性的人。对于其他所有人来说，你只是雷达荧光屏上的一个光点。所以，只管前行吧。

- - - - - - - - - - - - - - - - - - - -

The real thing is great. It's just not so easy with actual human beings, but if you work at it and you get it right, it will make you happier than anything else you do in your life.

真正的爱是伟大的。做人不容易，但是如果能为人生不断奋斗，并且朝着正确的方向前进，你就会比做其他任何事情更感觉幸福。

- - - - - - - - - - - - - - - - - - - -

As you begin your new journey, you can try to remove everything that you find distasteful in the world, or you can just pour in more love. It's the only thing that the more you give away, the more you have.

就像你开始一段新的旅程一样，你可以费力去把所有令人不快的东西都清除掉，也可以倾注更多的爱。付出越多，得到的就越多，这是唯一的真理。

清华大学

校训：自强不息 厚德载物（Self-discipline and Social Commitment）

总 括

　　清华大学，地处北京西北郊繁盛的园林区，是在几处清代皇家园林的遗址上发展而成的，是中华人民共和国教育部直属高等学校，名列 211 工程、985 工程，是中国最杰出的高等学府，也是亚洲和世界最重要的大学之一。清华大学是世界上最美丽的大学之一，是莘莘学子希望与梦想的摇篮！

Keep Your Dreams

执着于你的梦想

Tsinghua University Addressed by Arnold Alois Schwarzenegger Nov. 16, 2005

背景资料

　　2005 年 11 月 16 日，在世界影坛被誉为"超级硬汉"的阿诺德·施瓦辛格来到清华大学发表演讲。时任加州州长的他已年届 58 岁，依然风度翩翩，一上场就博得了热烈的掌声。以"执着于你的梦想"为主题，施瓦辛格与学生们畅谈理想，并分享了自己的成长故事。他说，自己在追逐梦想的过程中，常受到一些人的嘲讽和质疑，但他没有为此动摇，始终坚持通过自己取得的每一点进步去改变生活、改变未来。他的这种"执着于梦想"的精神是否让我们的目标更加坚定呢？

Some of your families maybe don't believe in your dreams. But let me tell you something, my young friends. Keep your dreams. No matter what, keep your dreams. Don't give up on them, even when you are temporarily defeated or denied. Keep your dreams.

　　你们的家人也许不相信你们的梦想，但是，朋友们，让我告诉你们，执着于你的梦想！无论如何，坚持你们的梦想。即使你们遭遇暂时的失败或被否定，也不要放弃你们的梦想。执着于你的梦想。

—— 阿诺德·施瓦辛格

姓　　名：	阿诺德·施瓦辛格（Arnold Alois Schwarzenegger）
性　　别：	男
职　　业：	美国加州州长 电影演员 健身运动员
国　　籍：	美国
出生日期：	1947 年 7 月 30 日
毕业学校：	威斯康辛大学苏必略分校
成功点睛：	施瓦辛格最大的特点是他办任何一件事都抱有极强的自信，并且始终坚持自己的梦想。
个人成就：	《终结者》《真实的谎言》

名人 简介

　　阿诺德·施瓦辛格 1947 年 7 月 30 日生于奥地利，1983 年加入美国籍。施瓦辛格在好莱坞是个传奇人物，没有受过专门的表演训练，但却跻身好莱坞主流影星之列。他在其他领域的建树同样引人注目。而最重要的是，那种百折不挠、坚韧不拔的意志贯穿了他各个时期的奋斗历程。阿诺德·施瓦辛格是当今国际影坛娱乐片领域里当之无愧的王者，但他最令人钦佩的不是他的王者之气，也不是他的肌肉、他的演技、他的精明，而是他那股永远向上的精神。

　　施瓦辛格总是充满自信。他在 1973 年出版的自传小说《阿诺德，一个健美运动员的成长》中说："我知道我是一个赢者，我知道我一定要做伟大的事情。"在洛杉矶定居后，他不满足于只是个健美冠军，立即向世界富豪的目标前进。无穷的抱负和充沛的精力使施瓦辛格永远迎接新的挑战。施瓦辛格的名字如同原子弹爆炸一样响遍全球，已经有人用"神话"来形容他的成功故事。在美国，在这个性、吸毒、摇滚乐流行的地方，施瓦辛格的影迷竟可以排在第四位。施瓦辛格简直成了大众文化的代表，美国人的偶像。

哈佛
大学

斯坦福
大 学

牛津
大学

耶鲁
大学

杜兰
大学

杜克
大学

威斯康
辛大学

清华
大学

北京
大学

亚利桑
那州立
大 学

加利福
它 亚
大 学

Well, thank you very much, President. First of all, I want to thank President Gu for having me here, and I want to thank Mr. Qizhi for your kind introduction. Thank you very much.

It is wonderful to be here at this university. What a special place. I just looked around a little bit here, it's a **gorgeous**, gorgeous place. I want to congratulate you for going to this **magnificent** university here.

Now, the last time I was here in China was five years ago, and then I was promoting my movies. They had a movie festival here, the Arnold Schwarzenegger Movie Festival. I remember they showed all my movies for a week — which was a **rarity**, may I remind you — and they also showed the movies on television. But we also were here to promote Special Olympics, which is an organization that helps people with mental disabilities, so I was here for both reasons.

But this time I'm here as the governor of the great state of California. I'm here representing the people of California, and we're here on a trade mission to see how we can do more business with China and to help each other, because both California is a very fast growing state, and China is a very fast growing country, and there are a lot of things that we can do for one another.

But I didn't want to miss the opportunity to come here today and to talk with the young people; as a matter of fact, to the brightest young people of China. And this is why it is so great to be here at the Tsinghua University, and I'm honored that I was invited here.

Now, I read a little bit about the history of Tsinghua, and I learned that actually this school originally prepared students to attend universities in America.

Now, I also know that since the **attack** on our World Trade Centers it has become more and more difficult to go to the universities in America because you need to fill out all kinds of **paperwork** now and you have to get **visas**, and it's very complicated, and you have to wait a much longer period of time to go over there. But let me tell you, things are improving already.

非常感谢。首先，我要感谢顾校长邀我至此，我还要感谢奇志先生对我的热心引荐。谢谢你们。

能来到清华大学让我感到万分荣幸。这个地方真的很特别！仅稍作环顾，我就发现，这里绚丽多彩。祝贺你们能来到这所宏伟壮观的大学学习。

上次我来中国是五年前的事了，当时是为了宣传我的电影。他们在这里举办了一个电影节——阿诺德·施瓦辛格电影节。我还记得他们整整一个星期都在放映我主演的电影，这并不常见。此外，他们还在电视上放映这些电影。当时我们来这里的另一个目的是宣传帮助智障人士的特殊奥林匹克运动会。因此，当时我来这里有双重目的。

但是，这一次我作为加利福尼亚州州长，谨代表加利福尼亚州的人民来到中国，肩负如何能与中国建立更多贸易往来并互利合作的重要使命。因为加利福尼亚是一个高速发展的州，而中国也是一个高速发展的国家，我们的合作是双赢的。

但我也不想错失今天来这里与你们这些年轻人交谈的机会。事实上，你们是中国最杰出的年轻人。这就是我为能来到清华而感到无比高兴的原因，也是我为能被贵校邀请而感到无比荣幸的原因。

现在，我对清华的历史略有了解了，我还了解到，这所学校最初实际上是为那些准备前往美国上大学的学生创立的院校。

同时我也知道，自从我们的世贸大厦遭遇空袭以来，去美国的大学深造越来越难了，因为你们现在需要填写各种各样的书面材料，还必须获得签证。这个过程非常复杂，你们得等很长的时间才能去美国。但让我告诉你们，情况已在不断改善。

热词空间

gorgeous ['gɔ:dʒəs] *adj.* 华丽的，极好

magnificent [mæg'nifisənt] *adj.* 壮丽的

rarity ['reərəti] *n.* 罕见

attack [ə'tæk] *n.* 攻击，袭击

paperwork ['peipə,wə:k] *n.* 文书工作

visa ['vi:zə] *n.* 签证

I've heard that it's **easing up** the restrictions, and it's easier to get a visa. My young Chinese friends, I want to tell you that **in case** no one from America has ever invited you, let me do this right now here personally. I want to warmly invite all of you here to come to the United States, and especially to come to California, because that's the happening place. California is the best place.

Please come and visit us, we will welcome you. I invite you all to come there and to travel, to meet the American people, and to come there and study in our universities, and some day hopefully you will come and do business over there, or maybe you'll want to move over there. Whatever your goal is, you're always welcome. America, after all, let's not forget, is the land of opportunity. And it's not only the land of opportunity for Austrians like me, but for Chinese people as well. Remember that.

I know that beginning with this century, China is also becoming a land of opportunity.

It's a fast growing place, and as the students of this great university and the citizens of a rising China, I think that you have a great future also here in this country.

And today I want to talk to you a little bit about the dreams, about the dreams of your future, and dreams for this country.

I want to talk to you a little bit about dreams, because it seems to me that I'm somewhat of an expert in dreams, because I had a lot of my dreams become a reality.

So let me just briefly tell you my story, and tell you a little bit about how I started with my career. I think that this story kind of relates a little bit also to you, and also to China.

I started way back as a weightlifter. I always liked the idea of lifting weights and being a bodybuilder. From the first moment when I **gripped** a **barbell** and held it around the bar and lifted the steel above my head, I felt this **exhilaration**, and I knew then that this is something that I'm going to do; that I was in love with that, and this is going to be something that I'm going to do. I'm going to pursue the sport of **weightlifting** and **bodybuilding**.

我听说，限制条件已趋于宽松，获得签证更容易了。年轻的中国朋友们，我想告诉你们，如果美国还没有人邀请你们，那么我现在就以个人名义邀请你们。我想诚挚地邀请你们所有人到美国，尤其要来加利福尼亚州，因为那里上演着许多传奇。加利福尼亚州是首选之地。

来吧，我们将欢迎你们来访。我邀请在座的各位去那里旅游，去结识美国人民，去我们的大学学习，希望你们有朝一日能在那里做生意，你们或许想要移居那里。无论你们的目标是什么，我们都欢迎你们的到来。不要忘了，美国毕竟充满了机遇，不仅对像我这样的奥地利人是这样，对中国人也是如此。请大家记住这一点。

我知道自本世纪以来，中国这片大地上也开始充满机遇。

中国正在快速发展，而你们作为这所出类拔萃的大学的学生，作为这个正在崛起的国家的公民，我相信你们在这个国家也会有一个光辉灿烂的未来。

今天，我想跟你们谈谈梦想，关于畅想你们未来的梦想，关于中国的梦想。

我之所以想跟你们略谈梦想，是因为我觉得自己似乎是这方面的专家，因为我的许多梦想都已经实现。

因此，让我简单地讲述一下我的故事，告诉你们我是怎样开始我的职业生涯的。我想这个故事多多少少会对你们甚至对中国有所启示。

我出道时是个举重运动员。我一直都喜欢举重运动，渴望能成为一名健美运动员。自从第一次抓紧杠铃、将其高高举过头顶之际，我就为此感到异常兴奋。那时我知道，我迷上了这项运动，这将是我要做的事情，我将从事举重和健美运动。

Now, I remember the first real **workout** that I had. Eight miles away from my home village in Austria there was a **gymnasium**, and I rode to that gymnasium with a bicycle. And there I trained for half an hour, because they said that after half an hour you should stop because otherwise your body will get really **sore**. But after half an hour I looked at my body, and nothing had happened. So I said, "I'd better work out for another half hour." So I lifted some more. My strength didn't improve, I didn't see the muscles **pop out** or anything like that, so I trained for another half an hour. And then after another half hour I trained another half hour, and all together I trained two and a half hours.

Well, let me tell you something. After two and a half hours — I left the gymnasium, even though they told me that I shouldn't train that much or I would get really sore — I rode my bicycle home. And after the first mile I got **numb**, and I couldn't feel anymore the **handle** of the bicycle, and I fell off the bike and I fell into the **ditch** on the side of the road. So I got up again and I tried it again. Another few yards, I fell off the bicycle again. And I tried it three, four more times, and I just couldn't ride my bicycle because my body was so numb and my legs felt like noodles.

Well, let me tell you something. The next morning when I got up, my body was so sore that I couldn't even lift my arms to comb my hair. I had to have my mother comb my hair, and you know how embarrassing that is. But you know something? I learned a very important lesson, that pain means progress. Pain is progress. Each time my muscles were sore from a workout I knew that they were growing and they were getting stronger.

I think there is a real life lesson in that. After two or three years of **discipline** and determination and working out hard, I actually changed my body, and I changed my strength. And that told me something, that if I could change my body that much, and if I could change the strength of my body that much, then I could also change anything else. I could change my habits, I could change my intelligence, I could change my attitude, my mind, my future, my life. And this is exactly what I have done. I think

我还记得最初那次真正的训练。当时我骑着自行车前往一家健身房，那儿离我在奥地利一个小村庄里的家有八英里之遥。在那里我训练了半个钟头，因为他们告诉我，训练必须半小时一停，否则你会全身酸痛。但半小时之后，我看看自己的身体，一点变化也没有！于是我说，"最好再练半小时吧。"就又多举了几下。可是我的力气并未因此增强，也不见肌肉鼓起来。然后我又练了半小时，再加半小时……结果总共练了两个半小时。

让我告诉你们，尽管他们告诉我不能练那么久，否则会浑身酸痛，但我训练了两个半小时，然后离开健身房骑车回家。刚走一英里，我顿觉四肢麻木，连车把都感觉不到了，结果整个人从车上摔下来，掉进了路边的水沟里。我站起了，又试了一次，但没骑多远又摔了下来。接下来我又试了三四次，但依旧不行，因为我全身异常酸麻，感觉腿就像面条一样软弱无力。

第二天早上起床，我浑身酸痛，连举手梳头都无能为力，只好叫我母亲帮我梳头——这真令人难堪！可你们知道吗，我获得了一个非常重要的教训：疼痛意味着进步。要想进步就得吃苦。每次我因过度训练而感觉肌肉酸痛时，我都知道，我的肌肉在增长、在强壮。

我认为，那其中蕴含着人生真谛。经过两三年意志上的磨练和体力上的锻炼，我最终改变了我的身体，我的力气也变大了。这件事告诉我，如果能在很大程度上改变我的身体，增强我的力气，我就能改变其他的一切：我能改变不好的习惯，能增强我的智慧，能改变我的态度、思想以及我的未来

that that lesson applies to people, and it also applies to countries. You can change; China can change; everyone in the world can change.

My parents, of course, I have to tell you, didn't understand my dreams at all. They were always wondering. They said, "What is he doing? When are you going to get a job, a real job? When are you going to make money?" And all of those questions I got. And they said, "I hope we didn't raise a **bum**, someone that doesn't make money and just wants to live in a gymnasium and think about their bodies." Well, I **endured** all of this negative thinking, and the more negative the thinking got, and the more negative the questions got, the stronger and the more positive I became, the stronger I became inside.

So of course some of your families maybe think the same way, and this is why I'm mentioning that. Some of your families maybe don't believe in your dreams. But let me tell you something, my young friends. Keep your dreams. No matter what, keep your dreams. Don't give up on them, even when you are **temporarily defeated** or denied. Keep your dreams.

I remember the first time I went to the United States and I was competing in a competition. It was the World **Championship** in Bodybuilding. I lost. I came in second, and I was **devastated**. I was **crushed**. I felt like a loser, a major loser, let me tell you. I cried, as a matter of fact, because I felt like I disappointed my friends and I disappointed myself. But the next day I **got my act together**, I **shifted gears**, and I said, "I'm going to learn from that lesson. I'm going to stay here in America. I'm not going to go back to Europe. I'm going to stay in America and I'm going to train with the American champions. I'm going to train the American way. I'm going to eat the American food. I'm going to train with the American machines and the principles. And a year later, in America, I became the World Champion in Bodybuilding. So I think this is a very, very important lesson.

And from then on, I continued. My career took off, and everything that I wanted to do I accomplished. First it was to become a champion in bodybuilding. Later on I

和我的人生。事实上我已经做到了。我想，这一教训也适用于任何人，也适用于任何国家。你们可以改变，中国可以改变，世界上每一个人都可以改变。

当然，我得告诉你们，我父母根本无法理解我的梦想。他们总是疑惑地问，"他在做什么呢？你什么时候能得到一份工作、一份真正的工作？你什么时候能挣钱？"还有一些类似的疑惑。他们会说，"希望我们养的不是一个寻欢作乐的儿子，一个不挣钱却只想在健身馆里考虑他的身材的人。"我承受了所有这一切消极的想法，而且这些想法越消极，我就变得越积极；这些疑虑越多，我就变得越坚强，我的内心也变得更强大。

当然你们中有些人的家人可能也会这么想，这也是我提起这件事的原因。你们的家人也许不相信你们的梦想，但是，朋友们，让我告诉你们，执着于你的梦想！无论如何，坚持你们的梦想。即使你们遭遇暂时的失败或被否定，也不要放弃你们的梦想。执着于你的梦想。

我还记得第一次到美国参加世界健美锦标赛。当时我输了，我仅得了第二，感觉非常绝望，彻底崩溃了。让我告诉你们，我当时就像一个失败者，一个遭受惨败的人。我哭了，事实上因为我感觉自己让朋友失望了，也让自己失望了。但第二天，我重振旗鼓，改变了态度，并对自己说，"我要吸取教训。我要留在美国。我不会再回欧洲。我要留在美国与美国的冠军一起训练，以美国的方式训练。我要吃美国的食物，用美国的健美器材和原则来训练。"一年后，我成了世界健美冠军。所以，我认为这是一次非常非常重要的教训。

从那时起，我不断努力，我的事业从此飞黄腾达，我实

热词空间

bum [bʌm] *n.* 能力差的人

endure [in'djuə] *vt.* 容忍

temporarily ['tempərərili] *adv.* 临时地

defeat [di'fi:t] *vt.* 战胜，打败

championship ['tʃæmpiənʃip] *n.* 锦标赛

devastate ['devəsteit] *vt.* 使不知所措

crush [krʌʃ] *vt.* 击垮

got one's act together 恢复镇静，克制，稳定情绪，振作精神

shift gears 改变态度

哈佛
大学

斯坦福
大 学

牛津
大学

耶鲁
大学

杜兰
大学

杜克
大学

威斯康
辛大学

清华
大学

北京
大学

亚利桑
那州立
大 学

加利福
尼 亚
大 学

became a movie star, to do all the great movies, the *Conan* movies and the *Terminator* movies and all this. Then I became the governor of the great state of California, of the sixth largest economy in the world.

All of this happened because of my dreams, even though other people told me that those dreams were **bogus** and they were crazy, but I held onto my dreams.

And people would always say, no matter what, even in bodybuilding they said I would never make it. And later on in the movies, in Hollywood they said I would not make it. They said, "You will never make it. You have a German **accent**. No one in Hollywood has ever made it with a German accent. Yeah, maybe you can play some Nazi roles or something like that, but you cannot become a leading star with an accent. Plus your body. You're overdeveloped. You have all these muscles. They did **Hercules** movies 20 years ago; that's outdated. Now it's Woody Allen. Woody Allen is in, his body is in." And those were the messages. "And Al Pacino, the **skinny** guy, he is in. But not your body, it's too big. And your name, Schwarzenegger, it will never fit on a movie **poster**. Forget it. Forget it. You will never make it. Go back to bodybuilding."

Well, the rest is history. After *Terminator 3*, I became the highest paid movie star in Hollywood. And let me tell you something, it continued on. Even when I ran for governor people said, "Arnold, you will never make it. You will never become governor of California. What do you know about government?" Well, the fact is, I knew exactly as much about government as the rest of the people knew in California, which is that government is out of touch, and it's **out of sync** with the people, and it needed a **shakeup**. So I didn't listen to all those people that said I would never make it. I continued campaigning, I listened to my dreams, and the rest also is history. I became governor.

So always it just carried me on, those dreams. So bodybuilding gave me the confidence, movies gave me the money, and pubic service and being a governor gave me a purpose larger than myself. And that is the brief story of my dreams and a brief

现了自己想做的一切——首先成为健美冠军，接着成为电影明星，拍所有的大片，如《柯南》、《终结者》等一系列电影。后来我当上了世界第六大经济体——加利福尼亚州的州长。

这一切的实现都是因为我的梦想，即使别人说我的那些梦想都是虚假而荒唐的，但是我仍坚持不懈。

不管做什么，人们总会说我不会成功，在健美事业上如此，在好莱坞的电影事业上也是如此。他们曾说，"你绝不可能成功，你一口德国音。在好莱坞还没有一个说话带德国口音的人能成为主角的。扮演一些纳粹或类似的角色你倒是可以，但说话带德国口音的人想成为主角是不可能的。还有你的体形，一身肌肉，太过发达了！20年前他们是拍过大力士的影片，不过那早过时了。现在当红的是伍迪·艾伦。伍迪·艾伦走红，他的体形也走红。还有阿尔·帕西诺，那个充满骨感美的家伙也很走红。且不说你的体格过大，再听听你的名字，施瓦辛格，根本不适合登在电影海报上。算了，算了，你不会成功的。还是回去搞你的健美运动去吧！"

其余的都成了往事。演完《终结者Ⅲ》之后，我便成了好莱坞片酬最高的影星，但外界的质疑从未中断过。我竞选州长时还有人说，"阿诺德，你不会成功的，你永远当不上加州州长。你对政治了解多少？"而事实上，我对政治的了解绝不亚于加利福尼亚的其他人，知道政府高高在上，与人民群众相脱离，需要进行改革。我没把那些说我不能成功的人的话放在心上，我依然参加了竞选。我相信自己的梦想，其余的都已成明日黄花。我最终当上了州长。

因此，那些梦想总引导着我不断向前——健美运动给了我信心，拍摄电影给了我财富，而公共服务以及当州长让我有了超越自身的更大的目标。这就是关于我的梦想和我的早

热词空间

bogus ['bəugəs] *adj.* 无知的

accent ['æksənt] *n.* 口音

hercules ['hə:kjuli:z] *n.* 大力王；巨人

skinny ['skini] *adj.* 皮包骨的

poster ['pəustə] *n.* 海报

out of sync 不同步

shakeup ['ʃeikʌp] *n.*（政策等的）剧变

story of my early life, and how my dreams made me successful.

A person, of course, should not be **stingy** with their dreams. So I, of course, don't just think and dream about myself, but I also have dreams for you, and dreams for China. So let me just talk a little bit about that. China's economy has become an **engine** of human progress, lifting millions of people out of poverty. This is a moral and economic good for China and for the rest of the world. I often read that China's economy is likely to become the largest in the world over the next 50 years, and I think this is **terrific**. This does not mean, of course, that America will get poorer; it just means that China will get richer, and the United States will benefit from China's progress as much as the U.S. benefited from the rise of Western Europe after World War II.

Some in my country fear that China's research and development will **overtake** America's, but I believe that America and the world will benefit from China's scientific and technological advances. I think we will benefit from that. If China makes advances in **stem cell** research, the rest of the world will benefit from that. If China discovers an energy **breakthrough**, this is good for the rest of the world, such as the benefit of a free market.

Some fear that China will **buy up** American companies, but that fear also existed in the 80s, when America feared that Japan was going to buy up American companies. So what? It was just good, and to the benefit of America. We should welcome China's investment in American companies, just as we welcome the billions of dollars that China has invested in U.S. **treasury bonds**. This shows that China has faith in America, and American investment in China shows that we have faith in you. So I believe that China and U.S. economic relations will become even closer in the years ahead. Certainly I realize that we do not agree on everything, but who does? Certainly I realize that China has major **hurdles** to overcome, but it is not for me to say how China should overcome those hurdles and achieve its dreams.

But I can tell you, however, what has given America such energy and strength

期生活的简短故事，以及我的梦想如何使我获得了成功。

当然，一个人不能缺乏梦想。而我当然也不只是为自己着想，只是追随自己的梦想，我对你们、对中国也有梦想。所以我想简单谈一下这个问题。中国的经济已经成为人类进步的动力，让千千万万的人们摆脱了贫困。这无论从道德上还是从经济上都让中国和世界其他国家受益匪浅。我经常读到一些报道，说中国在未来 50 年很可能成为世界最大经济体，我认为这非常了不起。这并不是说，美国会变穷，这只是说中国会更加富有，而美国也会从中国的进步中获益，就像二战后美国从欧洲的崛起中获益一样。

一些美国人担心中国的科研与发展将会超越美国，但我认为美国和世界其他国家都能从中国的科技进步中受益。我相信我们会从中受益。如果中国在骨髓干细胞研究方面取得进展，世界其他国家都会从中受益。如果中国在能源方面取得突破，这会像开放自由市场一样使世界其他国家受益。

一些人担心中国将收购美国公司，类似的担忧在 80 年代也存在，当时美国担心日本会收购美国公司。而结果又怎么样呢？一切都好，美国只是从中受益。我们应该欢迎中国投资美国公司，就像欢迎中国投资亿万美元购买美国国债一样。这表明，中国信任美国，而美国在中国的投资也表明美国对中国有信心。因此，我相信中美经济关系在未来将会更加密切。当然，我们无法在任何事情上都达成共识，但谁又能做到这一点呢？当然，我知道中国需要克服很多障碍，但关于中国应如何克服这些困难并实现它的梦想，我不会去评头论足。

但不管怎样，我想说，在过去的 200 年促使美国变得这么强大而充满活力的因素也能为中国提供一些借鉴。美国是

热词空间

stingy ['stindʒi] *adj.* 吝啬的，缺乏的

engine ['endʒin] *n.* 发动机

terrific [tə'rifik] *adj.* 极好的

overtake [əuvə'teik] *vt.* 超过

stem cell 干细胞

breakthrough ['breik.θru:] *n.* 突破

buy up 收购

treasury ['treʒəri] *n.* 国库

bond [bɔnd] *n.* 债券

hurdle ['hə:dl] *n.* 障碍

over the last 200 years, and perhaps there are some insights in this for China. America is a nation that believes in the power of the individual, and what the individual can accomplish, no matter the color, no matter the religion, no matter the ethnic background of the individual.

Recently, as you probably maybe have read, Rosa Parks, a former **seamstress** married to a barber, married to a hairdresser, died, and she lay in honor in the **Rotunda** of the U.S. **Capitol** in Washington. People from around America came to say farewell to her and to thank her for changing our history and for changing our society. Now, what did this 92-year-old black woman do that deserved such great honor? What did she do? Well, in 1955, the days of **racial segregation**, she had refused to give up her seat on the bus to a white man. She had refused. Her simple refusal to move to the back of the bus put into motion events that led to my country's great civil rights movement. The small **protest** of a woman that maybe weighed less than 100 pounds brought down a **racist** system. As you can see, the individual can make a difference.

Let me tell you about another individual, Ken Behring, a millionaire California businessman who found his **passion** in giving wheelchairs to poor and physically disabled people all around the globe, including China. He says that he has met people who have spent years in rooms with no window, just lying there and staring up at the ceiling, never seeing the outside world unless someone was willing to pick up that person and take them outside to show them the world. He says that it's no wonder so many of those physically disabled people dream about being a bird. Mr. Behring says that most of us think that a wheelchair would be a **confinement**, but to millions of people it is not a confinement, it is freedom, freedom to move and to go to school, freedom to vote, freedom to get a job, and freedom for hope for the future. He has given freedom and wheelchairs to 400,000 people around the world. The individual can make a difference.

一个相信个人能力的国家，美国相信个人能取得很多成就，不论其肤色、宗教信仰及种族背景。

最近罗莎·帕克斯去世了，你们可能已经看到了相关报道。她曾是一名裁缝，嫁给了一个理发师，但现在她却长眠于美国首都华盛顿国会大厦的圆形大厅里，受世人敬仰。来自美国各个州的人们都来向她告别，感谢她改变了我们的历史、改变了我们的社会。这位92岁的黑人妇女到底做了什么竟能获得如此殊荣？她做过什么？1955年，美国那时还处于种族隔离时期，罗莎·帕克斯在公交车上拒绝把座位让给一个白人。没错，她拒绝让座给白人。她拒绝到公交车车尾这一简单的举动推动了美国伟大的民权运动的进展。一位体重不足100磅的女人的一个小小的抗议竟瓦解了种族主义制度。由此你们可以看到，个人可以产生深远的影响。

让我再给你们讲述一个人，这个人就是加利福尼亚州的百万富翁肯·贝林，他是一位商人，他对援助轮椅情有独钟，曾向包括中国在内的全世界各个国家的贫困残疾人捐助轮椅。他说他曾见过一些残疾人连续数年待在没有窗户的屋子里，只是躺在那儿盯着天花板看，看不到外面的世界，除非有人愿意扶起他们，带他们去看外面的世界。他说难怪那么多残疾人都梦想着自己能成为一只小鸟呢。贝林先生说，我们大多数人认为轮椅是一个禁锢，但对于无数残疾人而言，轮椅不是禁锢，而是迈向自由的工具。有了轮椅，他们可以自由行动，自由地去学校，自由地去投票，自由地得到一份工作，甚至自由地畅想未来。他给全世界40万残疾人提供了轮椅和自由。个人可以产生深远的影响。

我总是很乐意提起我的岳母尤尼斯·肯尼迪·施莱弗，因

热词空间

seamstress ['si:mstris] n. 女裁缝师

rotunda [rəu'tʌndə] n. 圆形大厅

capito ['kæpitəl] n.（美国）国会大厦

racial segregation 种族隔离

protest [prəu'test] n. 抗议

racist ['reisist] n. 种族主义者

passion ['pæʃən] n. 热情，激情

confinement [kən'fainmənt] n. 限制；监禁

哈佛
大学

斯坦福
大 学

牛津
大学

耶鲁
大学

杜兰
大学

杜克
大学

威斯康
辛大学

清华
大学

北京
大学

亚利桑
那州立
大 学

加利福
尼 亚
大 学

My mother-in-law, Eunice Kennedy Shriver — I always like to mention her, because it gets me on the good side of her — she, for instance, started an organization called Special Olympics. She started Special Olympics which is for people with mental disabilities. And of course when she started that organization she was told by the experts, "Don't do it. You cannot take people with mental disabilities out of mental institutions and have them **participate** in sports events. They will **drown** in the swimming pools. They will kill each other out there, they will hurt each other. Don't do it." But Eunice Kennedy Shriver had a dream and a passion, and today millions of people compete in Special Olympics around the world, including right here in China. This is why I was here five years ago. Five years ago you had 50,000 participants in the Special Olympics. Today, five years later, you have 500,000 participants in Special Olympics. 500,000 people are getting a chance to participate in sports programs, getting a chance to have health care, have a chance to be treated equally, with respect and with **tolerance**. So Eunice Kennedy Shriver **exemplifies** that the individual can make a difference.

And I think what I'm trying to say to you is that each and every one of you can make a difference. So as you study and as you become smarter, and as you become richer, think about that, that there are millions of people that need your help. Now, you maybe ask yourself the question, what can I do? Well, let me tell you. Even though you maybe have no money or nothing, you can go out and help a child that has not yet learned yet how to read. You maybe can go out and help a person that is physically **handicapped**, to lift them up and to take them outside so they can see the world. There are so many different things that you can do. You maybe can take a person that is mentally disabled, to take them to a soccer game. There are all kinds of things that the individual can do to reach out and to help.

Imagine what could be accomplished if the dreams of China's 1.3 billion individuals could be **unleashed**. Imagine what could happen. Each of you here has the power of the individual within you, you have the power of your dreams within you, and these are **tremendous** powers. You're young, you're educated, and you are the very best China has to offer. My young Chinese friends, I believe in your dreams.

为这让我看到她善良的一面。她创立了特殊奥林匹克运动会。她专门为智障人士创立了这一组织。当然，在她创立这一运动会时，也有专家告诉她，"不要那样做，你不可能把智障人士带出精神病院，让他们参加运动会。他们会在游泳池溺水。一旦出了精神病院，他们就会相互伤害、相互残杀。不要去做。"但尤尼斯·肯尼迪·施莱弗有梦想，也有激情，如今全世界数百万人参加残奥会，包括中国在内。这也是我五年前来这儿的原因。五年前中国有5万人参加了残奥会。今天，中国参加残奥会的有50万人。50万残疾人有机会参加体育比赛、有机会享受医疗保健，能受到在尊重和宽容的基础上的平等对待。因此尤尼斯·肯尼迪·施莱弗向我们证明了：个人可以产生深远的影响。

我想跟你们说的就是，你们每一个人都可以产生深远影响。所以，当你们不断学习变得更加精明时，当你们变得富有时，想想有数百万人还需要你们的帮助。现在你们或许会问自己，我能做什么呢？让我来告诉你们，即使现在你没有金钱，你什么都没有，你们仍然可以去帮助那些甚至还不会读书识字的孩子。你们可以去帮助残疾人，把他们扶起来，带他们出去看看外面的世界。你们可以做许许多多不同的事情。你们可以带一位智障人士去足球场观看比赛。每个人都可以用各种方式伸出自己的援助之手。

试想一下，如果中国13亿人，每个人都去实现自己的梦想的话，将会创造出什么？将会发生什么？你们每一个人都有个人能力，都拥有自己的梦想，而这些就是巨大的力量。你们风华正茂，受过良好的教育，你们是中国最优秀的年轻人。年轻的中国朋友们，我相信你们的梦想。我相信你们能

热词空间

participate [pɑː'tisipeit] vi. 参加，参与

drown [draun] vi. 淹死，淹没

tolerance ['tɔlərəns] n. 宽容

exemplify [ig'zemplifai] vt. 例证；作为……的例证

handicapped ['hændikæpt] adj. 残废的

unleash [ˌʌn'liːʃ] vt. 把……释放出来

tremendous [tri'mendəs] adj. 极大的

I believe that you can achieve them, and I believe you can make a difference, a big difference. All you have to do is just make the **commitment**. All you have to do is create the action and commit, and say, "Let's do it." Go out and do it. I'm asking you. Do it for yourself, do it for China, and do it **for the good of** the world. Thank you very much for listening. Thank you.

施瓦辛格给我们的 启示

I learned a very important lesson, that pain means progress. Pain is progress.

我获得了一个非常重要的教训：疼痛意味着进步。要想进步就得吃苦。

I endured all of this negative thinking, and the more negative the thinking got, and the more negative the questions got, the stronger and the more positive I became, the stronger I became inside.

我承受了所有这一切消极的想法，而且这些想法越消极，我就变得越积极；这些疑虑越多，我就变得越坚强，我的内心也变得更强大。

All of this happened because of my dreams, even though other people told me that those dreams were bogus and they were crazy, but I held onto my dreams.

这一切的实现都是因为我的梦想，即使别人说我的那些梦想都是虚假而荒唐的，但是我仍坚持不懈。

My young Chinese friends, I believe in your dreams. I believe that you can achieve them, and I believe you can make a difference, a big difference. All you have to do is just make the commitment. All you have to do is create the action and commit, and say, "Let's do it." Go out and do it. I'm asking you. Do it for yourself, do it for China, and do it for the good of the world.

年轻的中国朋友们，我相信你们的梦想。我相信你们能够实现这些梦想。我相信你们可以有所作为，而且大有作为。你们必须要做的就是作出承诺。你们要做的就是付诸实际行动并全力以赴，并要说："让我们去做！"去实现你们的梦想吧！我恳请你们，为你们自己而努力，为中国而努力，为全世界的利益而努力。

够实现这些梦想。我相信你们可以有所作为，而且大有作为。你们必须要做的就是作出承诺。你们要做的就是付诸实际行动并全力以赴，并要说："让我们去做！"去实现你们的梦想吧！我恳请你们，为你们自己而努力，为中国而努力，为全世界的利益而努力。非常感谢大家听我讲话。谢谢大家。

热词空间

commitment [kə'mitmənt] *n.*
承诺，保证

for the good of 为了……的利益；为了……的好处

Everything Is Possible

一切皆有可能

Tsinghua University Addressed by Andrea Jung Oct.23, 2003

背景 资料

2003 年 10 月 23 日，雅芳全球董事会主席兼首席执行官钟彬娴走进了中国著名学府清华大学，与清华大学的莘莘学子倾情对话。在一个多小时的精彩演讲中，钟女士以多年美国商界拼搏的切身体验、满怀激情的表述和睿智自信的个人魅力赢得了清华学子的满堂喝彩。清华大学一位学生深受鼓舞，"她给了我们一个成功的梦想，甚至是非常完美的梦想。她是一个懂得坚持的女人，很有自信，演讲时从头到尾都保持微笑，这真的特别难。她对梦想特别执着，她从前也没有想过要做什么 CEO，就是从很平实的方面努力。我觉得未必要有特别远大的梦想，但是执着的人会有特别的收获。她以前想做律师，进入营销业其实是想为做律师做准备，不知道她当初选择雅芳算不算是捡到宝。"

Anything you choose to do is within your reach. How far you go will depend on how high you set your dreams and how hard you work to achieve them.

无论你们想做什么样的事业，你们都可以做得很出色。你们的梦想有多大，你们就能走多远；你们为梦想付出得越多，你们就会越成功。

—— 钟彬娴

姓　　名：	钟彬娴 (Andrea Jung)
性　　别：	女
职　　业：	雅芳全球董事会主席兼首席执行官
国　　籍：	美国
出生日期：	1958 年
毕业学校：	普林斯顿大学
成功点睛：	凭着深厚的中国传统文化底蕴和对梦想的执着追求，她成为全球最有影响力的商界女性
个人成就：	1999 年，出任雅芳首席行政长官，雅芳股票市值因此上涨 23% 2001 年，被《时代》杂志评选为"全球 25 位最有影响力的商界领袖" 2002 年，第五次入选《财富》"全美最有影响力的 50 位商界女性"

名人简介

　　钟彬娴，美籍华人，雅芳公司总裁和首席执行官。1958 年生于加拿大多伦多一个中产阶级移民家庭，20 岁时她从普林斯顿大学毕业。钟彬娴加入雅芳，曾任公司总裁和首席执行官，她还在《财富》杂志 2004 年公布的"全美最有影响力的 50 位商界女性"排行榜中连续 6 年榜上有名。

　　1993 年与雅芳前首席执行官吉姆的一次会面，钟彬娴还历历在目。当时，吉姆办公室的饰板上印有四个足印：猿猴、赤足男人、男皮鞋和女高跟鞋。上面的题词很简单：领导权的演变。当时，美国《财富》杂志评出的 500 强企业还没有一家是由女性领衔；因为那时在各个行业都有一块透明的、限制女性上升的天花板。吉姆看着钟彬娴，说："我完全相信，在未来的 10 年一定会有一位女性来领导雅芳。"钟彬娴根本没有想到：这个打破了玻璃天花板的女人，就是自己。

Good afternoon, everyone. I can't tell you how honored I am to be here with you to talk about my thoughts on leadership and to share my experiences as one of only a handful of women today running a major global corporation.

As I look out at all of you ... some at the beginning stages of your careers... some well along the road to your future ... wherever you are on your own personal path I can promise you a world of opportunity and excitement. Anything you choose to do is within your reach. How far you go will depend on how high you set your dreams and how hard you work to achieve them. But whatever path you take, the **foundation** provided by a good education will make success come that much easier, I promise you.

I have shared my experiences on leadership with many different groups of people all over the world. But being here in the country where my parents and grandparents were born — a country to which I continue to feel strong emotional and intellectual ties — is an **enormous** privilege and a dream comes true.

I consider myself a relatively recent member of a new generation of business leaders faced with a **dizzying** pace of change and a global economic and political environment that are redefined by the day in this **tumultuous** 21st century.

I was offered the job as CEO of Avon four years ago, and it has certainly been an experience of a lifetime for me ever since. We've had a **spectacular** success, modernizing everything about the company from top to bottom.

With sales this year that will top $6.7 billion USD and a stock price which is at an all-time high, we've certainly had some **incredible** results. Avon has been named one of *Fortune* magazine's most admired companies and we've made *Business Week*'s list of the world's most valuable brands for three years in a row.

Today, Avon is proudly known as "The Company for Women" in every country in which we do business. And our ability to provide women with both quality products and a significant earning's opportunity has become an important competitive advantage. It is one of the reasons our business in China has grown so rapidly right from the start.

Going forward, our strategy for Avon recognizes China as the number one

各位下午好！能来到这里和大家探讨对领导力的认识，并分享作为目前管理着一家大型跨国企业的为数不多的女性所走过的历程，我感到无比荣幸。

我注视着你们大家，你们中间有些人正处在职业生涯的起点，有些人已经在通向未来的道路上前进了，不管你在自己的道路上走了多远，我向你们保证，前面有无数的机遇和令人兴奋的事物。无论你们想做什么样的事业，你们都可以做得很出色。你们的梦想有多大，你们就能走多远；你们为梦想付出得越多，你们就会越成功。但无论你们选择哪条路，我保证，有良好的教育背景作为基础，成功会来得更容易。

我曾和来自全世界不同的人群分享过我的经历。但是在这个我祖父母和父母出生的国度，这个我一直被强烈的情感和文化纽带所维系的国度，能同各位分享我的成功感受，是我极大的荣幸，也圆了我的一个梦。

我认为自己属于相对新一代的商业领导者，我们面对的是令人目眩的变化节奏，以及被充满动荡的 21 世纪重新定义的全球经济和政治环境。

四年前我被任命为雅芳集团的首席执行官，从那个时候起开始了我一生难得的经历。我们取得了令人瞩目的成功，全方位地将整个公司推向现代化。

我们今年的销售额将达 67 亿美元，股票价格达到了历史新高，我们的确取得了骄人的业绩。雅芳被《财富》杂志评选为最令人敬佩的公司之一，并连续三年被《商业周刊》评为全球最有价值的品牌之一。

今天，在所有销售雅芳产品的国家，我们很自豪地被公认为"比女人更了解女人的公司"。为女性用户提供优质产品和有可观收入的创业机遇成为我们的一个重要竞争优势。这也是我们在中国的业务一开始就高速发展的原因之一。

展望未来，雅芳的战略是把中国作为全球第一的市场进

热词空间

foundation [faun'deiʃən] n. 基础

enormous [i'nɔːməs] adj. 巨大的，庞大的

dizzying ['dizi:iŋ] adj. 令人昏乱的

tumultuous [tju:'mʌltjuəs] adj. 动荡的，纷乱的

spectacular [spek'tækjulə] adj. 引人注目的，惊人的

incredible [in'kredəbl] adj. 难以置信的

market in the world for future **expansion**, reflecting our strong **commitment** to bring new business opportunities to **entrepreneurial** women in every corner of this great country.

As I look back to all that we have accomplished over the past decade and particularly over the past four years, it has been a real period of breakout success for our company ... **breathtaking**, but also **exhausting**. The roller coaster ride has opened my eyes to many things ... about the increasingly complex demands of running a business today, about my own **competencies** and the need to constantly challenge and renew my own commitment to being a better leader.

I had no idea at the moment I became CEO that I would experience such great fortune and such great challenge both at the same time ... and how enormously my life would change as a result. No idea what privilege, yet what responsibility comes with being the first woman to lead the company, to be constantly **scrutinized** as one of less than a handful of women CEOs today — what it would be like to balance my Chinese cultural background — what the responsibilities of the office would **entail** in this **unparalleled** environment. And what it would mean to be a business leader that could distinguish him or herself in today's world where the game is changing by the minute.

As I reflect on my rapid rise to the top as one of the few women running a major global corporation, I have found myself thinking a great deal about my Chinese **heritage** and how enormously fortunate I am to have been given this very precious gift.

I was raised in a traditional Chinese family where achievement was not demanded, but expected. My father, born in Hong Kong, was a successful architect. My mother, born in Shanghai, was the first female chemical engineer in her graduating class at the University of Toronto in Canada. They arrived in America not speaking a word of English but through hard work, both were able to fulfill their potential, and their success has set a wonderful example for me.

My parents were always, and continue to be today, the single biggest influence in my life. They raised my brother and I with a respect for the values and traditions of our Chinese heritage, yet also with an **unwavering** commitment to bring us up

行拓展，这一战略也体现了我们的坚定承诺，即为身处这个伟大国家的所有具有企业家精神的女性同胞带来新机遇。

过去十年尤其是最近四年，无疑是雅芳获得突破性成功的阶段，回首这一阶段，既波澜壮阔又充满坎坷。犹如乘坐过山车一般的感觉令我见识了很多有关当今经营企业所面临的复杂的要求，关乎我自身能力和不断挑战自己的需要，以及要做一名更优秀的领导者需要不断更新的自我期望。

刚成为首席执行官的时候，我从未想到我会如此幸运但同时又面临这么大的挑战，也从未想到这会给我的生活带来如此大的变化。我不知道作为领导这家公司的第一位女性意味着怎样的特殊性和责任；或者是作为当今为数不多的女性首席执行官该怎样为我的华裔文化背景取得平衡、并时刻被审视；或者是在前所未有的环境下担任这一职位所肩负的责任；还有在今天这个瞬息万变的世界做一名优秀的商业领袖所代表的意义。

作为极少数领导着大型跨国企业的女性中的一员，回顾自己快速成长的历程，我总是联想到我的中国文化传统，以及自己拥有这一宝贵的馈赠是多么的幸运。

我在一个传统的中国家庭里成长，家人不强求我取得多大成就，但期望我能成功。我父亲出生在香港，是一名成功的建筑师。我母亲生于上海，是当时加拿大多伦多大学研究生班里培养出来的第一位女性化学工程师。他们刚到美国时一句英语都不会讲，但他们通过努力，都充分发挥了自己的潜力。他们的成功为我树立了很好的榜样。

我的父母从过去到现在始终是我唯一的最大影响力的来源。他们用中国的传统文化和价值观教育我和弟弟，但也不遗余力地把握所有让我们接受教育的机会，帮助我们适应美国社会，并在这个变幻无常的世界里获得成功。

我和弟弟同我们的美国同龄人获得的机会是均等的：同一

热词空间

expansion [iks'pænʃən] n. 扩张，扩展

commitment [kə'mitmənt] n. 信奉，支持

entrepreneurial [ˌɔntrəprə'nɜːriəl] adj. 企业家的

breathtaking ['breθteikiŋ] adj. 惊人的，惊险的

exhausting [ig'zɔːstiŋ] adj. 使筋疲力尽的

competency ['kɔmpitənsi] n. 能力（等于 competence）

scrutinize ['skruːtinaiz] vt. 详细检查

entail [in'teil] vt. 必需，使承担

unparalleled [ʌn'pærəleld] adj. 无比的；空前的

heritage ['heritidʒ] n. 遗产，继承物

unwavering [ʌn'weivəriŋ] adj. 坚定的

with all the opportunities for higher education and a desire to prepare us to adapt to American society and to succeed in this world of great change.

My brother and I were given all the opportunities of our American friends — the same schools, the same tennis lessons, the same piano teachers ... but we had the wonderful advantage in my mind of a cultural heritage that we were always taught to be proud of. Mom and Dad always wanted us to be proud of being Chinese — my brother and I smile today when we reminisce on growing up in our house. We grew up believing that being Chinese was the greatest advantage in life; in our house, everything important in life came from China, was invented in China, owed all to the Chinese.

We went on elementary school field trips to pulp plants, where they taught us how paper was made. Paper was invented in China, Mom said, after we relayed the process in awe. Our favorite neighbors were Italian and invited us over for spaghetti. When we came home and raved, Dad would remind us that Marco Polo brought pasta home from China. Not Italian ... Chinese ... and so it went. And how wonderful they were to instill in us the sense of pride in our heritage that we have never forgotten.

When I first became CEO, a famous American television journalist interviewed my Dad and asked him if he always knew I would be successful in business. No, he said, quite to the contrary, he worried for years that raising me to be a respectful Chinese daughter would hinder my ability to compete in a world with what he considered the aggressive, cut throat traits of typical America CEO's. In fact, he passed on a letter to me that I keep, translated from Chinese to English, in my desk drawer.

The letter reads: "Remember, there are distinctive qualities that set apart the successful Chinese ... strive to excel in all you do; be a superb parent willing to curtail your own pleasure for the sake of better nurturing your children; be generous, fair, tolerant, eager to learn from other cultures while sharing your own. But beyond these attributes, remember to have an absence of arrogance and boastfulness; have unfailing courtesy, forbearance, sensitivity of others' feelings and above all, the ability to diffuse your anger and grievance, not by suppressing them but by transforming them into helpful, positive emotions. In an age and environment of

所学校、同样的网球课、相同的钢琴老师……但我们被中国传统文化熏陶的思想是一个很大的优势，我们为此感到骄傲。父亲和母亲一直教导我们要为自己是中国人感到自豪。如今，我和弟弟回想起在家的成长历程还会由衷地微笑。我们始终相信作为中国人是生活中最大的优势。在我家，生活中所有重要的东西都来自中国，都是在中国发明的，都归功于中国人。

读小学时，我们去纸浆厂参观，在那里他们教我们纸是怎样生产的。回家之后，我们崇拜地描述了一番，然后母亲告诉我们，纸是中国人发明的。我们最喜欢的邻居是意大利人，他们邀请我们去吃意大利面。我们吃完饭回到家极力赞美，父亲提醒我们，马可波罗是从中国把面团带回去的，不是意大利的，而是中国的……不断如此。我的父母很伟大，他们不断地向我们灌输对中国传统文化的自豪感，我们从未忘记中国文化。

当我刚担任首席执行官时，一个著名的美国电视记者采访我的父亲，问他是否早就知道我会在商界取得成功。不，他回答，恰恰相反，他多年来一直担心把我教育成一个孝顺的中国女儿会妨碍我在一个他认为充满了攻击性和残酷无情的典型美国首席执行官的圈子里和别人竞争。实际上，他写了封信给我，我还保存在我办公桌的抽屉里。信是由中文翻译成英文的。

信里这样写道："记住，成功的中国人具有和其他人不同的特质……所有事情都要努力做得最好；做一个愿意为培育子女放弃自己的快乐的杰出母亲；要慷慨、公正、宽容；不仅要乐于和别人分享你自己的文化，还要热情学习别人的文化。除此之外，切记不要骄傲自大、自吹自擂；要时刻保持礼节，容忍别人，理解别人的感受；最重要的是，要化解你的怒气和悲痛，不是压抑它们，而是把它们转变成积极的、有利的情感。在浮夸的年代和环境中，你有珍贵的中国文化传统，

热词空间

reminisce [ˌremiˈnis] *vi.* 回忆

a field trip 实地考察旅行，实习

pulp [pʌlp] *n.* 纸浆

relay [riˈlei] *vt.* 转述

awe [ɔ:] *n.* 敬畏，惊叹

spaghetti [spəˈgeti] *n.* 意大利式细面条

rave [reiv] *vi.* 极力赞美

pasta [ˈpɑ:stə] *n.* 面团

instill [inˈstil] *vt.* 逐渐灌输；徐徐滴入

aggressive [əˈgresiv] *adj.* 好斗的

trait [treit] *n.* 特性，品质

excel in 在……方面胜过

curtail [kə:ˈteil] *vt.* 缩减

attribute [ˈætribju:t] *n.* 特质

arrogance [ˈærəgəns] *n.* 自大；傲慢

boastfulness [ˈbəustfulnis] *n.* 浮夸，自吹自擂

courtesy [ˈkə:tisi] *n.* 礼貌

forbearance [fɔ:ˈbeərəns] *n.* 容忍

diffuse [diˈfju:s] *vt.* 分散

suppress [səˈpres] *vt.* 抑制

pretension, you have a precious Chinese cultural heritage which we are proud to pass down to you..."

And so, with my parents definition of distinguished leadership in my drawer at all times, I have pushed forward to redefine aggressive as assertive, yet hopefully never abrasive, to insure that I'm tough enough to make the hard decisions, but never unfairly, always treating people well ... reminding myself at all times to have the humility and sensitivity which is expected in the Chinese culture, adapted to the needs of the pressing business environment which requires a healthy dose of outwardly expressed confidence and courage.

In a way, my own experiences reflect those of many women in the business arena who struggle to retain the best of who they are while carving out a successful management career. During my visit here, I have met and talked with so many women, and I am truly heartened that the doors of opportunity are beginning to open for women in every field. But I also know that real change is a slow process, so I am hopeful that my own experiences as a woman and as a leader will provide a valuable perspective.

As the company for women, Avon's commitment to providing developmental opportunities for women is second to none. As you might expect, Avon has a solid representation of women in senior management. In fact, this was one of the reasons I joined the company a decade ago, working my way up the ranks through areas of increasing responsibility.

But interestingly, it has only been in recent years that "the company for women" has also emerged as the company for women in senior leadership positions. Until the last decade, women were not well represented in the executive suite. With few exceptions, middle management was about as far as they could go. Here was a company with virtually 100% women customers and sales representatives, yet capable women simply could not get to the top.

This not only proved unfair, it also proved to be a poor business decision. The lack of women in management came to hurt Avon. Between 1975 and 1985, more than twelve and a half million women entered the United States work force. These working women had to be served in new ways. But, at that time, Avon's leadership

我们为能把它传递给你而骄傲……"

于是，伴随着抽屉里我父母对杰出领导力的定义，我敢于将攻击性重新定义为决断性，但希望避免伤及他人，来确保我在做出艰难的决定时能足够强硬，但又不失公正，始终善待别人……提醒自己既要时刻保持中国文化所倡导的谦逊和感性，同时也要有商界高压力环境所要求的外显的自信和勇气。

在某种意义上，我自己的经历映射了商界中的许多女性，她们也在为保持最佳的自我和追求成功的管理生涯而奋斗。在我来访期间，我遇见了很多女性，同她们交谈，令我感到欣慰的是，在所有领域，机会的大门已经为女性敞开。但我也知道真正的改变需要一个漫长的过程，因此，我希望我自己作为女性领导者的经历能够提供一个有价值的视角。

作为一家"比女人更了解女人"的企业，雅芳的首要承诺就是为女性提供发展机会。你们可能知道雅芳的高级管理层很多是女性。实际上，这也是我十年前加入这家公司的原因之一，然后不断努力工作，得到升迁，承担更多的责任。

但有意思的是，只有在近几年这家"比女人更了解女人"的公司才让女性出现在高层管理者的职位上。十年前，执行层队伍中几乎没有女性，而中层管理人员中也只有零星几个。这是一个客户和销售代表几乎100%是女性的公司，但有能力的女性偏偏无法上升到高层职位。

这不仅不公平，也是一个很糟糕的决策。没有女性参与的管理层开始给雅芳的业务带来损害。在1975年到1985年间，超过1250万妇女加入美国的就业大军。这些职业妇女需要新的服务。但是，那时雅芳的领导团队还是全部由男性组成，我们规划市场战略时听不到女性的声音，结果便是我们在美国这个最大市场上的销售情况受到冲击。

幸运的是，雅芳学会了改变。男性和女性现在作为平等

热词空间

pretension [pri'tenʃən] n. 自负
assertive [ə'sə:tiv] adj. 决断的
abrasive [ə'breisiv] adj. 伤人感情的
humility [hju:'miləti] n. 谦逊
sensitivity [sensi'tiviti] n. 灵敏，敏感
dose [dəus] n. 剂量
arena [ə'ri:nə] n. 竞技场
retain [ri'tein] vt. 保持，保留
second to none 首屈一指
solid ['sɔlid] adj. 结实的，牢固的
emerge [i'mə:dʒ] vi. 出现，显露

team was still made up entirely of men. Women's voices weren't heard as we planned our marketing **strategy** and as a result, sales in our largest market suffered.

Fortunately, Avon learned to change. Men and women now work together as equal business partners. They learn from each other and respect each other. We still offer our male executives an **outstanding** career opportunity, but now women have an equal chance to succeed.

Today, six out of eleven of Avon's board of directors are women. My number two executive is a woman. Almost half of our management staff around the world are women. And importantly, we have put in place special programs to develop the next generation of women who are being trained and prepared to become General Managers in markets all over the world.

I am equally excited about our progress with the development of the next generation of Avon's women leaders in China. Women now account for 78% of our total **workforce** here. Even more impressive, 75% of our managers and **supervisors** are women, and 30% of our most senior executive are women.

With Avon's **reputation** for promoting women and my own career success, I am often asked for advice on how people can prepare themselves to be the leaders of tomorrow. In fact, over my career, I have come to believe that there are indeed some very special qualities that **distinguish** all leaders — and help them stand out in today's competitive arena.

First is Passion. You have to love the work you do. You have to be excited to come to work every day. They taught us the four principles of marketing when I went to school: product, price, place, **promotion**. But they didn't teach us the fifth, most **critical** principle which as far as I'm concerned is Passion, the key to being truly successful as a leader over the long run.

No matter what career path you choose, I believe you have to love what you do. My own personal experience proves this point. There was a time in my Avon career when I was passed over for a promotion to be the CEO. I had a job offer to be the head of another company, but a woman I respected gave me some good advice. She told me always to follow my heart, not my head. So I followed my heart and stayed

的商业搭档一起工作。他们互相学习，互相尊重。我们仍向男性高级管理者提供最佳的职业发展机会，但现在，女性有了同样的成功的可能性。

今天，雅芳的 11 位董事会成员中有 6 位是女性，我的助手是一名女性，我们全球的管理层几乎一半是女性。重要的是，我们设立了专门的项目来培养下一代女性职员，准备把她们培养成全球各个市场的总经理。

我感到同样兴奋的是，雅芳在中国培养下一代女性领导者所取得的成果。这里有 78% 的成员是女性，更令人钦佩的是，女性更在经理和主管队伍里占 75%，在最高层的管理人员中占 30%。

随着雅芳在为女性服务方面的声誉和对我个人职业成功的宣传，我经常被问及如何成为明日的领导者。其实，回想我的职业生涯，我逐渐相信的确有一些非常特殊的品质决定了哪些人会成为领导者，并帮助他们在当今竞争激烈的环境中显露锋芒。

首先是热情。你必须热爱你所做的工作。你为每天去工作感到兴奋。我上学的时候老师教我们市场营销的四 P 原则：产品 (Product)，价格 (Price)，地点 (Place) 和促销 (Promotion)。但他们没有告诉我们第五个，也是我认为最重要的原则：热情 (Passion)——从长远来看，这是成为一个真正成功的领导者的关键因素。

不管你选择哪一条职业发展之路，我认为你必须热爱你的选择。我的个人经历证明了这一点。在雅芳我曾经错过了一次晋升为首席执行官的机会，那时我可以成为另一家公司的领导者。但一位令我敬重的女性给我提了一些很好的建议。她让我听从内心的选择，而不是头脑的。于是我听从了内心留在了雅芳。最终，我获得了晋升，但最重要的是，我始终热爱我的工作，这才是最主要的。

热词空间

strategy ['strætidʒi] *n.* 战略，策略

outstanding [aut'stændiŋ] *adj.* 突出的，显著的

workforce ['wə:kfɔ:s] *n.* 劳动力

supervisor ['su:pəvaizə] *n.* 管理人，指导者

reputation [ˌrepju'teiʃən] *n.* 名气，名声

distinguish [di'stiŋgwiʃ] *vt.* 区分，辨别

promotion [prə'məuʃən] *n.* 提升，促进

critical ['kritikəl] *adj.* 决定性的

哈佛
大学

斯坦福
大学

牛津
大学

耶鲁
大学

杜兰
大学

杜克
大学

威斯康
辛大学

清华
大学

北京
大学

亚利桑
那州立
大学

加利福
尼亚
大学

at Avon. In the end, I got the promotion, but most important, I have always loved my work, and that has made all the difference.

The next distinguishing quality of leadership is Compassion — caring about people. In my four years as CEO at Avon, I've had to make some tough decisions and difficult calls — **eliminating** jobs and closing factories. Actions that affect good people. The **horrible** part of the job. But I believe we **demonstrate** compassion and treat people fairly, with respect and **dignity** during those tough decisions. And it is the responsibility for those of us wanting the privilege of being tomorrow's corporate leaders to honor the commitment to compassion and the protection of the human spirit, in spite of the pressures and demands of business today.

Along with compassion comes Humility. Many people are surprised to learn this is one of Avon's **core** values. None of us has all the answers. And all of us must listen to each other, because listening makes us stronger. One of the things I've learned about myself is that I tend to be **impatient** in solving problems. Instead of listening to the opinions of others, I try right away to find solutions. I have had to learn that other people can give me valuable input and that listening makes me a better leader.

To be a better listener, I now bring employees from all over the world — including China — to New York City four times a year to hear their suggestions for how to improve our business. I meet with them for a full day and spend most of my time listening. This is one of the most important things I do.

Balance is another essential leadership quality in today's complex world, and it's a quality that is especially critical for women who are **juggling** many and sometimes competing roles. As a working mother with two children — my daughter Lauren is 14 and my son Jamie is 6 — I constantly struggle with the issue of balance. People always ask me how I do it, and my answer is — it's never easy to balance work and family.

I'll give you an example. I belong to an executive committee of CEOs from the business world. Recently we were invited to Washington for a meeting with the President of the United States. This was very exciting to me. What an incredible opportunity. The only problem was, the meeting occurred at the same time as my daughter's first big trip away from home. It was a big moment for her and her friends

领导力的第二个特质是有同情心：关心别人。我在雅芳任首席执行官的四年里，有时不得不做出一些艰难的决定和通知，例如取消某个职位和关闭某个工厂。这些都会伤害一些无辜的员工。这也是工作中残忍的一面。但我相信在做这些决定时我们表现出了同情心和公平性，以及对他人尊严的尊重。尽管面临商界的压力和要求，但那些希望成为明天的企业领导者的人有责任怀有对人类的同情心，有责任呵护他人的心灵。

　　作为领导者，除了要有同情心，谦卑心也非常重要。许多人在得知这是雅芳的核心价值观之一时感到很惊讶。我们没有人能回答所有问题。我们必须相互倾听，因为倾听让我们更强大。就我对自己的了解，其中有一点就是，我在解决问题时会很不耐烦。我直接去寻找解决方案而不是先听别人的意见。我必须要懂得其他人能给我有价值的建议，而倾听会使我成为更好的领导者。

　　为了成为一个好的倾听者，我现在每年4次把员工从世界各地（包括中国）集合到纽约，以便听他们对改进业务的建议。我会花一整天的时间与他们见面，而我大多数时间主要是倾听。这是我做的最重要的事情之一。

　　在当今复杂的世界中，获取平衡是另一个重要的领导能力，尤其对于女性这个挣扎于许多角色中的群体，有时这些角色还是相互矛盾的。我是一个有着两个孩子的职业母亲，我的女儿 Lauren 今年 14 岁，儿子 Jamie 今年 6 岁，我经常在如何求得平衡中摸索。别人总问我是怎么做的，我的回答是——在工作和家庭之间取得平衡绝非一件容易的事情。

　　我举个例子。我是一个商界首席执行官委员会的成员。最近我们应邀到华盛顿去和总统见面，这令我很兴奋。这个机会太难得了。唯一的问题是，这次会见的时间正好是我女儿第一次离家去旅行，这对她和她的朋友们很重要。她希望参加几天的旅行，更需要我和她在一起。

热词空间

eliminate [i'limineit] vt. 消除，取消

horrible ['hɔrəbl] adj. 令人畏惧的

demonstrate ['demənstreit] vt. 证明，说明

dignity ['digniti] n. 庄严，端庄

core [kɔ:] n. 核心

impatient [im'peiʃənt] adj. 不耐烦的，急躁的

juggle ['dʒʌgl] vt. 尽力应付

哈佛
大学

斯坦福
大学

牛津
大学

耶鲁
大学

杜兰
大学

杜克
大学

威斯康
辛大学

清华
大学

北京
大学

亚利桑
那州立
大 学

加利福
尼 亚
大 学

— to go on a **multiple** day trip — and my daughter needed me to be there.

What should I do? There was never a doubt in my mind. The president wouldn't know if I was there or not. But my daughter would. So I went to the bus with her and I never looked back. It didn't affect Avon that I didn't go to the White House. But I also tell women that it is even all right if your job does sometimes come second to your personal **priorities**. Sometimes the job is more important. But sometimes your family has to be more important.

There are two final qualities of distinguished leadership that I want to share with you today. These may be the most important qualities of all and how lucky we are that both are a **fundamental** part of our Chinese culture — something we all learn from our parents **virtually** from the day we are born.

First is **Perseverance**. I'm talking about simple hard work and a commitment to stay the course even when times are tough. In today's fast-pace business environment, unexpected challenges come at you from all directions, with no end in sight. Sometimes I read articles about myself and my career path and it makes it sound so easy. But believe me, it hasn't been easy for a single day. I work far harder now than I ever have in my life. I've had to **embrace** constant change, and every time I think I've finally mastered the situation a new challenge comes along I hadn't anticipated.

There will be many days when the challenges each of you confront will seem **overwhelming**. We all have those days; they go with the territory when you are trying to achieve something great.

Perseverance and hard work will see you through the tough times. My parents instilled these qualities in me and it has made all the difference. Sometimes I watch young Americans quit when things are difficult, and I always advise them to try again ... and again ... and again. Never give up until you achieve your goal. That's what distinguishes those who make it to the top from those who don't.

Hard work is essential ... but all the hard work in the world won't take you anywhere unless you know where it is you want to go.

That's why it's so important to have a dream. This is the final important quality of leadership. Everything great that has ever happened in this world began with a dream.

我怎么办？其实我心里从来没有犹豫。总统并不知道我是否在场，但我女儿需要我的陪伴。所以我义无反顾地和她一起去了车站。不去白宫不会影响雅芳。但我也要告诉女性朋友，有时候你的工作排在你的私人事情之后是完全可以的。有时候，工作更重要，但有时候，你的家庭更重要。

我今天和你们分享的最后两点优秀领导力的特质可能是所有特质中最重要的，而我们如此幸运，因为这两点都是我们中华民族文化的根基，是我们几乎从出生那天起就开始向父母学习的。

第一是坚持。我所谈的是最基本的努力工作和面临困境时也能如此的信念。在如今快节奏的商业环境下，意料之外的挑战来自四面八方，看不到尽头。有时候我读一些关于我和我的职业生涯的文章，看上去好像一切都很容易。但相信我，没有一天是容易的。我现在要比以往任何时候都还要努力工作。我必须接纳不断的变化，而且每次我认为终于掌握局面的时候，一项新的没有预计到的挑战就会冒出来。

很多时候你们会感觉自己所面对的挑战令人无法招架。我们每个人都会经历这样的阶段。当你设法要取得一些成就的时候，这些挑战就会随之而来。

坚持和勤奋会帮助你渡过困境。我的父母给我灌输了这些特质，的确很有意义。有时候我看到年轻的美国人在遇到困难时就放弃了，我总是建议他们一次又一次地尝试。没有达到目标决不要放弃。这就是为什么有人能够到达顶峰，而有人却没有。

勤奋工作是最基本的，但仅仅有勤奋是不行的，除非你知道自己的目标是什么。

这也是为什么胸怀梦想非常重要。梦想是我要讲的领导力的最后一个要素。这个世界上所有的伟大成就都始于一个梦想。

热词空间

multiple ['mʌltipl] *adj.* 多种多样的

priority [prai'ɔriti] *n.* 优先权，重点

fundamental [fʌndə'mentl] *adj.* 基本的

virtually ['və:tʃuəli] *adv.* 实际上，事实上

perseverance [ˌpə:si'viərəns] *n.* 坚持不懈

embrace [im'breis] *vt.* 拥抱，包括

overwhelming [ˌəuvə'hwelmiŋ] *adj.* 势不可挡的

Avon has big dreams. In fact our company theme this year is "Dream Bigger". We want to be number one in beauty worldwide and number one in satisfying our customers and sales representatives. We want to be the best place to work. We want to be the leader in **philanthropy**. And we want to be one of the world's most successful companies.

I have a personal dream as well. My dream is to make a real difference for women all over the world and to help transform lives. Every time a woman opens an Avon Beauty **Boutique**, we are making her dream of business ownership come true. This is the dream of unlimited opportunity. This is the dream of hope. It is also the dream of China — where everything is possible and success can be as great as the size of your imagination.

In many ways the dream of China is really the biggest dream of all — and it's a dream we all share. And we're not alone. The dream of China has **captured** the world's imagination since the beginning of history. From Columbus to Marco Polo, explorers have traveled long and far to unlock China's mystery and discover its riches.

The dream of China is a gift given to each of us as part of our cultural heritage. As China emerges as one of the world's leading powers, this dream grows stronger and brighter every day. The world is looking on in awe. And nothing makes me prouder than to watch this growth and success. Nothing makes me prouder than to know that this is my culture. Like all of you, I am very proud to be Chinese, and very grateful that I have been given the gift of this wonderful heritage. It is a gift that serves as a source of strength and as a guiding **compass** every single day in my life and in my career.

In closing, I encourage all of you to take full advantage of the gifts you have been given. You have the benefit of a precious cultural heritage, including a respect for the value of hard work. You know what is important and you work to achieve it. And you are **tenacious** in pursuing your goals.

As you pursue these goals, I encourage you to **aspire** high.

Dream big dreams. Dream **bold** dreams. Dream as far as your imagination will take you. Whatever it is you dream of, there is no doubt in my mind you can do it. The world is open to you. So go out there and make all your dreams come true.

雅芳有很大的梦想。其实我们公司今年的主题就是"拥有更大的梦想"。我们想在美容方面成为世界第一；在客户和销售代表满意度方面也成为第一；我们想成为最佳的雇主；我们想成为慈善事业的领导者；我们想成为世界最成功的企业之一。

我个人也有一个梦想。我的梦想是为全球的女性带来一个全新的体会，帮助她们改变生活。每次一位女性开设一家雅芳产品专卖店，我们就在帮助她实现创业的梦想。这是一个蕴含着无限机遇的梦想。这是充满希望的梦想。这也是中国梦：一切皆有可能，你的想象力有多大，你的成功就会有多大。

在很多方面，中国梦的确是最大的梦想，这是我们共有的梦想。我们并不孤独。有史以来，中国的梦想就吸引着世界的想象力。从哥伦布到马可波罗，探险家长途跋涉为了揭开中国的神秘面纱、发现这里的财富。

中国梦是我们文化传统的一部分，是馈赠给我们每一个人的礼物。在中国逐渐成为占据领导地位的大国时，这个梦想会变得更大更明确。世界投以崇敬的目光。我为能目睹这样的成长和成功而感到无比自豪。我为这是我们自己的传统文化而无比自豪。和你们所有人一样，作为中国人我很自豪，也为拥有这样的美好传承而无比感激。在生活和事业中，这一传承是我力量的源泉，指引着我每次前行的方向。

讲话即将结束，我鼓励大家充分利用你们拥有的优势。你们拥有这份宝贵的传承，包括对勤奋工作的价值的尊重。你们知道什么是重要的，并且努力去完成。你们在追求目标的时候会坚持不懈。

在你们追求这些目标的时候，要树立更高的理想。

大胆地梦想，拥有更大的梦想，极尽你们的想象力去梦想。不管你们有什么梦想，我相信你们都可以做到。世界向你们敞开大门。大胆地走出去，去实现你们的梦想吧。

哈佛大学

斯坦福大学

牛津大学

耶鲁大学

杜兰大学

杜克大学

威斯康辛大学

清华大学

北京大学

亚利桑那州立大学

加利福尼亚大学

钟彬娴给我们的 启示

First is Passion. You have to love the work you do. You have to be excited to come to work every day. They taught us the four principles of marketing when I went to school: product, price, place, promotion. But they didn't teach us the fifth, most critical principle which as far as I'm concerned is Passion, the key to being truly successful as a leader over the long run.

首先是热情。你必须热爱你所做的工作。你为每天去工作感到兴奋。我上学的时候老师教我们市场营销的四 P 原则：产品 (Product)，价格 (Price)，地点 (Place) 和促销 (Promotion)。但他们没有告诉我们第五个，也是我认为最重要的原则：热情 (Passion)——从长远来看，这是成为一个真正成功的领导者的关键因素。

None of us has all the answers. And all of us must listen to each other, because listening makes us stronger.

我们没有人能回答所有问题。我们必须相互倾听，因为倾听让我们更强大。

I always advise them to try again ... and again ... and again. Never give up until you achieve your goal. That's what distinguishes those who make it to the top from those who don't.

我总是建议他们一次又一次地尝试。没有达到目标决不要放弃。这就是为什么有人能够到达顶峰，而有人却没有。

Everything great that has ever happened in this world began with a dream.

这个世界上所有的伟大成就都始于一个梦想。

This is the dream of unlimited opportunity. This is the dream of hope. It is also the dream of China — where everything is possible and success can be as great as the size of your imagination.

这是一个蕴含着无限机遇的梦想。这是充满希望的梦想。这也是中国梦：一切皆有可能，你的想象力有多大，你的成功就会有多大。

Dream big dreams. Dream bold dreams. Dream as far as your imagination will take you. Whatever it is you dream of, there is no doubt in my mind you can do it. The world is open to you. So go out there and make all your dreams come true.

大胆地梦想，拥有更大的梦想，极尽你们的想象力去梦想。不管你们有什么梦想，我相信你们都可以做到。世界向你们敞开大门。大胆地走出去，去实现你们的梦想吧。

北京大学

校训：爱国 进步 民主 科学 （Patriotism Progress Democracy Science）

总 括

　　北京大学，创建于 1898 年，初名京师大学堂，辛亥革命后，于 1912 年改为现名。北京大学是中国近代第一所国立大学，被公认为中国的最高综合性学府，也是亚洲和世界最重要的大学之一。在中国现代史上，北大是中国"新文化运动"与"五四运动"等运动的中心发祥地，也是多种政治思潮和社会理想在中国的最早传播地，有"中国政治晴雨表"之称，享有极高的声誉和重要的地位。

Challenge of the 21st Century

21 世纪的挑战

背景资料

　　1998年6月29日，美国总统克林顿访问北京大学并发表演讲。由于此次访问对中美关系影响深远，因此受到中外媒体的高度关注，也引起了北大校方的高度重视。克林顿在北京大学发表演讲时说，中国日新月异，美国希望在新世纪里与中国建立一种新关系，共创和平、繁荣的未来。他说，"当今世界正发生着变化，你们年轻一代是中国的未来，因此更有必要向你们阐述中美之间建立伙伴关系的重要性。我们更重视未来。中国度过的千年比美国度过的百年还要多。我们已经看到了新世纪的曙光。你们不仅以过去的伟大而自豪，以目前的成就而自豪，而且以未来更伟大的事业而自豪。"

In the 21st century, your generation must make it your mission to ensure that today's progress does not come at tomorrow's expense.

在21世纪，你们年轻一代的使命是必须保证今天的进步发展不以明天为代价。

——克林顿

最名人档案

姓　　名：	威廉·杰斐逊·克林顿 (William Jefferson Clinton)
性　　别：	男
职　　业：	美国第 42 任总统
国　　籍：	美国
党　　派：	民主党
出生日期：	1946 年 8 月 19 日
毕业学校：	耶鲁法学院
成功点睛：	用魅力谱写多彩的人生，用智慧创造美国经济的神话
代表作品：	自传《我的生活》
荣　　誉：	美国第 42 任总统。他在任内创造了美国 8 年的长期经济繁荣，并使美国高科技行业飞速发展，奠定今日美国高科技大国的地位。克林顿是历史上得到最多公众肯定的总统之一。

名人简介

　　威廉·杰斐逊·克林顿，也可以称为比尔·克林顿，美国律师、政治家，美国民主党成员。1946 年 8 月 19 日出生于阿肯色州的霍普，然后在温泉城长大。克林顿在学校时成绩出色，而且是个很好的萨克斯演奏手，他曾一度想要成为一名专业的音乐家。在高中时他作为全国学生代表到白宫与当时的美国总统约翰·肯尼迪见面。这次的白宫之旅让他下定决心要成为一名公务员。出身贫寒的克林顿在乔治城大学外交学院拿到国际关系学位后，又获得了罗兹奖学金，得以到英国牛津大学深造，1973 年又获得了耶鲁法学院的法学学位。在耶鲁他遇到了希拉里，两人在 1975 年结婚。他们育有一个女儿切尔西（1980年出生）。克林顿曾任阿肯色州州长，并于 1993 年成功竞选美国第 42 任总统，1997 年成功连任。在克林顿的执政下，美国经济空前繁荣昌盛，没有受到战争的困扰，也没有经济的不景气，华尔街三大股指屡次创新高，克林顿总统是美国最成功的总统之一，他执政的八年被誉为"黄金八年"。

Thank you. Thank you, President Chen, Chairmen Ren, Vice President Chi, Vice Minister Wei. We are delighted to be here today with a very large American delegation, including the First Lady and our daughter, who is a student at Stanford, one of the schools with which Beijing University has a relationship. We have six members of the United States Congress; the Secretary of State; Secretary of Commerce; the Secretary of Agriculture; the Chairman of our Council of Economic Advisors; Senator Sasser, our Ambassador; the National Security Advisor and my Chief of Staff, among others. I say that to illustrate the importance that the United States places on our relationship with China.

I would like to begin by congratulating all of you, the students, the faculty, the administrators, on celebrating the centennial year of your university. Gongxi, Beida.

As I'm sure all of you know, this campus was once home to Yenching University which was founded by American missionaries. Many of its wonderful buildings were designed by an American architect. Thousands of American students and professors have come here to study and teach. We feel a special kinship with you.

I am, however, grateful that this day is different in one important respect from another important occasion 79 years ago. In June of 1919, the first president of Yenching University, John Leighton Stuart, was set to deliver the very first commencement address on these very grounds. At the appointed hour, he appeared, but no students appeared. They were all out leading the May 4th Movement for China's political and cultural renewal. When I read this, I hoped that when I walked into the auditorium today, someone would be sitting here. And I thank you for being here, very much.

Over the last 100 years, this university has grown to more than 20,000 students. Your graduates are spread throughout China and around the world. You have built the largest university library in all of Asia. Last year, 20 percent of your graduates went abroad to study, including half of your math and science majors. And in this anniversary year, more than a million people in China, Asia, and beyond have logged on to your website. At the dawn of a new century, this university is leading China into the future.

I come here today to talk to you, the next generation of China's leaders, about the

谢谢。陈校长、任书记、迟副校长、韦副部长，谢谢你们。今天，我很高兴率领一个庞大的美国代表团来到这里，代表团中有第一夫人和我们的女儿。我的女儿是斯坦福大学的学生，该校是和北大具有交流关系的学校之一。此外，我们的代表团中还包括6位美国国会议员、国务卿、商务部长、农业部长、经济顾问理事会理事长、我国驻华大使参议员尚慕杰、国家安全顾问和我的办公厅主任等。我提到这些人是为了说明美国极为重视对华关系。

在北大百年校庆之际，我首先要向北大的所有学生、全体教职员工、各位管理人员表示祝贺。恭喜，北大！

各位知道，这个校园曾经是由美国传教士建立的燕京大学。学校许多美丽的建筑物都是由一位美国建筑师设计的。成千上万的美国学生和教授来到北大求学和教课。我们对你们有一种特殊的亲近感。

我很庆幸，在某种重要意义上今天和79年前的一个重要的日子大不相同。1919年6月，就在这里，燕京大学首任校长约翰·雷登·斯图尔特准备在此地发表第一个毕业典礼致辞。他准时出场，但学生一个未到。学生们为了振兴中国的政治和文化，全部走上街头领导"五四运动"去了。我读到这个故事后，希望今天当我走进这个礼堂时，会有人坐在这里。非常感谢大家前来听我演讲。

一百年以来，北大已经发展到拥有两万多学生。贵校的毕业生遍及中国和全世界。贵校建成了亚洲最大的大学图书馆。去年贵校有20%的毕业生去国外深造，其中包括一半的数理专业学生。在这个百年校庆之年，中国、亚洲和全世界有100多万人访问贵校的网址。在新世纪即将来临之际，北大正在率领中国奔向未来。

你们是中国下一代的领导者。我今天要跟你们讲的是，

critical importance to your future of building a strong partnership between China and the United States.

The American people deeply admire China for its thousands of years of contributions to culture and religion, to philosophy and the arts, to science and technology. We remember well our strong partnership in World War II . Now we see China at a moment in history when your **glorious** past is matched by your present sweeping transformation and the even greater promise of your future.

Just three decades ago, China was virtually **shut off** from the world. Now, China is a member of more than 1,000 international organizations — enterprises that affect everything from air travel to agricultural development. You have opened your nation to trade and investment **on a large scale**. Today, 40,000 young Chinese study in the United States, with hundreds of thousands more learning in Asia, Africa, Europe, and Latin America.

Your social and economic transformation has been even more remarkable, moving from a closed command economic system to a driving, increasingly market-based and driven economy, generating two decades of **unprecedented** growth, giving people greater freedom to travel within and outside China, to vote in village elections, to own a home, choose a job, attend a better school. As a result you have lifted literally hundreds of millions of people from poverty. **Per capita income** has more than doubled in the last decade. Most Chinese people are leading lives they could not have imagined just 20 years ago.

Of course, these changes have also brought **disruptions** in settled patterns of life and work, and have **imposed** enormous **strains** on your environment. Once every urban Chinese was guaranteed employment in a state enterprise. Now you must compete in a job market. Once a Chinese worker had only to meet the demands of a central planner in Beijing. Now the global economy means all must match the quality and creativity of the rest of the world. For those who lack the right training and skills and support, this new world can be **daunting**.

In the short-term, good, hardworking people — some, at least will find themselves unemployed. And, as all of you can see, there have been enormous environmental and economic and health care costs to the development pattern and the

建立中美两国牢固的伙伴关系，对于你们的未来至关重要。

在几千年的历史长河中，中国为人类文化、宗教、哲学、艺术和科技做出了贡献，美国人民非常钦佩你们。我们铭记着第二次世界大战期间中美两国牢固的伙伴关系。如今，我们看到中国正处在一个通过迅猛全面的改革赶超辉煌的往昔，并展现更加美好前景的历史时刻。

仅仅在30年前，中国还与世界隔绝。现在，中国加入了1000多个国际组织，这些组织的影响遍及我们生活的每一个方面，从航空到农业发展无所不包。贵国为大规模贸易和投资敞开了大门。如今，有40,000年轻的中国学生在美国留学，还有数十万中国学生在亚洲、非洲、欧洲和拉美国家留学。

贵国在社会和经济领域的变革更为显著，从一个封闭的指令性经济体制向一个日显生机、日趋注重市场性的经济转变，产生了连续20年史无前例的增长，赋予人民到国内外旅游、进行村委会选举、拥有住房、选择职业以及上更好学校的更大自由。因此，贵国帮助成千上百万的人们摆脱了贫困。在过去的10年中人均收入翻了一番以上。大多数中国人民过上了20年前还难以想象的美好生活。

当然，这些变化也打乱了固有的生活和工作格局，给贵国的环境造成了巨大压力。以前，每个城市居民到国有企业就业都有保障。现在，你们必须到就业市场上去竞争。以前，每个中国工人只要满足北京中央计划人员的要求，现在，全球性经济一体化意味着必须跟上世界其他地区的质量和创造力。对于缺乏适当训练、技能和支持的人们来说，这个新世界的确令人生畏。

在短期内，一些善良勤快的人会失业。正如你们所见，过去20年的开发模式和能源使用模式，造成了空气污染、滥

热词空间

glorious ['glɔ:riəs] *adj.* 光荣的，壮丽的

shut off 切断，隔绝

on a large scale 大规模地

unprecedented [ʌn'presidəntid] *adj.* 空前的

per capita ['kæpitə] **income** 人均收入

disruption [dis'rʌpʃən] *n.* 破坏，分裂

impose [im'pəuz] *vt.* 强加

strain [strein] *n.* 拉紧，紧张

daunting ['dɔ:ntiŋ] *adj.* 使人畏缩的

energy use pattern of the last 20 years — from air pollution to **deforestation** to **acid rain** and water shortage.

In the face of these challenges, new systems of training and social security will have to be devised, and new environmental policies and technologies will have to be introduced with the goal of growing your economy while improving the environment. Everything I know about the intelligence, the **ingenuity**, the enterprise of the Chinese people and everything I have heard these last few days in my discussions with President Jiang, Prime Minister Zhu and others give me confidence that you will succeed.

As you build a new China, America wants to build a new relationship with you. We want China to be successful, secure and open, working with us for a more peaceful and **prosperous** world. I know there are those in China and the United States who question whether closer relations between our countries is a good thing. But everything all of us know about the way the world is changing and the challenges your generation will face tell us that our two nations will be far better off working together than apart.

The late Deng Xiaoping **counseled** us to seek truth from facts. At the dawn of the new century, the facts are clear. The distance between our two nations, indeed, between any nations, is **shrinking**. Where once an American **clipper** ship took months to cross from China to the United States. Today, technology has made us all virtual neighbors. From laptops to **lasers**, from **microchips** to **megabytes**, an information revolution is lighting the landscape of human knowledge, bringing us all closer together. Ideas, information, and money cross the planet at the stroke of a computer key, bringing with them extraordinary opportunities to create wealth, to prevent and conquer disease, to **foster** greater understanding among peoples of different histories and different cultures.

But we also know that this greater openness and faster change mean that problems which start beyond one nation's borders can quickly move inside them — the spread of weapons of mass destruction, the threats of organized crime and **drug trafficking**, of environmental **degradation**, and severe economic **dislocation**. No nation can isolate itself from these problems, and no nation can solve them alone.

伐森林、酸雨和缺水，使环境、经济和医疗保健方面付出了巨大代价。

面对这些挑战，必须建立培训和社会保障的新体系，推出保护环境的新政策和采用新技术，以便在促进经济增长的同时改善环境。我对中国人民智慧、独创性和开发精神的所见所闻，以及过去几天我和江主席、朱总理及其他人的会谈中的所见所闻，给了我信心，相信你们一定会取得成功。

在你们建设新中国的同时，美国希望同你们建立新关系。我们要看到一个成就非凡、安全开放的中国，和我们携手为一个更加和平繁荣的世界而努力。我知道，无论在中国还是在美国，都有人怀疑两国之间的紧密关系是否是好事。但是，世界在变化，我们面临着种种挑战，我们了解的这一切告诉我们，我们两国携手合作比各自为政要有利得多。

已故的邓小平告诫我们要实事求是。新世纪来临之际，事实显而易见。我们两国间的距离在缩短，实际上是所有国家间的距离在缩短。以前，美国的快速帆船从中国开到美国要花几个月。今天，高科技使我们天涯若比邻。从笔记本电脑到激光技术、从微芯片到兆字节储存器，信息革命正在照亮人类知识领域，将我们更紧密地联结起来。人们只要敲一下电脑的键盘，观念、信息和资金就能跨越全球，为人们创造财富、预防和征服疾病、加深具有不同历史和文化背景的人民之间的了解带来了极大的机会。

但我们也知道，更大的开放和更快的变革也意味着，别国产生的问题会很快蔓延到本国境内，如大规模毁灭性武器的扩散、有组织的犯罪和贩卖毒品的威胁、环境的恶化和严重的经济混乱等问题。没有哪个国家能避免这些问题，没有哪个国家能独自解决这些问题。我们，特别是中美两国的年

热词空间

deforestation [di:ˌfɔri'steiʃən] n. 采伐森林

acid rain 酸雨

ingenuity [ˌindʒi'njuːəti] n. 心灵手巧，独创性

prosperous ['prɔspərəs] adj. 兴旺的

counsel ['kaunsəl] vt. 劝告

shrink [ʃriŋk] vi. 收缩，畏缩

clipper ['klipə] n. 快速帆船

laser ['leizə] n. 激光

microchip ['maikrəutʃip] n. 微芯片

megabyte ['megəbait] n. [计] 兆字节

foster ['fɔstə] vt. 培养，促进

drug trafficking ['træfikiŋ] 贩毒，毒品走私

degradation [ˌdegrə'deiʃən] n. 降低，恶化

dislocation [ˌdisləu'keiʃən] n. 脱节，动乱

哈佛
大学

斯坦福
大 学

牛津
大学

耶鲁
大学

杜兰
大学

杜克
大学

威斯康
辛大学

清华
大学

北京
大学

亚利桑
那州立
大 学

加利福
尼 亚
大 学

We, especially the younger generations of China and the United States, must make common cause of our common challenges, so that we can, together, shape a new century of brilliant possibilities.

In the 21st century — your century — China and the United States will face the challenge of security in Asia. On the Korean Peninsula, where once we were adversaries, today we are working together for a permanent peace and a future freer of nuclear weapons.

On the Indian subcontinent, just as most of the rest of the world is moving away from nuclear danger, India and Pakistan risk sparking a new arms race. We are now pursuing a common strategy to move India and Pakistan away from further testing and toward a dialogue to resolve their differences.

In the 21st century, your generation must face the challenge of stopping the spread of deadlier nuclear, chemical, and biological weapons. In the wrong hands or the wrong places, these weapons can threaten the peace of nations large and small. Increasingly, China and the United States agree on the importance of stopping proliferation. That is why we are beginning to act in concert to control the world's most dangerous weapons.

In the 21st century, your generation will have to reverse the international tide of crime and drugs. Around the world, organized crime robs people of billions of dollars every year and undermines trust in government. America knows all about the devastation and despair that drugs can bring to schools and neighborhoods. With borders on more than a dozen countries, China has become a crossroad for smugglers of all kinds.

Last year, President Jiang and I asked senior Chinese and American law enforcement officials to step up our cooperation against these predators, to stop money from being laundered, to stop aliens from being cruelly smuggled, to stop currencies from being undermined by counterfeiting. Just this month, our drug enforcement agency opened an office in Beijing, and soon Chinese counternarcotics experts will be working out of Washington.

In the 21st century, your generation must make it your mission to ensure that today's progress does not come at tomorrow's expense. China's remarkable growth

轻一代，必须以迎接这些共同的挑战为共同的事业，共创一个光辉灿烂的新世纪。

二十一世纪是你们的世纪。中美两国将面临亚洲安全的挑战。我们两国曾在朝鲜半岛为敌，现在我们携手合作，为一个永久和平和无核武器的未来而努力。

当世界上大多数国家都在摆脱核威胁时，印度和巴基斯坦却甘冒挑起新一轮军备竞赛的风险。我们正在谋求一个共同的策略，以使印巴两国停止进一步的核试验，并为解决分歧进行对话。

在二十一世纪，你们年轻一代必须承担制止更加致命的核武器、化学武器和生化武器扩散的重任。如果这种武器落入坏人之手或流入不适当的场所，无论大小国家，其安全都会受到威胁。中美两国日益认识到制止这类武器扩散的重要性，因此我们已开始齐心协力，控制世界上最危险的武器。

在二十一世纪，你们年轻一代一定要扭转犯罪和毒品的国际逆流。全世界有组织的犯罪分子每年从人民手中掠夺的财产达数十亿美元，破坏了人民对政府的信任。美国人民深知毒品给学校师生和社区居民造成的破坏和绝望。中国的边境和十几个国家相邻，已成了各种走私分子的通道。

去年，我和江主席请求中美双方的高级执法官员加强合作，打击这些犯罪分子，防止洗钱，防止在恶劣的条件下走私人口，防止伪币破坏货币的信用。就在本月，我们的缉毒署在北京开设了办事处。不久，中国的缉毒专家也将在华盛顿开展工作。

在二十一世纪，你们年轻一代的使命是必须保证今天的进步发展不以明天为代价。中国过去 20 年来的快速增长以遭受有毒污染物的危害为代价，贵国人民的饮用水和呼吸的空

热词空间

peninsula [pi'ninsjulə] *n.* 半岛

adversary ['ædvəsəri] *n.* 敌手, 对手

permanent ['pə:mənənt] *adj.* 永久的, 固定的

spark [spɑ:k] *vt.* 引起, 激发

proliferation [prəu,lifə'reiʃən] *n.* 扩散

in concert 一致, 一齐

undermine [,ʌndə'main] *vt.* 破坏

devastation [devəs'teiʃən] *n.* 破坏

smuggler ['smʌglə] *n.* 走私船, 走私者

predator ['predətə] *n.* 捕食者, 掠夺者

launder ['lɑ:ndə] *vt.* 清洗, 洗黑钱

alien ['eiljən] *n.* 外国人

counterfeit ['kauntəfit] *vi.* 仿造

counternarcotics [,kauntənɑ:'kɔtiks] *n.* 缉毒专家

in the last two decades has come with a toxic cost, pollutants that foul the water you drink and the air you breathe — the cost is not only environmental, it is also serious in terms of the health consequences of your people and in terms of the drag on economic growth.

Environmental problems are also increasingly global as well as national. For example, in the near future, if present energy use patterns persist, China will overtake the United States as the world's largest emitter of greenhouse gases, the gases which are the principal cause of global warming. If the nations of the world do not reduce the gases which are causing global warming, sometime in the next century there is a serious risk of dramatic changes in climate which will change the way we live and the way we work, which could literally bury some island nations under mountains of water and undermine the economic and social fabric of nations.

We must work together. We Americans know from our own experience that it is possible to grow an economy while improving the environment. We must do that together for ourselves and for the world.

Building on the work that our Vice President, Al Gore, has done previously with the Chinese government, President Jiang and I are working together on ways to bring American clean energy technology to help improve air quality and grow the Chinese economy at the same time.

But I will say this again — this is not on my remarks — your generation must do more about this. This is a huge challenge for you, for the American people and for the future of the world. And it must be addressed at the university level, because political leaders will never be willing to adopt environmental measures if they believe it will lead to large-scale unemployment or more poverty. The evidence is clear that does not have to happen. You will actually have more rapid economic growth and better paying jobs, leading to higher levels of education and technology if we do this in the proper way. But you and the university, communities in China, the United States and throughout the world will have to lead the way.

In the 21st century your generation must also lead the challenge of an international financial system that has no respect for national borders. When stock markets fall in Hong Kong or Jakarta, the effects are no longer local; they are global.

气都已遭受污染。这种代价不仅仅体现在环境方面，对人民的健康也造成了严重的危害，而且还会阻碍经济的发展。

环境问题正在变得日趋全球化和全国化。例如，在不久的将来，如果目前的能源使用模式不改变，中国将超过美国成为世界最大的温室气体排放国。温室气体是全球变暖的主要原因。如果世界各国不减少排放造成全球变暖的气体，下世纪的某个时候就会出现气候急剧变化的严重威胁，这将改变我们的生活和工作方式，某些岛国就会被大水淹没，某些国家的经济和社会结构就会遭到破坏。

我们必须共同协作。经验告诉我们美国人，在促使经济成长的同时改善环境是有可能的。为了我们自己也为了世界，我们必须做到这一点。

我国副总统戈尔已同中国政府合作开展了不少工作。在此基础上，我和江主席正在一起探讨方法，在中国引入美国的清洁能源技术，在促进中国经济发展的同时提高其空气质量。

但我还要重申——这话不在我的讲稿上——在这一点上你们这一代还要有更多的作为。这对你们、对美国人民和世界的未来都是一个巨大的挑战。这个问题必须在大学里提出，因为如果政治领导人认为采取环保措施会导致大规模的失业或严重的贫困，他们就不愿意这样做。事实证明环保不会造成失业和贫困。如果我们的方法得当，人们将取得更快的经济增长，拥有薪水更高的工作，促进教育和科技向更高水平发展。但是，你们大学生和你们的大学，中美两国以及全世界的人民都必须带这个头。

在二十一世纪，你们面临的挑战还包括一个：不分国界的国际金融系统。当香港和雅加达的股票市场下跌时，其影响再也不是局部的，而是全球性的。因此，贵国充满生机的经济增长同整个亚太地区恢复稳定和经济发展紧密相连。

热词空间

toxic ['tɔksik] adj. 有毒的
foul [faul] vt. 弄脏
drag [dræg] n. 拖，拖累
persist [pə'sist] vi. 坚持
emitter [i'mitə] n. 释放者，发射者
principal ['prinsəpəl] adj. 主要的，首要的
fabric ['fæbrik] n. 构造，组织

The **vibrant** growth of your own economy is tied closely, therefore, to the **restoration** of stability and growth in the Asia Pacific region.

China has **steadfastly shouldered** its responsibilities to the region and the world in this latest **financial crisis** — helping to prevent another cycle of dangerous **devaluations**. We must continue to work together to counter this threat to the global financial system and to the growth and prosperity which should be embracing all of this region.

In the 21st century, your generation will have a remarkable opportunity to bring together the talents of our scientists, doctors, engineers into a shared **quest** for progress. Already the breakthroughs we have achieved in our areas of joint cooperation — in challenges from dealing with **spina bifida** to dealing with extreme weather conditions and earthquakes — have proved what we can do together to change the lives of millions of people in China and the United States and around the world. Expanding our cooperation in science and technology can be one of our greatest gifts to the future.

In each of these vital areas that I have mentioned, we can clearly accomplish so much more by walking together rather than standing apart. That is why we should work to see that the productive relationship we now enjoy **blossoms** into a fuller partnership in the new century.

If that is to happen, it is very important that we understand each other better, that we understand both our common interest and our shared aspirations and our honest differences. I believe the kind of open, direct exchange that President Jiang and I had on Saturday at our press conference — which I know many of you watched on television — can both clarify and narrow our differences, and, more important, by allowing people to understand and debate and discuss these things can give a greater sense of confidence to our people that we can make a better future.

From the windows of the White House, where I live in Washington, D.C., the monument to our first President, George Washington, dominates the skyline. It is a very tall **obelisk**. But very near this large monument there is a small stone which contains these words: The United States neither established titles of nobility and royalty, nor created a **hereditary** system. State affairs are put to the vote of public opinion.

在最近的一次金融危机中，中国坚定不移地承担了对本地区和全世界的责任，帮助避免了又一个危险的货币贬值周期。我们必须继续携手合作，对抗全球金融系统面临的威胁以及对整个亚太地区本应有的发展和繁荣的威胁。

在二十一世纪，你们这一代将有极大的机会，将我们的科学家、医生、工程师的各种才能结合起来，用于追求共同的发展。我们早就在一些合作领域中取得了突破，从医治脊柱裂到对抗极端天气和地震等。这些突破证明，我们的合作能改变中美乃至全世界数百万人的生活。扩大我们在科技领域的合作是我们给未来奉献的厚礼之一。

在我以上列举的每一个关键领域，显然，只要我们相互合作而不是分道扬镳，我们就能取得更大的成就。因此，我们应该努力，确保双方之间目前的建设性关系在下个世纪结出圆满的协作果实。

要做到这一点，我们就必须更好地相互了解，了解我们的共同利益、共有的期望和真实的差异。我相信，正如大家在电视上看到的，我和江主席星期六在联合记者招待会上公开直接的交流，有助于澄清和缩小我们的分歧。更为重要的是，让人们理解、辩论和探讨这些问题，能使他们对我们建设美好的未来更加充满信心。

从我居住的华盛顿特区白宫的窗口向外眺望，我们的第一任总统乔治·华盛顿的纪念碑俯视全城。那是一座高耸的方形尖塔。在这个庞大的纪念碑旁，有一块很小的石碑，上面刻着这样的文字：美国决不设立贵族和皇室头衔，也不建立世袭制度。国家事务由舆论公决。

美国就是这样建立了一个从古至今史无前例的崭新政治

热词空间

vibrant ['vaibrənt] adj. 充满生机的

restoration [.restə'reiʃən] n. 修复

steadfastly ['stedfa:stli] adv. 固定地

shoulder ['ʃəuldə] vt. 肩负，承担

financial crisis 经济危机

devaluation [di:vælju'eiʃən] n. 货币贬值

quest [kwest] n. 寻求，探索

spina bifida [,spainə'bifidə] 脊柱裂

blossom ['blɔsəm] n. 全盛期

obelisk ['ɔbəlisk] n. 方尖塔

hereditary [hi'reditəri] adj. 世袭的

This created a new political situation, unprecedented from ancient times to the present. How wonderful it is! Those words were not written by an American. They were written by Xu Jiyu, governor of Fujian Province, inscribed as a gift from the government of China to our nation in 1853.

I am very grateful for that gift from China. It goes to the heart of who we are as a people — the right to life, liberty, and the pursuit of happiness, the freedom to debate, to dissent, to associate, to worship without interference from the state. These are the ideals that were at the core of our founding over 220 years ago. These are the ideas that led us across our continent and onto the world stage. These are the ideals that Americans cherish today.

As I said in my press conference with President Jiang, we have an ongoing quest ourselves to live up to those ideals. The people who framed our Constitution understood that we would never achieve perfection. They said that the mission of America would always be "to form a more perfect union" — in other words, that we would never be perfect, but we had to keep trying to do better.

The darkest moments in our history have come when we abandoned the effort to do better, when we denied freedom to our people because of their race or their religion, because there were new immigrants or because they held unpopular opinions. The best moments in our history have come when we protected the freedom of people who held unpopular opinions, or extended rights enjoyed by the many to the few who had previously been denied them, making, therefore, the promises of our *Declaration of Independence* and *Constitution* more than faded words on old parchment.

Today we do not seek to impose our vision on others, but we are convinced that certain rights are universal — not American rights or European rights or rights for developed nations, but the birthrights of people everywhere, now enshrined in *the United Nations Declaration on Human Rights* — the right to be treated with dignity; the right to express one's opinions, to choose one's own leaders, to associate freely with others, and to worship, or not, freely, however one chooses.

In the last letter of his life, the author of our *Declaration of Independence* and our third President, Thomas Jefferson, said then that "all eyes are opening to the rights of man." I believe that in this time, at long last, 172 years after Jefferson wrote those

体系。这是多么奇妙的事物呀！然而，这些话不是美国人写的，而是出自福建省巡抚徐继畲之手，并于 1853 年由中国政府刻成碑文，作为礼物送给美国。

我很感激中国送的这份礼物。它道出了全美人民的心声，即人人有生命和自由的权利、追求幸福的权利，有不受国家的干涉发表言论和持不同政见的自由，有结社的自由和宗教信仰的自由。这些就是 220 年前美国立国的核心理想。这些理想指引我们跨越美洲大陆，走向世界舞台。这些仍然是美国人民今天珍视的理想。

正如我在和江主席举行的记者招待会上所说，我们美国人民正在不断寻求实现这些理想。美国宪法的制定者了解，我们不可能做到尽善尽美。他们说，美国的使命始终是要"建设一个更为完美的联邦"。换言之，我们永远不可能尽善尽美，但我们必须不断改进。

每当我们放弃努力去改进，每当我们由于种族或宗教原因、由于是新移民，或者由于有人持不受欢迎的意见，而剥夺人民的自由，我们的历史就出现最黑暗的时刻。每当我们保护持不同政见者的自由，或者将大多数人享受的权利给予以前被剥夺权利的人们，从而实践《独立宣言》和《宪法》的诺言，而不是使其成为一纸空文时，我们的历史就出现最光明的时刻。

今天，我们并不试图将自己的见解强加于人，但我们坚信，某些权利具有普遍性，它们不是美国的权利或者欧洲的权利或者是发达国家的权利，而是每个人与生俱来的权利。这些权利现在载于《联合国人权宣言》。这些就是待人以尊严、各抒己见、选举领袖、自由结社、自由选择信教或不信教的权利。

《独立宣言》的作者、美国第三任总统托马斯·杰斐逊在他一生的最后一封信中写道："人们正在睁开眼睛关注人权。"在杰斐逊写了这句话 172 年之后，我相信，人们现在终于睁

热词空间

inscribe [in'skraib] vt. 题写，雕
liberty ['libəti] n. 自由
dissent [di'sent] vi. 不同意
worship ['wə:ʃip] vi. 崇拜
cherish ['tʃeriʃ] vt. 珍爱
abandon [ə'bændən] vt. 遗弃，抛弃
parchment ['pɑ:tʃmənt] n. 羊皮纸
enshrine [in'ʃrain] vt. 珍藏

words, all eyes are opening to the rights of men and women everywhere.

Over the past two decades, a rising tide of freedom has lifted the lives of millions around the world, sweeping away failed dictatorial systems in the Former Soviet Union, throughout Central Europe; ending a vicious cycle of military coups and civil wars in Latin America; giving more people in Africa the chance to make the most of their hard-won independence. And from the Philippines to South Korea, from Thailand to Mongolia, freedom has reached Asia's shores, powering a surge of growth and productivity.

Economic security also can be an essential element of freedom. It is recognized in *the United Nations Covenant on Economic, Social, and Cultural Rights*. In China, you have made extraordinary strides in nurturing that liberty, and spreading freedom from want, to be a source of strength to your people. Incomes are up, poverty is down; people do have more choices of jobs, and the ability to travel — the ability to make a better life. But true freedom includes more than economic freedom. In America, we believe it is a concept which is indivisible.

Over the past four days, I have seen freedom in many manifestations in China. I have seen the fresh shoots of democracy growing in the villages of your heartland. I have visited a village that chose its own leaders in free elections. I have also seen the cell phones, the video players, the fax machines carrying ideas, information and images from all over the world. I've heard people speak their minds and I have joined people in prayer in the faith of my own choosing. In all these ways I felt a steady breeze of freedom.

The question is, where do we go from here? How do we work together to be on the right side of history together? More than 50 years ago, Hu Shi, one of your great political thinkers and a teacher at this university, said these words: "Now some people say to me you must sacrifice your individual freedom so that the nation may be free. But I reply, the struggle for individual freedom is the struggle for the nation's freedom. The struggle for your own character is the struggle for the nation's character."

We Americans believe Hu Shi was right. We believe and our experience demonstrates that freedom strengthens stability and helps nations to change.

One of our founding fathers, Benjamin Franklin, once said, "Our critics are our

开眼睛关注着世界各地男女老少应享受的人权。

过去 20 年以来，一个高涨的自由浪潮解放了全世界成千上百万的生灵，扫除了前苏联和中欧那种失败的独裁统治，结束了拉美国家军事政变和内战的恶性循环，使更多的非洲人民有机会享受来之不易的独立。从菲律宾到南朝鲜，从泰国到蒙古，自由之浪已冲到亚洲的海岸，给发展和生产力注入了动力。

经济保障也是自由的一个基本要素。这在《联合国经济社会文化权益公约》中获得承认。在中国，你们为培育这种自由已迈出了大步，并将这种自由不断扩展，使之成为贵国人民的力量源泉。中国人的收入增加了，贫困现象减少了；人们有了更多选择就业的机会和外出旅游的机会，有了创造更好生活的机会。但真正的自由不仅仅是经济的自由。在美国，我们认为这是一个不可分割的概念。

在过去的四天中，我在中国看到了自由的许多表现形式。我看到民主的萌芽在贵国心脏地带的村庄迸发。我访问了一个自由选举村委领导的村庄。我也看到了移动电话、录像机和传真机，这些机器带来了来自世界各地的信息和影像。我听到人们谈论自己的想法，我还同当地与我有着相同宗教信仰的人一起祈祷。在所有这些方面，我感觉到自由的微风在吹拂。

但人们不禁要问，我们的发展方向是什么？我们怎样相互合作走上历史的正确一面？中国伟大的政治思想家、曾在北大任教的胡适教授在 50 多年前说过："有些人对我说，为了国家的自由你必须牺牲自己的个人自由。但我回答，为了个人自由而奋斗就是为了国家的自由而奋斗。解放个性就是解放民族。"

我们美国人认为胡适是对的。我们相信，并且我们的经验表明，自由可以加强稳定，自由有助于国家的变革。

热词空间

dictatorial [ˌdiktəˈtɔːriəl] *adj.* 独裁的

vicious [ˈviʃəs] **cycle** 恶性循环

coup [kuː] *n.* 政变

stride [straid] *n.* 大步，步伐

nurture [ˈnəːtʃə] *vt.* 培育，培养

freedom from want 免于匮乏的自由

indivisible [ˌindiˈvizəbl] *adj.* 不可分割的，不可分裂的

manifestation [ˌmænifeˈsteiʃən] *n.* 表现；显示

breeze [briːz] *n.* 微风

friends, for they show us our faults." Now, if that is true, there are many days in the United States when the President has more friends than anyone else in America. But it is so.

In the world we live in, this global information age, constant improvement and change is necessary to economic opportunity and to national strength. Therefore, the freest possible flow of information, ideas, and opinions, and a greater respect for divergent political and religious convictions will actually breed strength and stability going forward.

It is, therefore, profoundly in your interest, and the world's, that young Chinese minds be free to reach the fullness of their potential. That is the message of our time and the mandate of the new century and the new millennium.

I hope China will more fully embrace this mandate. For all the grandeur of your history, I believe your greatest days are still ahead. Against great odds in the 20th century China has not only survived, it is moving forward dramatically.

Other ancient cultures failed because they failed to change. China has constantly proven the capacity to change and grow. Now, you must re-imagine China again for a new century, and your generation must be at the heart of China's regeneration.

The new century is upon us. All our sights are turned toward the future. Now your country has known more millennia than the United States has known centuries. Today, however, China is as young as any nation on Earth. This new century can be the dawn of a new China, proud of your ancient greatness, proud of what you are doing, prouder still of the tomorrows to come. It can be a time when the world again looks to China for the vigor of its culture, the freshness of its thinking, the elevation of human dignity that is apparent in its works. It can be a time when the oldest of nations helps to make a new world.

The United States wants to work with you to make that time a reality.

Thank you very much.

我国的一位开国先贤本杰明·富兰克林曾经说过："我们的批评者是我们的朋友，因为他们指出我们的缺点。"如果这话正确，在美国很多时候，总统的朋友比其他任何人都多。但确实如此。

在我们生活的世界，在这个全球性的信息时代，不断的改进和变革是增加经济机会和增强国力的必要条件。因此，最大限度地自由交换信息、观念和看法，更多地尊重不同的政治和宗教信仰，实际上将增加实力，推动稳定。

因此，为了贵国和世界的根本利益，中国的年轻人必须享有心灵上的自由，以便最充分地发挥自己的潜力。这是我们时代的信息，也是新的世纪和新的千年的要求。

我希望中国能更充分地赞同这个要求。尽管贵国历史上有过辉煌的功绩，我认为，贵国最伟大的时代仍在前头。中国不仅在20世纪的种种艰难险阻中生存了下来，而且正在迅速向前迈进。

其他的古老文化消亡了，因为它们没有进行变革。中国始终显示出变革和成长的能力。你们必须重新想象新世纪的中国，你们这一代必然处于中国复兴的中心。

我们即将进入新世纪。我们所有的目光瞄向未来。中国经过的千年比美国经过的百年还要多。然而，今天的中国和世界上任何一个国家一样年轻。新世纪将是新的中国的黎明，贵国为历史上的辉煌而自豪，为你们正在进行的事业而自豪，更为明天的到来而自豪。在新世纪中，世界可能再次转向中国寻求她文化的活力、思想的新颖、人类尊严的升华，这在中国的成就中显而易见。在新世纪中，最古老的国家有可能帮助建设一个新世界。

美国希望与贵国合作，使那个时刻成为现实。

感谢大家。

热词空间

divergent [dai'və:dʒənt] *adj.* 相异的，分歧的

conviction [kən'vikʃən] *n.* 坚信，信服

breed [bri:d] *vt.* 培育，产生

profoundly [prə'faundli] *adv.* 深刻地，深深地

mandate ['mændeit] *n.* 授权；命令

millennium [mi'leniəm] *n.* 千禧年，一千年

grandeur ['grændʒə] *n.* 庄严，伟大

vigor ['vigə] *n.* 活力

elevation [ęli'veiʃən] *n.* 提高，提升

哈佛
大学

斯坦福
大 学

牛津
大学

耶鲁
大学

杜兰
大学

杜克
大学

威斯康
辛大学

清华
大学

北京
大学

亚利桑
那州立
大 学

加利福
尼 亚
大 学

克林顿给我们的 启示

We would never be perfect, but we had to keep trying to do better.

我们永远不可能尽善尽美，但我们必须不断改进。

It is, therefore, profoundly in your interest, and the world's, that young Chinese minds be free to reach the fullness of their potential. That is the message of our time and the mandate of the new century and the new millennium.

因此，为了贵国和世界的根本利益，中国的年轻人必须享有心灵上的自由，以便最充分地开发自己的潜力。这是我们时代的信息，也是新的世纪和新的千年的要求。

For all the grandeur of your history, I believe your greatest days are still ahead. Against great odds in the 20th century China has not only survived, it is moving forward dramatically.

尽管贵国历史上有过辉煌的功绩，我认为，贵国最伟大的时代仍在前头。中国不仅在 20 世纪的种种艰难险阻中生存了下来，而且正在迅速向前迈进。

This new century can be the dawn of a new China, proud of your ancient greatness, proud of what you are doing, prouder still of the tomorrows to come. It can be a time when the world again looks to China for the vigor *of its culture, the freshness of its thinking, the elevation of human dignity that is apparent in its works. It can be a time when the oldest of nations helps to make a new world.*

新世纪将是新的中国的黎明，贵国为历史上的辉煌而自豪，为你们正在进行的事业而自豪，更为明天的到来而自豪。在新世纪中，世界可能再次转向中国寻求她文化的活力、思想的新颖、人类尊严的升华，这在中国的成就中显而易见。在新世纪中，最古老的国家有可能帮助建设一个新世界。

亚利桑那州立大学

校训：A New American University（一所新型的美国大学）

总　括

  亚利桑那州立大学，简称 ASU，是一所男女兼收的四年制公立大学，是全美最大最佳的五所"大学城"之一，是国际认可的研究型大学。ASU 成立于 1885 年，是亚利桑那州第一所师范学院，后因稳定的成长与发展，在 1958 年，改名为亚利桑那州立大学。ASU 由分散于菲尼斯大都会区各地的校区组成，学术力量雄厚，教学一流。开设有 150 个本科专业，硕士学位专业多达 97 个，博士学位专业 52 个。亚利桑那州立大学的商学院和教育学院分别在全美排第 34 位和第 29 位。

To Make the World a Better Place: Go Beyond the Boundary of Material Comfort

跨越物质的藩篱，让世界今非昔比

Arizona State University
Commencement Address
Barack Hussein Obama
May 13, 2009

背景 资料

　　这是奥巴马在亚利桑那州立大学 2009 年 5 月 13 日毕业典礼上的演讲。他在演讲中提到如今闪耀着理想之光的美国梦在人们心中被物化为靓车豪宅、锦衣玉食，本应多元化的成功定义被浓缩成了名望地位、权力利益，以此对年轻人表以期望，希望所有困惑着的年轻人都能够在理想的指引下，坚持梦想，迎接挑战，帮助他人，让世界今非昔比！

Each of them, at one point in their life, didn't have any title or much status to speak of. But they had passion, a commitment to following that passion wherever it would lead, and to working hard every step along the way. And that's not just how you'll ensure that your own life is well-lived. It's how you'll make a difference in the life of our nation.

　　他们中的每一个人，在生命中的某一时刻，都没有响亮的头衔和显赫的地位值得炫耀。但他们有激情，他们追随着这种激情，并在整个过程中努力走好每一步。不仅努力过好自己的生活，更重要的是，努力让自己的国家今非昔比。

　　　　　　　　　　　　　　　　　　　　　　—— 奥巴马

姓　　名：	贝拉克·侯赛因·奥巴马二世 (Barack Hussein Obama Ⅱ)
性　　别：	男
职　　业：	美国第 44 任总统
国　　籍：	美国
党　　派：	民主党
出生日期：	1961 年 8 月 4 日
毕业学校：	1983 年获哥伦比亚大学文学学士学位（曾经在美国加州西方学院攻读两年，后转至哥伦比亚大学）1991 年获哈佛大学法学院法学博士学位
成功点睛：	他是第一个立志要完成所有竞选承诺的总统，他是美国梦的完美诠释。

名人 简介

　　贝拉克·侯赛因·奥巴马二世，美国第 44 任总统，1961 年 8 月 4 日出生于美国夏威夷州火奴鲁鲁，祖籍肯尼亚。1979 年进入加州西方学院攻读，1981 年转至哥伦比亚大学学习，并于 1983 年获得文学学士学位。在 1988 年下半年，进入哈佛大学法学院，1991 年获得"极优等"法学博士学位。他也是第一个担任《哈佛法学评论》主编的非洲裔美国人，并在此期间获得了全国范围的认可。奥巴马是首位拥有黑人血统，并且童年在亚洲成长的美国总统，有着与不同地方不同文化背景的人共同生活的经历。2010 年 5 月 27 日美国白宫发布了"国家安全战略报告"。奥巴马在该报告中将军事作为外交努力无效的最后手段。新国家安全战略认为世界充满了多种威胁，放弃了布什政府"反恐战争"的说法。

　　奥巴马具有强大的人格魅力，包括优秀的演讲能力，草根背景，平民色彩，乐观的精神，诚实的外表和品质等。

Well, thank you, President Crow, for that extremely generous introduction, for your inspired leadership as well here at ASU.

And I want to thank the entire ASU community for the honor of attaching my name to a scholarship program that will help open the doors of higher education to students from every background. What a wonderful gift. Thank you.

That notion of opening doors of opportunity to everybody, that is the core mission of this school; it's a core mission of my presidency; and I hope this program will serve as a model for universities across this country. So thank you so much.

I want to obviously congratulate the Class of 2009 for your unbelievable achievement. I want to thank the parents, the uncles, the grandpas, the grandmas, cousins — Calabash cousins — everybody, who was involved in helping these extraordinary young people arrive at this moment. I also want to apologize to the entire state of Arizona for stealing away your wonderful former governor, Janet Napolitano. But you've got a fine governor here and I also know that Janet is now applying her extraordinary talents to serve our entire country as the Secretary of Homeland Security, keeping America safe. And she's doing a great job.

Now, before I begin, I'd just like to clear the air about that little controversy everybody was talking about a few weeks back. I have to tell you, I really thought this was much ado about nothing, but I do think we all learned an important lesson. I learned never again to pick another team over the Sun Devils in my NCAA bracket. It won't happen again. President Crow and the Board of Regents will soon learn about being audited by the IRS.

Now, in all seriousness, I come here not to dispute the suggestion that I haven't yet achieved enough in my life. First of all, Michelle concurs with that assessment. She has a long list of things that I have not yet done waiting for me when I get home.

But more than that, I come to embrace the notion that I haven't done enough in my life; I heartily concur; I come to affirm that one's title, even a title like President of the United States, says very little about how well one's life has been led — that no

非常感谢克罗校长，感谢您精彩的介绍，感谢您对亚利桑那州立大学的英明领导。

同时，我要感谢贵校以我的姓名重新命名学校的奖学金项目，这一项目将有助于使高校的大门对来自不同背景的学生敞开，这令我倍感荣幸。这个礼物真是太棒了！谢谢你们。

给予每个人同等的机会，这是贵校的核心使命；也是我担任总统期间的核心使命。我希望贵校的这个项目能为美国的其他高校树立榜样。为此，我非常感谢你们。

2009 届的毕业生们，我要祝贺你们取得了令人难以置信的成绩。我要感谢你们的父母、叔伯、爷爷奶奶、表兄表弟以及你们的好友，感谢所有帮助你们这些卓越的年轻人顺利完成学业的人。我还要向亚利桑那州的所有人们致歉，因为我调走了你们杰出的前州长珍娜·奈帕利塔诺。但你们现在拥有另一位出色的州长。珍娜现在担任国土安全部部长，她正在用她非凡的才智服务全国，确保美国国土安全。她工作得非常出色。

首先，我想澄清一点，几周以来，人们一直在争论贵校是否应授予我荣誉学位，我真的觉得这有点儿小题大做，但我们都从中得到了很宝贵的教训。我得到的教训是，我再也不会在美国大学联盟锦标赛篮球队里挑一支比 Sun Devils 更厉害的球队了。（注：NCAA 是美国大学联盟锦标赛。奥巴马是篮球迷，而且大选时曾许诺：如果当选总统就预测一下今年的 NCAA 最后四强。奥巴马兑现承诺，预测了前四强，但只预测对了北卡罗来纳大学队，并言中了北卡会夺冠；Sun devils 是 ASU 的篮球队，而奥巴马预测的最后四强里有一支是 路易斯维尔大学队，该队在十六进八赛时就把 Sun Devils 淘汰掉了，但是路易斯维尔大学并未像奥巴马预测的那样进入四强。所以奥巴马有点自嘲似地说我不会再挑一支比 Sun Devils 厉害的球队了，因为路易斯维尔大学虽然击败了 Sun Devils，但没进四

热词空间

notion ['nəuʃən] n. 观念

core [kɔː] n. 核心

presidency ['prezidənsi] n. 总统（或大学校长等）的职位（任期）

extraordinary [iks'trɔːdnri] adj. 非凡的

steal away vt. 偷走

Secretary of Homeland Security 美国国土安全部部长

controversy ['kɔntrə,vəːsi] n. 争论

ado [ə'duː] n. 纷扰，麻烦

audit ['ɔːdit] vi. 审计

in all seriousness 严肃地

dispute ['dispjuːt] vt. 争论

concur [kən'kəː] vi. 同意；一致

assessment [ə'sesmənt] n. 评定

embrace [im'breis] vt. 接受

matter how much you've done, or how successful you've been, there's always more to do, always more to learn, and always more to achieve.

And I want to say to you today, graduates, Class of 2009, that despite having achieved a remarkable milestone in your life, despite the fact that you and your families are so rightfully proud, you too cannot rest on your laurels. Not even some of those remarkable young people who were introduced earlier — not even that young lady who's got four degrees yet today. You can't rest. Your own body of work is also yet to come.

Now, some graduating classes have marched into this stadium in easy times — times of peace and stability when we call on our graduates simply to keep things going, and don't screw it up.

Other classes have received their diplomas in times of trial and upheaval, when the very foundations of our lives, the old order has been shaken, the old ideas and institutions have crumbled, and a new generation is called upon to remake the world. It should be clear to you by now the category into which all of you fall. For we gather here tonight in times of extraordinary difficulty, for the nation and for the world. The economy remains in the midst of a historic recession, the worst we've seen since the Great Depression; the result, in part, of greed and irresponsibility that rippled out from Wall Street and Washington, as we spent beyond our means and failed to make our choices. We're engaged in two wars and a struggle against terrorism. The threats of climate change, nuclear proliferation, and pandemic defy national boundaries and easy solutions.

For many of you, these challenges are also felt in more personal terms. Perhaps you're still looking for a job — or struggling to figure out what career path makes sense in this disrupted economy. Maybe you've got student loans — oh, you definitely have student loans — or credit card debts, and you're wondering how you'll ever pay them off. Maybe you've got a family to raise, and you're wondering how you'll ensure that your children have the same opportunities you've had to get an

强。）这样的事绝不会再发生了。克罗校长和董事会很快因此受到国税局的审查。

　　现在，我要很严肃地告诉大家，我并不是来这儿争论业绩多寡的。首先，米歇尔就认为我做的还不够。她那儿有一大堆我还未完成的事情等着我回家做。

　　不仅如此，我也觉得我做的还不够。我由衷地赞同这一观点。我想申明一点，一个人的头衔，即使是美国总统的头衔，也不能说明他在生活中有多么成功——无论你做了多少，无论你有多么成功，也总还有更多的事情要做，更多的东西要学，更多的理想要去实现。

　　今天，我想跟你们说，2009 届的毕业生们，虽然你们的生命已经达到了一个重要的里程碑，虽然你和你的家人都理所应当为此感到自豪，你们也不能仅仅满足于这些已经获得的荣誉。甚至先前介绍过的那些杰出的年轻人也不能就此满足，包括那位迄今为止已获得四个学位的年轻女士。你们不能停滞不前。因为你们的任务尚未开始。

　　如今，一些毕业班赶上了和平稳定的时代，这个时代只需要他们保持现状，不要把局面搞砸就可以了。

　　而有些毕业班赶上了时局变革，生活的基础动荡不安，旧的秩序动摇了，陈旧的观念和体系崩溃坍塌，这一切呼吁新的一代重新改造这个世界。大家都应该清楚自己现在所处的局势。因为今晚我们聚集在这里，面对的是一个困难重重的时期，不管是对于美国还是对于整个世界来说，都是如此。经济空前萧条，整个国家面临着自"大萧条"以来最严重的经济危机。这一局面从某种程度上归咎于华尔街和华盛顿散播开来的贪婪和不负责任，归咎于我们的过度消费和决策失误。我们参与了两场战争，还肩负着反恐的重任。气候变化、核扩散和流行疾病的传播无视国界，我们无法轻而易举解决这些问题。

热词空间

remarkable [ri'ma:kəbl] adj.
卓越的；非凡的

milestone ['mailstəun] n. 里程碑；划时代的事件

laurel ['lɔ:rəl] n. 桂冠；殊荣

screw [skru:] vt. 拧

upheaval [ʌp'hi:vəl] n. 剧变

crumble ['krʌmbl] vi. 崩溃

category ['kætigəri] n. 种类；分类；范畴

ripple ['ripl] vt. 使……起涟漪

nuclear proliferation
[prəu,lifə'reiʃən] 核扩散

pandemic [pæn'demik] n. 大流行病 adj. 全国流行的；普遍的

defy [di:'fai] vt. 藐视

disrupted [dis'rʌptid] adj. 分裂的，混乱的

education and pursue their dreams.

Now, in the face of these challenges, it may be tempting to fall back on the formulas for success that have been pedaled so frequently in recent years. It goes something like this: You're taught to chase after all the usual brass rings; you try to be on this "who's who" list or that top 100 list; you chase after the big money and you figure out how big your corner office is; you worry about whether you have a fancy enough title or a fancy enough car. That's the message that's sent each and every day, or has been in our culture for far too long — that through material possessions, through a ruthless competition pursued only on your own behalf — that's how you will measure success.

Now, you can take that road — and it may work for some. But at this critical juncture in our nation's history, at this difficult time, let me suggest that such an approach won't get you where you want to go; it displays a poverty of ambition — that in fact, the elevation of appearance over substance of celebrity over character, of short-term gains over lasting achievement is precisely what your generation needs to help end.

Now, ASU, I want to highlight — I want to highlight two main problems with that old, tired, me-first approach to life. First of all, it distracts you from what's truly important, and may lead you to compromise your values and your principles and your commitments. Think about it. It's in chasing titles and status — in worrying about the next election rather than the national interest and the interests of those who you're supposed to represent — that politicians so often lose their ways in Washington. They spend time thinking about polls but not about principle. It was in pursuit of gaudy short-term profits, and the bonuses that came with them, that so many folks lost their way on Wall Street, engaging in extraordinary risks with other people's money.

In contrast, the leaders we revere the businesses and institutions that last — they are not generally the result of a narrow pursuit of popularity or personal advancement, but of devotion to some bigger purpose — the preservation of the Union or the

你们中的许多人也已经感受到了这些挑战对你们自身的影响。也许你们还在找工作，也许你还在苦苦思考在这个经济衰落的时期，什么样的职业道路才行得通。或许你使用了助学贷款，喔，你一定使用了学生贷款或有信用卡债务，你不知道如何偿还这些债务。或许，你们需要供养一个家庭，你不知道如何能确保你的孩子能像你一样拥有接受教育追求梦想的机会。

现在，面对这些挑战，很容易落入最近几年很是流行的成功秘诀的俗套。这个套路大概是这样的：你应该追逐功名利禄；想方设法跻身"名人录"或者"前100强"；应该想着赚大钱，想想自己的高级办公室该有多大；此外，你还要担心自己有没有尊贵的头衔，有没有高级的轿车。这些就是我们衡量成功的标准，日复一日，我们都会收到这样的讯息，这已在我们的文化中根深蒂固——通过物质财富占有的多少，通过仅仅为了一己之利的残酷竞争来衡量成功与否。

当然，你们可以选择这条路——而且这条路可能会让一些人成功。但是，在国家历史上这一关键时刻，在这个困难的时期，我要说，这种选择无法带你到理想的彼岸；它只能表明你缺少雄心壮志——事实上，你们这一代人需要摒弃这样的风气：重表面而轻实质，重名气而轻品质，重短期利益而轻长远发展。

同学们，就这种过时的、陈腐的、以自我为中心的人生观，我想重点说明它存在的两个问题。首先，这种人生观会使你无法集中于真正重要的东西，还会让你的价值观、做人的原则和责任心大打折扣。仔细想想，正是因为只是追逐头衔和地位，只是担心下次的选举而非国家和所应该代表的人们的利益，致使华盛顿的政客们经常迷失方向。这些政客们考虑的常是投票问题，而不是治国方略。正是因为对虚浮的短期收益和红利的追逐让众多的民众迷失在华尔街上，冒着巨大

热词空间

tempting ['temptiŋ] *adj.* 吸引人的；诱惑人的

formula ['fɔ:mjulə] *n.* 公式，准则

pedal ['pedl] *vi.* 踩踏板；骑车

ruthless ['ru:θlis] *adj.* 无情的，残忍的

juncture ['dʒʌŋktʃə] *n.* 关键时刻，紧要关头

elevation [,eli'veiʃən] *n.* 提高

substance ['sʌbstəns] *n.* 物质

celebrity [si'lebrəti] *n.* 名声

highlight ['hailait] *vt.* 突出；强调

distract [dis'trækt] *vt.* 转移；分心

polls [pəul] *n.* 民意调查；投票

gaudy ['gɔ:di] *adj.* 华而不实的

revere [ri'viə] *vt.* 尊敬；崇敬

determination to lift a country out of a depression; the creation of a quality product; a commitment to your customers, your workers, your shareholders and your community; a commitment to make sure that an institution like ASU is inclusive and diverse and giving opportunity to all. That's a hallmark of real success.

That other stuff — that other stuff, the trappings of success may be a byproduct of this larger mission, but it can't be the central thing. Just ask Bernie Madoff. That's the first problem with the old attitude.

But the second problem with the old approach to success is that a relentless focus on the outward markers of success can lead to complacency. It can make you lazy. We too often let the external, the material things, serve as indicators that we're doing well, even though something inside us tells us that we're not doing our best; that we're avoiding that which is hard, but also necessary; that we're shrinking from rather than rising to, the challenges of the age. And the thing is, in this new, hyper-competitive age, none of us — none of us — can afford to be complacent.

That's true whatever profession you choose. Professors might earn the distinction of tenure, but that doesn't guarantee that they'll keep putting in the long hours and late nights — and have the passion and the drive — to be great educators. The same principle is true in your personal life. Being a parent is not just a matter of paying the bills, doing the bare minimum — it's not just bringing a child into the world that matters, but the acts of love and sacrifice it takes to raise and educate that child and give them opportunity. It can happen to Presidents, as well. If you think about it, Abraham Lincoln and Millard Fillmore had the very same title, they were both Presidents of the United States, but their tenure in office and their legacy could not be more different. And this is not just true for individuals — it's also true for this nation. In recent years, in many ways, we've become enamored with our own past success — lulled into complacency by the glitter of our own achievements.

We've become accustomed to the title of "military super-power," forgetting the qualities that got us there — not just the power of our weapons, but the discipline and

的风险用他人的钱谋取私利。

相反，我们所尊敬的领导者，那些能持久经营的企业和社会机构，通常不会仅仅狭隘地追求名望或个人的提升，而是投身于更伟大的目标，比如维护联邦的利益，一心让国家摆脱经济萧条，创造优质产品，恪守对顾客、员工、股东和社会的承诺。承诺使得亚利桑那州立大学这样的机构具有包容性、多样性，使其能给予所有人平等的机遇。这才是真正成功的标志。

而其他的东西——成功的那些表象只是这个伟大使命的副产品，绝不可能成为核心。问问伯纳德·麦道夫（金融巨骗），你们就明白了。上面所说的是陈腐人生观所存在的第一个问题。

关于这种陈腐人生观的第二个问题是：过多地看重成功的表象会使人骄傲自满，不思进取。我们过多地把那些外在的、物质的东西看成是我们取得成就的标记，虽然我们内心明白自己并没有尽力；自己正在逃避必须经历的困难；自己面对时代的挑战，没有奋起迎接，而是选择了退缩。问题是，在这个竞争极度激烈的新时代，我们中没有任何人能够付得起自满的代价。

无论选择何种职业，都不能自满。教授可能会获得终身教授的荣誉，但这并不能保证他们夜以继日潜心工作，也不能保证他们拥有成为伟大教育家的激情和动力。这一原则也适用于你的个人生活。父母的职责不只是支付账单、做最低限度的事情，也不只是把孩子带到这个世界上来，而是用爱和奉献抚养教育孩子，并给他们提供机遇。纵使对于总统也是如此。你们想想看，亚伯拉罕·林肯（第十六任美国总统）和米勒德·菲尔莫尔（美国第十三任总统）有相同的头衔，他们都曾是美国总统，但他们的总统任期和为人类创造的价值却有天壤之别。个人如此，国家亦然。近些年，我们在许多方面沉湎于曾经取得的成功，为我们国家取得的辉煌成就而

热词空间

shareholder ['ʃɛəˌhəʊldə] n. 股东；股票持有人

inclusive [in'klu:siv] adj. 具有包容性的

diverse [dai'və:s] adj. 不同的；多种多样的

hallmark ['hɔ:lmɑ:k] n. 特点；标志

byproduct ['baiˌprɒdʌkt] n. 副产品

relentless [ri'lentlis] adj. 不间断的；残酷的

complacency [kəm'pleisənsi] n. 自满

shrink from 退避；在……前面畏缩

hyper-competitive 竞争激烈的

distinction [dis'tiŋkʃən] n. 区别；荣誉；勋章

tenure ['tenjə] n. 任期，终身职位

Millard Fillmore 米勒德·菲尔莫尔（1800 年 1 月 7 日—1874 年 3 月 8 日）美国第十三任总统。他被评为最差美国总统第十名，是因为他未能解决奴隶制危机。

become enamored with 醉心于、沉湎于

lull [lʌl] vt. 使平静

glitter ['glitə] n. 灿烂

哈佛
大学

斯坦福
大　学

牛津
大学

耶鲁
大学

杜兰
大学

杜克
大学

威斯康
辛大学

清华
大学

北京
大学

亚利桑
那州立
大　学

加利福
尼　亚
大　学

valor and the code of conduct of our men and women in uniform. The Marshall Plan, and the Peace Corps, and all those initiatives that show our commitment to working with other nations to pursue the ideals of opportunity and equality and freedom that have made us who we are. That's what made us a super power.

We've become accustomed to our economic dominance in the world, forgetting that it wasn't reckless deals and get-rich-quick schemes that got us where we are, but hard work and smart ideas — quality products and wise investments. We started taking shortcuts. We started living on credit, instead of building up savings. We saw businesses focus more on rebranding and repackaging than innovating and developing new ideas that improve our lives.

All the while, the rest of the world has grown hungry, more restless — in constant motion to build and to discover — not content with where they are right now, determined to strive for more. They're coming.

So graduates, it's now abundantly clear that we need to start doing things a little bit different. In your own lives, you'll need to continuously adapt to a continuously changing economy. You'll end up having more than one job and more than one career over the course of your life; you'll have to keep gaining new skills — possibly even new degrees; and you'll have to keep on taking risks as new opportunities arise.

And as a nation, we'll need a fundamental change of perspective and attitude. It's clear that we need to build a new foundation — a stronger foundation — for our economy and our prosperity, rethinking how we grow our economy, how we use energy, how we educate our children, how we care for our sick, how we treat our environment.

Many of our current challenges are unprecedented. There are no standard remedies, no go-to fixes this time around. And Class of 2009 that's why we're going to need your help. We need young people like you to step up. We need your daring, we need your enthusiasm, we need your energy, we need your imagination.

And let me be clear, when I say young, I'm not just referring to the date of your

沾沾自喜。

我们习惯了被称为"超级军事大国"，却忘记了我们之所以得到这个头衔不只是因为武器的威力，还有美国军人严守纪律、英勇无畏的品质和行为准则。马歇尔计划、维和部队、与其他国家积极合作，共同创造机遇、平等、自由，这使得我们获得了今天的荣誉，使我们成为超级大国。

我们习惯了在世界经济领域占主导地位，却忘记了一点：我们获得这一地位不是依靠草率的交易和速富计划，而是通过努力的工作、睿智的想法、优质的产品和英明的投资。之后，我们开始寻找捷径，开始超前消费，而不是节俭储蓄。企业已不再是为改善生活而进行产品创新和创意发掘，而把重点放在了重塑品牌形象，不断更新包装上。

一直以来，其他国家都在如饥似渴、永不停歇地创造和发现，他们不满足于现状，决心取得更大的发展。这些国家正在赶超我们。

因此，同学们，我们明显需要稍微改变一下做事的方式了。就个人的生活而言，你们需要不停地适应一个时刻在改变的经济环境。你们一生中可能会从事不止一项工作或者一种职业，因而需要不断学习新的技能——甚至考取新的学位。当新的机遇出现时，你们必须冒险去接受挑战。

作为一个国家，我们需要从根本上改变我们的观念和态度。很明显，为了经济的繁荣，我们必须建立一个崭新的、更加坚实的基础，重新思考如何发展经济、如何使用能源、如何教育孩子、如何照料老人以及如何对待我们的环境。

我们目前面临的许多挑战都是前所未有的。我们没有标准的补救措施，也没有力挽狂澜的手段。所以，2009届的毕业生们，我们需要你们的帮助。我们需要你们这样的年轻人行动起来。我们需要你们的果敢、热情、活力和想象力。

说得更清楚一点，我所指的"年轻"，并不是你们出生证

热词空间

valor ['vælə] n. 英勇；勇猛

dominance ['dɔminəns] n. 优势；统治；支配

reckless ['reklis] adj. 鲁莽的，不顾后果的

strive for 争取，奋斗

end up 最终成为，最后处于

fundamental [ˌfʌndə'mentəl] adj. 基本的，根本的

foundation [faun'deiʃən] n. 基础；地基

unprecedented [ʌn'presidəntid] adj. 空前的

remedy ['remidi] n. 补救；赔偿

enthusiasm [in'θjuːziæzəm] n. 热情，热心

birth certificate. I'm talking about an approach to life, a quality of mind and a quality of heart, a willingness to follow your passions regardless of whether they lead to fortune and fame, a willingness to question conventional wisdom and rethink old dogmas, a lack of regard for all the traditional markers of status and prestige, and a commitment instead to doing what's meaningful to you, what helps others, what makes a difference in this world.

That's the spirit that led a band of patriots not much older than most of you to take on an empire, to start this experiment in democracy we call America. It's what drove young pioneers west, to Arizona and beyond; it's what drove young women to reach for the ballot; what inspired a 30 year-old escaped slave to run an underground railroad to freedom — what inspired a young man named Cesar to go out and help farm workers; what inspired a 26 year-old preacher to lead a bus boycott for justice. It's what led firefighters and police officers in the prime of their lives up the stairs of those burning towers; and young people across this country to drop what they were doing and come to the aid of a flooded New Orleans. It's what led two guys in a garage — named Hewlett and Packard — to form a company that would change the way we live and work; what led scientists in laboratories, and novelists in coffee shops to labor in obscurity until they finally succeeded in changing the way we see the world.

That's the great American story: young people just like you, following their passions, determined to meet the times on their own terms. They weren't doing it for the money. Their titles weren't fancy — ex-slave, minister, student, citizen. A whole bunch of them didn't get honorary degrees. But they changed the course of history — and so can you ASU, so can you Class of 2009. So can you.

With a degree from this outstanding institution, you have everything you need to get started. You've got no excuses. You have no excuses not to change the world.

Did you study business? Go start a company. Or why not help our struggling non-profits find better, more effective ways to serve folks in need.

Did you study nursing? Go understaffed clinics and hospitals across this country that are desperate for your help.

明上的日期。我所指的是一种生活方式、一种精神和心理品格，愿意追随自己的激情，不管它是否能带来财富和名望，愿意质疑传统的价值观，重新思考陈旧的教条、蔑视一切代表地位和特权的传统标志，去做有意义的事，去做有利于他人的事，去做能改变世界的事。

正是由于这种精神，才涌现出了一群爱国者，那时他们并不比你们大多少，却肩负了国家的使命，开始在这个我们称之为美国的国家试行民主。正是由于这种精神，年轻的拓荒者开始向西部挺进，走向亚利桑那和更远的地方。正是由于这种信念，年轻的妇女开始争取选举权。这种力量给了一名 30 岁的奴隶通过地下铁路逃向自由的勇气，促使一位名叫塞萨尔的年轻人挺身帮助农场工人，促使一位 26 岁的牧师为了正义发起了一场拒乘公共汽车的运动。它使得风华正茂的消防队员和警察冲向熊熊燃烧的双子塔的楼梯；也使得全国的年轻人扔下手中的工作前来支援遭受洪灾的新奥尔良人。这种精神引领两个年轻人——休利特与帕卡德——在车库中组建了一个公司（今天的惠普公司），从而改变了我们的生活和工作方式；这种精神鼓舞着实验室里的科学家和咖啡厅里的小说家默默无闻地工作，直到最终成功地改变了我们看待这个世界的方式。

这就是伟大的美国故事：这些像你们一样的年轻人，追随自己的激情，决意用自己的方式迎接时代的挑战。他们这样做不是为了金钱。他们没有响亮的头衔——他们是从前的奴隶、牧师、学生、市民。他们中没有一个人得到过荣誉学位。但他们改变了历史的进程——亚利桑那大学的同学们，你们也可以！ 2009 届的毕业生们，你们也可以！

凭借从这所著名的学院获得的学位，你们具备了一切的起步条件。你们没有理由不去改变这个世界。

你们是学商务专业的吗？那就去开公司吧。或帮那些不景气的非盈利机构找到更有效的方法，去更好地帮助那些处

热词空间

democracy [di'mɔkrəsi] *n.* 民主国家，民主

ballot ['bælət] *n.* 投票，选举权

preacher ['priːtʃə] *n.* 传道者，讲道者

Hewlett 威廉·休利特（1913 年 5 月 20 日—2001 年 1 月 12 日）HP 惠普共同创始人，前主席兼 CEO

Parkard 帕卡德

HP 惠普公司创始人之一，硅谷创业的元老人物。一代产业巨子。曾担任过美国国防部副部长，树立了著名的"惠普之道"。

in obscurity [əb'skjuriti] 默默无闻

clinic ['klinik] *n.* 诊所

Did you study education? Teach in a high-need school where the kids really need you; give a chance to kids who can't — who can't get everything they need maybe in their neighborhood, maybe not even in their home but we can't afford to give up on them. Prepare them to compete for any job anywhere in the world.

Did you study engineering? Help us lead a green revolution — developing new sources of clean energy that will power our economy and preserve our planet.

But you can also make your mark in smaller, more individual ways. That's what so many of you have already done during your time here at ASU — tutoring children; registering voters; doing your own small part to fight hunger and homelessness, AIDS and cancer.

One student said it best when she spoke about her senior engineering project building medical devices for people with disabilities in a village in Africa. Her professor showed a video of the folks they'd been helping, and she said, "When we saw the people on the videos, we began to feel a connection to them. It made us want to be successful for them." Think about that: "It made us want to be successful for them."

That's a great motto for all of us — find somebody to be successful for. Raise their hopes. Rise to their needs.

As you think about your life after graduation, as you look into the mirror tonight after the partying is done — that shouldn't get such a big cheer — you may look in the mirror tonight and you may see somebody who's not really sure what to do with their lives. That's what you may see, but a troubled child might look at you and see a mentor. A homebound senior citizen might see a lifeline. The folks at your local homeless shelter might see a friend.

None of them care how much money is in your bank account, or whether you're important at work, or whether you're famous around town — they just know that you're somebody who cares, somebody who makes a difference in their lives.

So Class of 2009, that's what building a body of work is all about — it's about

于困境中的人们。

你们是学护理专业的吗？那就去一些人手不够的诊所和医院，那里正迫切需要你们的加入。

你们是学教育专业的吗？那就去那些师资力量严重匮乏的学校吧，那里的孩子非常需要你们。给孩子们一个机会。他们无法从街坊甚至家里得到他们所需要的一切，但我们不能因此而放弃他们。我们应该给予他们在世界的任何地方竞争任何工作的资本。

你们是学工程专业的吗？那就去领导一场绿色革命，开发清洁的、既能推动经济的增长又能保护我们地球的新能源。

你们还可以用更细致、更独特的方式服务社会。你们中的许多人在这儿读大学期间辅导孩子、进行选民登记，用自己微薄的力量去帮助那些挨饿的和无家可归的人们，为防止艾滋病和癌症做出力所能及的贡献。

一个学生在谈起她参与过的为非洲一个小村庄中的残疾人建造医疗设施的高级工程项目时，说过一段很精彩的话。在她的教授播放了一段他们帮助过的那些人们的录像后，那个女生说，"当我们看到录像上的那些人时，就感觉到自己与他们有着某种联系。这种感觉使得我们想为了他们而成功。"想想那句话，"这种感觉使得我们想为了他们而成功。"

这句话对于我们所有人来说都是至理箴言，寻找一些人，并为了他们的希望和需要而成功。

在今晚这场典礼结束后，你们考虑毕业后的人生时——好像不应该如此欢呼——你们对镜自照，在镜中看到的也许是一个不知该如何应对生活的人。或许你是这么看自己的，但当一个迷茫的孩子看着你时，他看到的也许是一个良师益友；一个困居家中的老人看到的也许是生命的希望；你们当地收容所里那些无家可归的人看到的也许是一个朋友。

他们不会去考虑你银行账户里有多少钱，你在工作上是否担任重要职务，你在镇里是否很有名气——他们只知道你

热词空间

be desperate for 迫切需要

preserve [pri'zɜːv] vt. 保护，维持

register ['redʒɪstə] vt. 登记，记录，注册

senior ['siːnjə] adj. 地位较高的，高级的

folk [fəuk] n. 人们，亲属

motto ['mɔtəu] n. 座右铭，箴言

mentor ['mentɔː] n. 指导者，良师益友

homebound ['həumbaund] adj. 闲居家中的

shelter ['ʃeltə] n. 避难所，庇护

the daily labor, the many individual acts, the choices large and small that add up over time, over a lifetime, to a lasting legacy. That's what you want on your tombstone.

It's about not being satisfied with the latest achievement, the latest gold star — because the one thing I know about a body of work is that it's never finished. It's cumulative; it deepens and expands with each day that you give your best, each day that you give back and contribute to the life of your community and your nation. You may have setbacks, and you may have failures, but you're not done — you're not even getting started, not by a long shot.

And if you ever forget that, just look to history. Thomas Paine was a failed corset maker, a failed teacher, and a failed tax collector before he made his mark on history with a little book called "Common Sense" that helped ignite a revolution. Julia Child didn't publish her first cookbook until she was almost 50. Colonel Sanders didn't open up his first Kentucky Fried Chicken until he was in his 60s.

Winston Churchill was dismissed as little more than a has-been, who enjoyed scotch a little bit too much, before he took over as Prime Minister and saw Great Britain through its finest hour.

No one thought a former football player stocking shelves at the local supermarket would return to the game he loved, become a Super Bowl MVP, and then come here to Arizona and lead your Cardinals to their first Super Bowl. Your body of work is never done.

Each of them, at one point in their life, didn't have any title or much status to speak of. But they had passion, a commitment to following that passion wherever it would lead, and to working hard every step along the way. And that's not just how you'll ensure that your own life is well-lived. It's how you'll make a difference in the life of our nation.

I talked earlier about the selfishness and irresponsibility on Wall Street and Washington that rippled out and led to so many of the problems that we face today. I talked about the focus on outward markers of success that can help lead us astray.

是一个关心他们的人，是一个改变他们生活的人。

所以，2009 届的毕业生们，这就是成就一项事业所需要的全部——日常的辛勤工作，各种大大小小的个人行为，长期的、甚至是一生积累下来的大大小小的选择，这一切构成一种永久的财富。这才是你们想要的墓志铭。

这就要求我们不满足于自己目前取得的成就，不满足于刚刚获得的金星荣誉奖章，因为我知道这样的事业是永无止境的。它需要日积月累，随着你每日竭尽全力地回报祖国并为社会做贡献而深化、拓宽。你们也许会遇到挫折和失败，但这并不意味着你们的工作已经结束，你们甚至还没有开始。

如果你忘记这一点，就请回头看看历史。托马斯·潘恩曾经是一个失败的紧身衣裁缝，一个失败的老师，一个失败的税务员，但他最后却名垂青史，他的那本名叫《常识》的小书引发了一场革命。朱莉娅·查尔德直到将近 50 岁时才出版了她的第一部烹饪书。桑德斯上校直到六十多岁才开办了第一家肯德基餐厅。

温斯顿·丘吉尔（英国政治家及作家）在担任首相之前曾遭罢免，只因为他有点过于偏爱苏格兰威士忌，并且输掉了达达尼尔海峡；接任首相后，他却带领英国步入了全盛时期。

谁也没有想到，整天忙着给超市货架上货的前足球运动员会重返他喜爱的赛场，一举成为美国橄榄球超级杯大赛最佳选手，然后来到亚利桑那，带领你们的红雀队首次冲进超级杯。所以，你们的事业永无止境。

他们中的每一个人，在生命中的某一时刻，都没有响亮的头衔和显赫的地位值得炫耀。但他们有激情，他们追随着这种激情，并在整个过程中努力走好每一步。不仅努力过好自己的生活，更重要的是，努力让自己的国家今非昔比。

先前我谈到了由于华尔街和华盛顿的人们的自私和不负责任致使今天我们面临着诸多问题。我也谈到了过分看重成功的外在标志会令我们误入歧途。

But here's the thing, Class of 2009: it works the other way too. Acts of sacrifice and decency without regard to what's in it for you — that also creates ripple effects — ones that lift up families and communities; that spread opportunity and boost our economy; that reach folks in the forgotten corners of the world who, in committed young people like you, see the true face of America: our strength, our goodness, our diversity, our enduring power, our ideals.

I know starting your careers in troubled times is a challenge. But it is also a privilege. Because it's moments like these that force us to try harder, and to dig deeper, and to discover gifts we never knew we had — to find the greatness that lies within each of us. So don't ever shy away from that endeavor. Don't stop adding to your body of work. I can promise that you will be the better for that continued effort, as will this nation that we all love.

Congratulations, Class of 2009, on your graduation.

God bless you.

And God bless the United States of America.

但是，2009 届的毕业生们，反过来也一样。正直无私的奉献，从不考虑自己能从中得到什么——这种行为也会产生涟漪效应——这种效应能鼓舞家庭和社会；可以传播机遇，繁荣经济；能影响世界上那些被遗忘在角落里的人们的生活，让他们从你们这些具有奉献精神的年轻人身上看到真实的美国，看到我们的力量，我们的美德、我们的多样性、我们的动力以及我们的理想。

我知道，在复杂的形势下开创你们的事业对你们而言是一个挑战。但也是一种特殊的荣幸。因为，只有在这样的时刻，我们才会更加努力，去发掘更深刻的东西，去发现自己从未发掘的天赋，发现我们内心的伟大之处。所以，千万不要逃避这种尝试。不要停止，为自己的事业增光添彩吧！我可以保证，通过不断地努力，你们将会有所进步，我们挚爱的祖国也会变得更加美好。

祝贺你们，2009 届的毕业生们，祝贺你们顺利毕业！

上帝保佑你们！

上帝保佑美利坚合众国。

热词空间

astray [əˈstrei] *adv.* 误入歧途地；迷途地

sacrifice [ˈsækrifais] *n.* 奉献

decency [ˈdiːsənsi] *n.* 正派；体面；礼貌

ripple effects 涟漪效应

boost [buːst] *vt.* 促进

diversity [daiˈvəsɪti] *n.* 多样

privilege [ˈprivilidʒ] *n.* 特权，特惠

endeavor [ɛnˈdɛvə] *n.* 努力，尽力

奥巴马给我们的 启示

And Class of 2009 that's why we're going to need your help. We need young people like you to step up. We need your daring, we need your enthusiasm and your energy, we need your imagination.

所以，2009届的毕业生们，我们需要你们的帮助。我们需要你们这样的年轻人行动起来。我们需要你们的果敢、热情、活力和想象力。

That's a great motto for all of us — find somebody to be successful for. Raise their hopes. Rise to their needs.

这句话对于我们所有人来说都是至理箴言，寻找一些人，并为了他们的希望和需要而成功。

You may have setbacks, and you may have failures, but you're not done — you're not even getting started, not by a long shot.

你们也许会遇到挫折和失败，但这并不意味着你们的工作已经结束，你们甚至还没有开始。

So don't ever shy away from that endeavor. Don't stop adding to your body of work. I can promise that you will be the better for that continued effort, as will this nation that we all love.

所以，千万不要逃避这种尝试。不要停止，为自己的事业增光添彩吧！我可以保证，通过不断地努力，你们将会有所进步，我们挚爱的祖国也会变得更加美好。

加利福尼亚大学

校训：Let there be light（让这里光芒闪耀）

总 括

　　加利福尼亚大学，简称加州大学（UC），是美国加州的一个公立大学系统。加州大学起源于 19 世纪 50 年代建立在奥克兰的加利福尼亚学院，如今已发展成一所拥有 10 个分校、对加州发展影响深远的巨型大学系统。加州大学是美国最具影响力的公立大学之一，其伯克利分校、旧金山分校、圣地亚哥分校和洛杉矶分校都是世界一流的学府。加州大学拥有诺贝尔奖得主 50 多位，美国国家科学院院士 350 多位，占美国国家科学院总院士人数的近 1/5。美国大学协会有成员 61 个，其中加州大学有 6 所分校为其成员。在建校之初，校方在发展目标上就达成了共识——采取兼收并蓄、自由开放的方针，容天下贤士于一堂，从而把大学建成为世界一流大学。加州大学素以学术自由和学生自治著称。

Service—the True Measure of Success

服务 —— 衡量成功的真正标准

University of
Califomia, Merced
Commencement Address
Michelle Obama
May 16, 2009

背景 资料

2009 年 5 月 16 日，现任美国第一夫人米歇尔在加利福尼亚大学摩赛德分校进行了她的第一场毕业演讲。米歇尔的这次演讲自始至终充满了对年轻人的鼓励，鼓励毕业生们带着梦想返回社区工作，以对社会所做的服务作为成功的标准。

Service is the rent we pay for living . . . it is the true measure, the only measure of our success.

服务是我们为生活而支付的租金……它是真正的标准，是衡量我们成功的唯一标准。

——米歇尔·奥巴马引语

姓　　名：	米歇尔·奥巴马 (Michelle Obama)
性　　别：	女
职　　业：	律师
国　　籍：	美国
党　　派：	民主党
出生日期：	1964 年 1 月 17 日
毕业学校：	普林斯顿大学及哈佛大学法学院
成功点睛：	她是时尚界的偶像，是一位健美的母亲，是毕业于哈佛大学法学专业的杰奎琳·肯尼迪，是来自芝加哥南区的智慧女性。

名人简介

　　米歇尔·奥巴马，是美国第 44 任总统巴拉克·奥巴马二世的妻子，是美国历史上第一位非洲裔美国籍总统夫人。米歇尔是土生土长的芝加哥人，她的父亲弗雷泽·罗宾逊是一位水管工，她的母亲玛丽安对子女教育很重视。米歇尔和哥哥克雷格的童年主要在读书、下国际象棋中度过。米歇尔还具有运动天赋，喜欢玩棒球、足球和篮球。

　　奥巴马的妻子米歇尔曾被评为最性感政治女性。在 1989 年认识贝拉克·奥巴马之前，米歇尔就是一位成功的黑人女性。

　　1981 年，米歇尔进入著名的普林斯顿大学读社会学。在普林斯顿读大学的时候，米歇尔是当时校园里少见的黑人女孩。米歇尔回忆说："我在普林斯顿的经历让我前所未有地注意自己的肤色。有时候我总觉得自己只是个访客，并不属于那里。

　　1985 年，从普林斯顿大学毕业后的米歇尔进入哈佛法学院学习，1988 年毕业后成为芝加哥悉尼·奥斯汀律师事务所的律师。1989 年，米歇尔认识了到悉尼·奥斯汀律师事务所工作的奥巴马。比米歇尔大 3 岁的奥巴马开始了对米歇尔的追求。但米歇尔最初拒绝了奥巴马的约会，因为她不喜欢办公室恋情。不过，两人最终于 1992 年结婚。

　　结婚后两人分别辞去律师工作，奥巴马开始进军政坛，米歇尔则开始做社会工作，成为一家著名非营利教育机构的负责人。后来米歇尔进入芝加哥大学工作。芝加哥大学医院是全美著名的大医院，但跟附近贫民区居民的关系很差，米歇尔被校方任命为负责社区事务的副院长，负责协调医院跟附近居民的关系。这个职务为米歇尔赢得巨大声誉，但为了丈夫的竞选，她不得不离开芝加哥大学的校园。

　　米歇尔的个人魅力得到美国媒体的普遍认可。在《花花公子》杂志的最性感政治女性评选中，米歇尔位居榜首，而希拉里屈居第四，排在二三位的则是赖斯和前第一夫人劳拉。在美国《名利场》杂志 2009 年 8 月评选年度全球最佳衣着人士中，米歇尔也榜上有名。

Class of 2009, all I can say is wow, and good afternoon, everyone. I am so proud of these graduates. We have to just give them one big round of applause before I start. This is just an amazing day. I want to thank Dick for that lovely introduction. He makes for a good companion when you have to go to an inauguration. So I'm glad he could be here with me today. I appreciate all that he has done to make this day so very special.

I want to acknowledge a few other people before I begin: Congressman Jerry McNerney, Lieutenant Governor John Garamendi, Attorney General Jerry Brown, and Assembly Speaker Karen Bass. I want to thank you all for your leadership and for being an example of what a life in public service can mean to us all.

And of course I have to thank Chancellor Kang for this incredible welcome, and as well as President Yudof and Provost Keith Alley for all that they've done to help make this event just such a wonderful day for us all.

And to the graduates and their families and the entire community of Merced, I am so pleased, so thrilled, so honored to be here with all of you today.

Now, I know we've got a lot of national press out there, and a few people may be wondering why did I choose the University of California-Merced to deliver my first commencement speech as First Lady. Well, let me tell you something, the answer is simple: You inspired me. You touched me. You know, there are few things that are more rewarding than to watch young people recognize that they have the power to make their dreams come true. And you did just that. Your perseverance and creativity were on full display in your efforts to bring me here to Merced for this wonderful occasion.

So let me tell you what you did. If you don't know, parents, because some of you were involved, my office received thousands of letters and, of course, Valentines cards from students; each and every one of them so filled with hope and enthusiasm. It moved not just me but my entire staff. They came up to me and said, "Michelle, you have to do this." "You have to go here!"

热词空间

2009届的毕业生们，我现在能说的就是：哇，大家下午好！我为在座的毕业生感到无比骄傲。因此，在我开始讲话前，让我们先用热烈的掌声祝贺你们！这是一个无比奇妙的日子。我要感谢迪克对我的热心介绍。因此如果你必须参加就职典礼的话，他会是一个很棒的陪同。他能够和我一起参加典礼让我非常高兴。真的很感激他，他所做的一切使得今天如此特别。

在开始之前，我还要感谢另外一些人，我要感谢国会议员杰瑞·麦克纳尼、副州长约翰·加拉曼蒂、首席检察官杰瑞·布朗以及议长凯伦·贝斯。你们有出色的领导能力，并在公众服务方面为我们做出了杰出榜样，因此，我要感谢你们。

当然，我还要感谢名誉校长康先生，他安排的欢迎仪式令人难以置信。同时还要感谢校长尤道夫先生和教务长凯斯·艾利。他们为准备毕业典礼的到来所做的一切，让这一天如此美好。

全体毕业生，各位家长，摩塞德社区的所有人们，感谢你们！非常高兴今天能来到这里和你们分享这一刻，我感到无比高兴，无比激动。

我知道这里有很多国内记者，而且一些人可能也很想知道：作为第一夫人我为什么会选择在加利福尼亚大学摩塞德分校进行我的第一次毕业典礼演讲呢？那么，让我告诉大家，我的答案非常简单：是因为你们激发了我，你们感动了我。你们知道，几乎没有什么能比看到年轻人认识到他们能够实现自己的梦想更有价值了。你们确实认识到了这一点。你们邀请我来见证这一美好时刻，期间你们所付出的努力充分展示了你们的坚韧和想象力。

那么，让我告诉大家你们都做了些什么。各位家长，你们可能不知道，你们中也有一些人参与其间。我收到了上千封学生们的来信，当然还有情人节明信片，每一封信每一张

campanion [kəm'pæniən] n. 同伴

inauguration [i,nɔ:gju'reiʃən] n. 就职典礼

lieutenant [lu:'tenənt] n. 副官

attorney [ə'tə:ni] general 首席检察官

incredible [in'kredəbl] adj. 难以置信的

community [kə'mju:niti] n. 社区，社会

thrill [θril] vt. (使) 激动

perseverance [,pə:si'viərəns] n. 不屈不挠，毅力

enthusiasm [in'θju:ziæzəm] n. 热情，热心

They were all terrific. Like the one from Christopher Casuga that read, "Dear Mrs. Obama: Please come to UC Merced's Commencement. We could really use the publicity." That really touched me.

Or then there was one from Jim Greenwood who wrote not on his behalf but on behalf of his wife and the mother of his two children, who is graduating with us today.

And then there was the one from Andrea Mercado. I think this was one of my favorites. Andrea said that the role of First Lady is — and I quote — "the balance between politics and sanity". Thank you, Andrea, for that vote of confidence.

I received letters from everyone connected to this university — not just students, but they came from parents, and grandparents, and cousins, and aunts, and uncles, and neighbors, and friends, all of them telling me about how hard you all have worked and how important this day is for you and for the entire Merced community.

And then there's that beautiful video, the "We Believe" video. Well, let me tell you, it worked, because I'm here!

And I want to thank in particular Sam Fong and Yaasha Sabba and all of the students who launched the "Dear Michelle" campaign. I am honored by your efforts and happy to be with you to celebrate this important milestone.

But I understand that this type of community-based letter writing campaign isn't unique to me. This community, this Merced community, employed the same strategy to help get the University of California to build the new campus here in Merced. Every school kid in the entire county, I understand, sent a postcard to the UC Board of Regents in order to convince them to select Merced, and I just love the fact that some of the graduates sitting in this audience today participating were involved in that campaign, as well, and then they used the same strategy to get me here. That is amazing. And what it demonstrates is the power of many voices coming together to make something wonderful happen. And I'm telling you, next year's graduation speaker better watch out, because Merced students know how to get what they want.

This type of activism and optimism speaks volumes about the students here,

明信片中都充满了期待和热情。这不仅感动了我，还感动了我所有的同事们。他们过来跟我说："米歇尔，你必须参加。""你必须到那里去。"

那些信和明信片都写得棒极了。比如，来自克里斯多夫·卡苏卡的信中写道："亲爱的奥巴马夫人，请来参加加州大学摩塞德分校的毕业典礼吧！我们真的可以使用公众舆论。"那真的触动了我的心灵。

来自吉姆·格林伍德的信中说，他不仅仅是代表他自己给我写信，还代表他的妻子。他的妻子已经是两个孩子的母亲了，她是今天在座的毕业生中的一员。

还有一封是来自安德里亚·梅尔卡多的信。我想这是我最喜欢的来信中的一封。安德里亚在信中写道："第一夫人的角色就是要在政治和理智之间寻求平衡。"谢谢你，安德里亚，谢谢你给我的信任投票。

我收到了所有与这个大学相关的人的来信——不只是学生，还有他们的父母、祖父母、堂表兄妹、姑舅叔姨以及他们的邻居和朋友，所有的人都告诉我，你们是多么地努力，而这一天对于你们和整个摩塞德分校多么重要。

我还收到了一段精彩的视频，名为"我们相信"。那么让我告诉你们，这一切真的很奏效，因为我最终来到了这里。

我要特别感谢萨姆·方和亚沙·萨巴以及所有发起"亲爱的米歇尔"活动的学生们。你们的努力让我感受到了极大的荣耀，我很高兴和你们一起庆祝这一重要时刻。

但是我明白，这种基于社区而写信的活动并不仅仅针对我。这个社区，默赛德社区用同样的方式使得加利福尼亚大学在摩塞德成立了新的分校。这个县城里的每一个学生都给加利福尼亚大学董事会寄了一张明信片，以说服他们在这里成立分校。我很高兴因为事实上，今天在座的一些毕业生当时也参与了那次活动，而他们用同样的方式说服我来到了这

热词空间

publicity [pʌbˈlisiti] *n.* 公众的注意

sanity [ˈsænəti] *n.* 明智；通情达理

in particular 特别，尤其

launch [ˈlɔːntʃ] *vt.* 发动

demonstrate [ˈdemənstreit] *vt.* 证明

optimism [ˈɔptimizəm] *n.* 乐观，乐观主义

speak volumes(for sth.) 明白表示，有力地说明

哈佛
大学

斯坦福
大学

牛津
大学

耶鲁
大学

杜兰
大学

杜克
大学

威斯康
辛大学

清华
大学

北京
大学

亚利桑
那州立
大学

加利福
尼亚
大学

the faculty, the staff, but also about the character and history of Merced — a town built by laborers and immigrants from all over the world: early settlers who came here as pioneers and trailblazers in the late 1800s as part of the Gold Rush and built the churches and businesses and schools that exist; African Americans who escaped slavery and the racism of the South to work on the railways as truck drivers up and down Route 99; Mexican Americans who traveled north to find work on the farms and have since become the backbone of our agricultural industry; Asian Americans who arrived in San Francisco and have slowly branched out to become a part of the community in the San Joaquin Valley.

Merced's make-up may have changed over the years, but its values and character have not — long, hot days filled with hard work by generations of men and women of all races who wanted an opportunity to build a better life for their children and their grandchildren; hardworking folks who believed that access to a good education would be their building blocks to a brighter future.

You know, I grew up in one of those communities with similar values. Like Merced, the South Side of Chicago is a community where people struggled financially, but worked hard, looked out for each other and rallied around their children. My father was a blue-collar worker, as you all know. My mother stayed at home to raise me and my brother. We were the first to graduate from college in our immediate family.

I know that many of you out here are also the first in your families to achieve that distinction, as well. And as you know, being the first is often a big responsibility, particularly in a community that, like many others around our country at the moment, is struggling to cope with record high unemployment and foreclosure rates; a community where families are a single paycheck or an emergency room visit away from homelessness.

And with jobs scarce, many of you may be considering leaving town with your diploma in hand. And it wouldn't be unreasonable. For those of you who come from

里。这真是太奇妙了。这说明一点，万众齐心必然能够创造奇迹。而且我也想说下一年的毕业演讲人，你可要当心了，摩塞德分校的学生可知道如何实现他们的愿望。

这种行动主义和乐观主义不仅诠释了这儿的学生和教职员工，也是摩塞德个性和历史的体现。摩塞德是由劳动者和来自全世界的移民共同建立的县城。早期的拓荒者以及19世纪末淘金热中的一些先驱来到这里建立了学校、商业区和教堂，这些现在依然存在。当时非裔美国人利用沿99号铁路线做卡车司机的机会逃离了南方的奴隶制度和种族主义的压迫。墨西哥裔美国人来到北边在这里的农场找工作，成为我们农业生产的支柱。还有亚裔美国人，他们来到旧金山，在这里扎根繁衍，逐渐成为圣华金河谷社区的一部分。

过去的这些年，摩塞德的人口结构虽发生了变化，但是它的价值观和品格没有改变——在漫长的炎炎烈日下一代又一代的男男女女辛勤劳作，不分种族，他们想得到的就是为子孙后代建设美好生活的机会；辛苦劳作的人们相信，接受良好的教育就是通往更加美好未来的阶梯。

你们知道，我在一个有着相似价值观的社区里长大。就像摩塞德一样，芝加哥南部是一个过去人们在经济困境中挣扎的社区，但是那里的人们辛勤工作，彼此照料，以子女为中心。你们都知道的，我的父亲是个蓝领工人。我的母亲在家里抚养我和哥哥。我们兄妹是我们的所有直系亲属中第一批从大学毕业的成员。

我知道你们中的很多人也是你们家族中第一位获得如此殊荣的成员。但正如你们所了解的那样，成为第一就常常意味着肩负更大的责任，特别是在一个和当前我们国家的很多其他社区一样面对创纪录的高失业率和高抵押房屋赎回权丧失率的社区，特别是一个家庭是单一收入来源或者家庭只是为了避免无家可归的紧急避难所的社区。

热词空间

immigrant ['imigrənt] n. 移民，侨民

trailblazer ['treil,bleizə] n. 开拓者

racism ['reisizəm] n. 种族歧视

backbone ['bækbəun] n. 脊骨，骨干

branch out 扩大范围

block [blɔk] n. 街区，大楼

financially [fai'nænʃəli] adv. 财政上（金融上）

rally ['ræli] vt. 集合，站在……的一边

immediate [i'miːdjət] adj. 直接的，最接近的

distinction [di'stiŋkʃən] n. 荣誉，差别

foreclosure [fɔː'kləuʒə] n. 丧失抵押品赎回权

paycheck ['peitʃek] n. 薪水支票，工资

diploma [di'pləumə] n. 文凭

communities facing similar economic hardships, you may also be wondering how you'll build decent lives for yourselves if you choose to return to those communities.

But I would encourage you to call upon the same hope and hard work that brought you to this day. Call upon that optimism and tenacity that built the University of California at Merced to invest in the future of Merced in your own home towns all across this country. By using what you've learned here, you can shorten the path perhaps for kids who may not see a path at all.

And I was once one of those kids. Most of you were once one of those kids. I grew up just a few miles from the University of Chicago in my hometown. The university, like most institutions, was a major cultural, economic institution in my neighborhood. My mother even worked as a secretary there for several years.

Yet that university never played a meaningful role in my academic development. The institution made no effort to reach out to me — a bright and promising student in their midst — and I had no reason to believe there was a place for me there. Therefore, when it came time for me to apply to college, I never for one second considered the university in my own backyard as a viable option.

And as fate would have it, I ultimately went on and accepted a position in student affairs at the University of Chicago more than a decade later. What I found was that working within the institution gave me the opportunity to express my concerns about how little role the university plays in the life of its neighbors. I wanted desperately to be involved in helping to break down the barriers that existed between the campus and the community.

And in less than a year, through that position, I worked with others to build the university's first Office of Community Service. And today, the office continues to provide students with opportunities to help reshape relationships between the university and its surrounding community. Students there today are volunteering in local elementary schools, serving as mentors at high schools, organizing neighborhood watches, and worshiping in local churches.

在这样的社区里，工作机会很少，你们中的很多人可能会考虑带着你们的学位证书离开城镇。这并非不合理。对于那些来自处于相似经济困境社区的同学而言，你们也许会有疑问：假如我回到了那些社区，我怎么才能过上体面的生活呢？

但是我要鼓励你们拿出过去让你们取得今日之成就的希望和努力，拿出建设加州大学摩塞德校区的乐观和不屈不挠的精神，将其投入到建设摩塞德的美好未来之中，投入到建设分布在全国各地的你们的家乡中去。运用你们在这所大学学到的知识，你们能够帮助那些也许根本看不到出路的孩子们找到通往成功的捷径。

我曾经就是那些看不到出路的孩子中的一员。你们中的大多数人也曾经是那些孩子中的一员。我的家乡距离芝加哥大学只有几英里。和大多数学校一样，芝加哥大学就是我邻近地区的一个文化经济中心。我的母亲甚至在那里做了几年秘书工作。

但是那所大学从来没有在我的学业发展中发挥积极的作用。它没做出任何努力来吸引我这样一个有着大好前途的学生，而我也没有任何理由相信在那里有我的一席之地。因此，当到了申请大学的时候，我根本没有考虑选择自己家门口的那所大学。

就像命中注定一样，十多年后我最终接受了芝加哥大学一个负责学生事务的职位。我发现在这所大学工作使得我有机会关注那个问题，即它在周围社区生活中扮演着多么渺小的角色。我当时迫切地想扫除挡在大学校园和社区之间的障碍。

在不到一年的时间里，我和他人一起努力建立了芝加哥大学的第一个社区服务办公室。今天，该办公室还在继续为学生们提供机会，让他们帮助重塑大学与周边社区的关系。如今，那里的学生们在当地小学做志愿者，到当地中学做辅导员，组织邻里监督，到当地教堂做礼拜。

热词空间

tenacity [tə'næsiti] n. 韧性；不屈不挠

invest [in'vest] vt. 投资，投入

academic [ækə'demik] adj. 学校（院）的

viable ['vaiəbl] adj. 可行的

ultimate ['ʌltimit] adj. 根本的，极限的

desperate ['despərit] adj. 急需要的

break down 损坏，崩溃

elementary [ˌelə'mentəri] adj. 基本的，初级的

But you know a little something about working with your community here, don't you, Merced? UC Merced, its faculty and its students seem to already have a handle on this need and it speaks once again to the character of this community. As I learned more about what you have done, I am so impressed with how the students, faculty and the community are collaborating to ensure that every child in this community understands there is a place for them at this big beautiful university if they study hard and stay out of trouble.

There are local leaders like police officer, Nick Navarette, who coordinates a program that brings about 60 UC Merced students to local elementary schools each week to mentor students from poor neighborhoods. Nick then brings kids to campus regularly so that they can do something special: see what it's like to be on a college campus, and begin to dream.

And then there is my friend and former law school professor, Charles Ogletree, a product of the Merced public schools. Now, he is an example of how you can bring your skills back. His ambitions took him far away from home, but he has never forgotten where he came from.

Each year, with his help, Merced's high schools are able to hand out scholarships, not just for the best and the brightest students, but also for many students who are just stuck in poverty and simply need a hand up to compete.

So the faculty, the students, local leaders, Merced alumni, everyone here is doing their part to help the children of Merced realize that access to a quality education is available to them as long as they work hard, study hard and apply themselves.

It is this kind of commitment that we're going to need in this nation to put this country back on a path where every child expects to succeed and where every child has the tools that they need to achieve their dreams. That's what we're aiming for. And we're going to need all of you, graduates, this generation, we need you to lead the way.

Now, let me tell you, careers focused on lifting up our communities — whether

你们多少知道一点和你们社区一起工作的事情，不是吗，摩塞德的同学们？加州大学摩塞德分校的教职员工和学生们似乎已经掌握了这种需求，这再次说明了这个社区的特性。随着我对你们所做的事情有更深一步的了解，我就更深刻地体会到学生们、教职员工以及社区居民如何通力合作以保证该社区的每个孩子都能明白，只要他们努力学习，不惹麻烦，在这样一个规模宏大而又美丽的大学里就有他们的一席之地。

本地的一些领导人，比如尼克·纳瓦莱特警官，他协调一个项目，该项目每周会分派大约 60 名加州大学摩塞德分校的学生到本地小学去辅导家境贫寒的学生。然后尼克会定期把孩子们带到大学校园，以便他们能够做一些特别的事情：看看在大学校园里是什么感觉，并开始塑造梦想。

还有我的朋友查理斯·奥格里特里，他以前是法学院的教授，他是摩塞德公立学校的"产品"。现在，他带着自己的技能回到社区，为他人树立了榜样。他的雄心壮志让他远离家乡，但是他从来没有忘记他来自哪里。

在他的帮助下，摩塞德中学每年，不但向那些最优秀最有前途的学生提供奖学金，也向很多被贫穷所困、需要别人的一臂之力助他们参与竞争的学生们提供。

因此，教职员工们、学生们、本地领导者、摩塞德的校友们以及这里的每个人都在做自己力所能及的事，来帮助摩塞德的孩子们认识到，只要他们勤奋工作、努力学习，他们就能够接受优质教育。

我们国家需要的正是这种承诺，让国家再次步入正轨，让每个孩子都期盼成功，让每个孩子都有实现梦想所需要的工具。这就是我们的目标。我们需要你们中的每一位，需要所有毕业生，需要你们这一代人，我们需要你们引航带路。

现在，让我来告诉你们，那些旨在提高我们社区生活水

热词空间

be impressed with 对……印象深刻

collaborate [kə'læbəreit] vi. 合作，通敌

coordinate [kəu'ɔ:dineit] vt. 调节，协调

ambition [æm'biʃən] n. 雄心，抱负

hand out 给予，分发

do one's part 尽自己的职责

available [ə'veiləbl] adj. 有效的，可用的

as long as 如果，只要

commitment [kə'mitmənt] n. 承诺，保证

focuse on 集中在……

it's helping transform troubled schools or creating after-school programs or training workers for green jobs — these careers are not always obvious, but today they are necessary. Solutions to our nation's most challenging social problems are not going to come from Washington alone. Real innovation often starts with individuals who apply themselves to solve a problem right in their own community. That's where the best ideas come from.

And some pretty incredible social innovations have been launched by young people all across this world.

Teach for America in this country is a great example. It was created by Wendy Kopp as a part of her undergraduate senior thesis in 1989. And now, as a result of her work then, more than 6,200 corps members are teaching in our country's neediest communities, reaching approximately 400,000 students.

And then there's Van Jones, who recently joined the Obama administration, as a special adviser to the President on green jobs. Van started out as a grassroots organizer and became an advocate and a creator of "green collar" jobs — jobs that are not only good for the environment, but also provide good wages and career advancement for both skilled and unskilled workers; jobs similar to the ones being created right here at UC Merced as this green campus continues to grow.

And then one of my heroes, Geoffrey Canada, grew up in the South Bronx. After graduating from Bowdoin and getting his masters at Harvard, he returned to New York City and used his education to ensure that the next generation would have a chance at the same opportunity. Geoffrey's Harlem Children's Zone is a nationally recognized program that covers 100 blocks and reaches nearly 10,000 children with a variety of social services to ensure that all kids are prepared to get a good education.

And in an effort to invest in and encourage the future Wendy Kopps, Van Joneses and Geoffrey Canadas, the Obama administration recently launched the Office of Social Innovation at the White House. The President has asked Congress to provide $50 million in seed capital to fund great ideas like the ones I just described.

平的职业——无论它是帮助改善陷入困境的学校，还是建立课外项目，还是培训工人从事绿色工作——这些职业常常并不显眼，但是今天我们确实需要这些职业。解决我们国家所面临的最具挑战性的社会问题的方法并不一定单单来自于华盛顿。真正的革新经常始于那些致力于解决他们自己社区问题的个人。最好的主意来自他们。

一些很有创意的社会革新已经由世界各地的青年人发动起来了。

"为美国而教书"就是很棒的一个例子。该口号是温迪·科普1989年在其本科毕业论文里提出来的。由于她当时的努力，现在有超过6200名队员正在我国最贫穷的社区教书，他们教授的学生数量大概有40万名。

还有凡·琼斯，他最近加入了奥巴马政府，成了总统在绿色工作方面的特别顾问。凡开始时是一名民间组织者，后来成了"绿领"工作口号的创始者和倡导者——这种工作不但对环境有利，而且技术工人和非技术工人都会得到不错的工资待遇及职业生涯，这种工作类似于加州大学摩塞德分校随着绿色校园面积的扩大而创造出的工作。

还有我心目中的英雄之———杰弗瑞·凯那德，他在南布朗克斯长大。在拿到鲍登学院的学士学位和哈佛大学的硕士学位后，他返回纽约，运用所学到的知识，确保下一代能够拥有平等的机会。杰弗瑞创办的"哈雷姆儿童地带"组织获得了全国性的认可；该项目覆盖100个街区，给近1万名儿童提供各种社会服务，以保证所有孩子们都能为接受良好的教育做好准备。

为了使温迪·柯璞、凡·琼斯以及杰弗瑞·凯那德所建的项目在未来得到投资和鼓励，奥巴马政府最近在白宫设立了"社会革新办公室"。总统已经请求国会拨款5千万美元作为种子资金来资助那些了不起的想法，就像我刚才所说的那些项目。

热词空间

transform [træns'fɔːm] vt. 改变，转换

innovation [ˌinəu'veiʃən] n. 创新，革新

approximate [ə'prɔksimit] adj. 近似的，大约的

administration [ədˌmini'streiʃən] n. 实施，管理，行政

Congress ['kɔŋgres] n. 代表大会，议会，国会

The Office is going to identify the most promising, results-oriented non-profit programs and expand their reach throughout the country.

And this university is blessed with some of the leading researchers and academics who are focusing already their attention on solving some of our nation's most critical issues, like the energy crisis, global warming, climate change, and air pollution.

And you, the students, the graduates and faculty on this campus, you're capable of changing the world, that's for sure. Where you are right now is no different from where Wendy and Van and Geoffrey were when they graduated, remember that. You too can have this same transformative effect on the community of Merced and our entire nation. We need your ideas, graduates. We need your resourcefulness. We need your inventiveness.

And as the students who helped build this school, I ask you, make your legacy a lasting one. Dream big, think broadly about your life, and please make giving back to your community a part of that vision. Take the same hope and optimism, the hard work and tenacity that brought you to this point, and carry that with you for the rest of your life in whatever you choose to do. Each and every single day, some young person is out there changing the ways — the world in ways both big and small.

But let me tell you something, as you step out into that big, open world, and you start building your lives, the truth is that you will face tough times, you will certainly have doubts, let me tell you, because I know I did when I was your age. There will be days when you will worry about whether you're really up for the challenge. Maybe some of you already feel a little of that right now. Maybe you're wondering: Am I smart enough? Do I really belong? Can I live up to all those expectations that everyone has of me?

And you will definitely have your share of setbacks. Count on it. Your best laid plans will be consumed by obstacles. Your excellent ideas will be peppered with flaws. You will be confronted with financial strains as your loans become due and salaries fall short of both expectations and expenses. You will make mistakes that will shatter your

该办公室将会认同那些最有前景、结果明确的非营利项目，并将扩大它们在全国的业务。

这所大学幸运地拥有一些一流的研究人员和专业学者，他们正把研究重点放在解决我们国家最迫切的问题上，例如能源危机、全球变暖、气候变化以及空气污染。

而你们——这所学校的大学生们、毕业生们以及教职员工们——你们有能力改变这个世界，这是肯定的。你们现在的起点和当年温迪、凡、杰弗瑞毕业的时候的起点并无二致，记住这一点。你们也能够给摩塞德社区乃至我们整个国家带来同样的转变效应。我们需要你们的想法，毕业生们。我们需要你们的智慧。我们需要你们发明创造的才能。

正如曾帮助建设这所大学的学生一样，我请求你们把你们的传统传承下去。要有更远大的梦想，思维要更开阔一些，你们的梦想应包含为社区服务。带着让你们取得今日成就的这种辉煌的希望和乐观精神、努力和坚韧，无论选择什么样的事业，让这些品格陪伴着你们的人生。每一天都有一些年轻人在或多或少地改变着世界。

但是让我来告诉你们，当你们走向那个广阔开放的世界时，你们就开始了建设自己人生的旅程，你们肯定会面对艰难时刻，当然也会有困惑，因为我在你们这个年龄时曾经也是如此。将来会有那么一天，你会担心自己是否真的有能力迎接挑战。也许你们中的一些人现在已经有了这种感觉。也许你们要问：我足够聪明吗？我真的能够适应吗？我能不辜负所有人对我的期待吗？

你们肯定会遇到挫折。要想到这一点。你们深思熟虑的计划可能因为挫折而泡汤。你们卓越的想法难免会有瑕疵。当你们的贷款到期、工资低于期望值而且不能满足花费时，你们将会遇到财务紧张的情况。你们难免会犯错误，这将摧毁你们的自信心。你们难免会妥协，这将挑战你们的信念。

热词空间

result-oriented 结果导向型的

transformative [,træns'fɔ:mətiv] adj. 起改造作用的

resourcefulness [ri'sɔ:sfəlnis] n. 足智多谋

inventiveness [in'ventivnis] n. 创造性

legacy ['legəsi] n. 遗赠物

tenacity [ti'næsiti] n. 坚韧，固执

expectation [,ekspek'teiʃən] n. 预料，期望

setback ['setbæk] n. 推迟，延缓

pepper ['pepə] vt. 不断打击

flaw [flɔ:] n. 瑕疵，缺陷

financial strain 资金紧张

shatter ['ʃætə] vt. 粉碎；破坏

confidence. You will make compromises that will test your **convictions**. You will find that there is rarely a clear and direct path to any of your visions. And you will find that you'll have to readjust again and again and again. And there may be times when you wonder whether it's all worth it. And there may be moments when you just want to quit.

But in those moments, those **inevitable** moments, I urge you to think about this day. Look around you. Look around you. There are thousands and thousands of hardworking people who have helped you get to this point, people who are celebrating with you today, who are praying for you every single day, and others who couldn't be here, for whatever reason. I want you to think of the people who **sacrificed** for you — you know that — family members who worked a third job to get you through, who took on the extra shifts to get you through, who put off doing something important for themselves to get you to this day.

And think about the friends who never got the chance to go to college but were still invested in your success — friends who talked you out of dropping out, friends who kept you out of trouble so that you could graduate on time, friends who forced you to study when you wanted to **procrastinate**.

Most importantly, though, think of the millions of kids living all over this world who will never come close to having the chance to stand in your shoes — kids in New Orleans whose schools are still recovering from the **ravages** of Katrina; kids who will never go to school at all because they're forced to work in a sweat shop somewhere; kids in your very own communities who just can't get a break, who don't have anyone in their lives telling them that they're good enough and smart enough to do whatever they can imagine; kids who have lost the ability to dream. These kids are desperate to find someone or something to **cling to**. They are looking to you for some sign of hope.

So, whenever you get ready to give up, think about all of these people and remember that you are blessed. Remember that you are blessed. Remember that in exchange for those blessings, you must give something back. You must reach back and pull someone up. You must **bend down** and let someone else stand on your

你们将会发现，几乎没有一条道路会明朗而直接地通向理想。你们将会发现不得不再三调整。也许你们在某些时刻怀疑自己的理想是否有价值。也许在某些时候你们想放弃。

但是在那些时候，在那些不可避免的时刻，我希望你们回想一下今天。看看你们周围。看看这成千上万为帮助你们走到今天而努力工作的人，还有今天和你们一起庆祝的人，每一天都为你们祈祷的人，以及不管出于什么原因不能来到这里的其他人。我要你们想想那些为你们做出牺牲的人——你们知道——他们就是你们的家人，为了让你们顺利毕业，他们身兼三职；为了让你们顺利毕业，他们加班加点地工作；为了你们能达到今天的成就，他们将自己的大事一拖再拖。

想想那些从来没有机会进入大学但依然为你们的成功出钱出力的朋友们吧——想想那些劝告你们不要辍学的朋友们，想想那些让你们远离麻烦以便你们能够准时毕业的朋友们，想想那些当你们想偷懒时强迫你们去学习的朋友们。

但是最为重要的，想想世界上还有数以百万计的孩子们，他们永远不会像你们一样离机会如此之近——想想纽奥良的那些孩子们，他们的学校遭受了卡特里娜飓风的肆虐，目前还在修复；想想那些将永远没有机会上学的孩子们，他们会被迫在世界某个角落的血汗工厂里做工；想想你们自己社区里的孩子们吧，他们没有这么好的运气，在他们的生命里没人告诉他们，他们聪明优秀，足以完成他们想象的任何事情；想想那些失去梦想的孩子们吧。这些孩子们迫切想找到可以依赖的人或事物。他们想要从你们那里看到希望的曙光。

所以当你们准备放弃的时候，想想所有这些人，记住你们是幸运的。记住你们是被祝福的。记住，得到了这些幸福后，你们必须拿出东西来回馈社会。你们必须回过身去拉别人一把。你们必须弯下腰来让别人站在你们的肩膀上，让他们看

热词空间

conviction [kən'vikʃən] n. 坚信，定罪
inevitable [in'evitəbl] adj. 不可避免的
sacrifice ['sækrifais] vt. 牺牲
procrastinate [prəu'kræstineit] vt. 耽搁，延迟
ravage ['rævidʒ] n. 破坏
cling to 依赖
bend down 屈身，弯腰

shoulders so that they can see a brighter future.

As advocate and activist Marian Wright Edelman says, "Service is the rent we pay for living... it is the true measure, the only measure of our success." So, graduates, when times get tough and fear sets in, think of those people who paved the way for you and those who are counting on you to pave the way for them. Never let setbacks or fear dictate the course of your life. Hold on to the possibility and push beyond the fear. Hold on to the hope that brought you here today, the hope of laborers and immigrants, settlers and slaves, whose blood and sweat built this community and made it possible for you to sit in these seats.

There are a lot of people in your lives who know a little something about the power of hope. Don't we, parents and grandparents? Look, I know a little something about the power of hope. My husband knows a little something about the power of hope.

You are the hope of Merced and of this nation. And be the realization of our dreams and the hope for the next generation. We believe in you. Thank you so much, and good luck. God bless you all.

到更加灿烂的未来。

正如儿童权利倡导者和社会活动家马琳·赖特·埃德曼所说："服务是我们为生活而支付的租金……它是真正的标准，是我们衡量成功的唯一标准。"因此，毕业生们，当世道艰险、恐惧来临的时候，想想那些为你们铺路搭桥的人们吧，想想那些期待你为他们铺路搭桥的人们吧。永远不要让挫折或恐惧占据你们的人生之路。只要有可能，就要坚持住并把恐惧抛诸脑后。坚守住那曾经把你们带到这里的希望，那是劳工和移民的希望，那是移居者和奴隶的希望，他们用血汗建设了这个社会，他们让你们有机会坐在了这里。

在你们的生命中有很多人知道希望的力量。难道不是吗？父母们，祖父母们。瞧，我知道希望的力量。我的丈夫知道希望的力量。

你们是摩塞德的希望，是我们国家的希望。实现我们的梦想吧，成为下一代的希望。我们相信你们。非常感谢大家，祝你们好运。上帝保佑你们。

热词空间

advocate ['ædvəkeit] *n.* 拥护者，提倡者

set in 开始，嵌入

pave the way for... 为……铺平道路

dictate ['dikteit] *vt.* 命令

米歇尔·奥巴马给我们的

Dream big, think broadly about your life, and please make giving back to your community a part of that vision. Take the same hope and optimism, the hard work and tenacity that brought you to this point, and carry that with you for the rest of your life in whatever you choose to do. Each and every single day, some young person is out there changing the ways — the world in ways both big and small.

要有更远大的梦想，思维要更开阔一些，你们的梦想应包含为社区服务。带着让你们取得今日成就的这种辉煌的希望和乐观精神、努力和坚韧，无论选择什么样的事业，让这些品格陪伴着你们的人生。每一天都有一些年轻人在或多或少地改变着世界。

So, whenever you get ready to give up, think about all of these people and remember that you are blessed. Remember that you are blessed. Remember that in exchange for those blessings, you must give something back. You must reach back and pull someone up. You must bend down and let someone else stand on your shoulders so that they can see a brighter future.

所以当你们准备放弃的时候，想想所有这些人，记住你们是幸运的。记住你们是被祝福的。记住，得到了这些幸福后，你们必须拿出东西来回馈社会。你们必须回过身去拉别人一把。你们必须弯下腰来让别人站在你们的肩膀上，让他们看到更加灿烂的未来。

Never let setbacks or fear dictate the course of your life. Hold on to the possibility and push beyond the fear. Hold on to the hope that brought you here today, the hope of laborers and immigrants, settlers and slaves, whose blood and sweat built this community and made it possible for you to sit in these seats.

永远不要让挫折或恐惧占据你们的人生之路。只要有可能，就要坚持住并把恐惧抛诸脑后。坚守住那曾经把你们带到这里的希望，那是劳工和移民的希望，那是移居者和奴隶的希望，他们用血汗建设了这个社会，他们让你们有机会坐在了这里。

读者反馈表

前**50**位

亲爱的读者：

　　您好！非常感谢您购买振宇图书，希望您抽出宝贵的时间填写这份反馈表，以便我们做进一步的改进，日后能为您提供更加优秀的图书。另外，我们将对每月前50位反馈的读者赠送振宇英语最新图书一本，获奖名单将刊登于振宇英语网（www.zhenglish.com）。谢谢！

读者档案

您所购买的图书的名称：_____　QQ：_____

您的姓名：_____　性别：_____　年龄：_____　职业：_____

教育程度：_____　联系电话：_____　E-mail：_____

通讯地址：_____　邮编：_____

1. **您是通过何种途径获知本书的？（可多选）**
   □ 书店　□ 网络　□ 老师介绍　□ 朋友推荐　□ 振宇英语官网　□ 其他

2. **您购买本书的原因是？（可多选）**
   □ 封面设计　□ 正文内容　□ 图书价格　□ 书评广告　□ 纸张　□ 出版社
   □ 振宇英语品牌　□ 其他 _____

3. **您对本书封面设计的满意程度？**
   □ 很满意　□ 比较满意　□ 一般　□ 不满意　□ 您的建议 _____

4. **您希望正文内容的哪些方面需要改进？（可多选）**
   □ 版式　□ 层次结构　□ 难易度　□ 内容丰富性　□ 印刷　□ 其他 _____

5. **本书最令您满意的地方是哪些？**
   □ 封面　□ 内文　□ 价格　□ 印装质量　□ 其他 _____

6. **您希望本书的定价是多少？**
   □ 20 元以下　□ 25 元左右　□ 30 元以下　□ 35 元左右　□ 其他 _____

7. **您的其他意见和建议：** _____
   _____

8. **填表日期：** _____ 年 _____ 月 _____ 日

请将本反馈表寄至：

北京市朝阳区北四环东路 108 号千鹤家园 10 号楼 1105 室

振宇英语编辑部　收

邮编：100029　　E-mail: zhenglish@126.com　　QQ: 1151372025

同步推出，敬请关注

《当幸福来敲门——心灵鸡汤精选》

　　本书共分为六卷，分别是：紫丁香的回忆；生活中，我们最幸福时；我们都可以成为天使；当幸福来敲门；人生的补丁；阳光总在风雨后；它们对应的主题分别是亲情、爱情、友情、幸福、人生、奋斗。一共60篇美文和18首英文歌曲。书中既包含很多感人的故事，也包含一些短小精悍的优美散文和哲理小论文。幸福是什么？通过读这本书，我们会对幸福有更深的领悟。我们想要幸福，就需要给别人去幸福。请记住：在你敲开别人的幸福之门时，幸福也将敲开你的门。

《生而为赢——心灵鸡汤精选》

　　本书按内容共分为六卷：如果我休息，我就会生锈；不抱怨的世界；生而为赢；给年轻人的建议；生活的理想是为了理想的生活；活在当下。本书精选了58篇励志美文和18首英文经典歌曲，是一本英汉对照的优秀励志读物。这是一本需要你用眼睛去看，用嘴巴去读，用耳朵去听，用心灵去感悟的好书。这里的每一则故事都会激发你的灵魂；每一个旋律都能净化你的心灵；每一篇美文都会是一对翅膀，能够带您飞向成功的远方……希望本书能成为你成长中的朋友，生活中的导航。

《影响你一生的名人励志演讲》

　　本书收录了19篇英语演讲，演讲者来自政治、经济、文化等各个领域。本书共分为五章，分别为国家领袖、政治人物、商界精英、作家记者和娱乐名人。精选出的这些演讲名篇题材涉猎广泛、风格迥异，有的气势恢宏、意蕴精深；有的轻松诙谐，令人捧腹；有的言辞恳切，语重心长。它们都有一个共同点：演讲者或立足于时代背景下，或从个人自身经历出发，鼓舞人奋发向上、积极进取，做出个人应有的成绩，为时代、为国家作贡献。本书配有原声音频，让你最近距离感受这些最有影响力的声音。

《影响你一生的名校励志演讲》

　　这是一本中英对照的世界名人在世界名校演讲的图书。共收录16篇演讲，涵盖12所世界一流大学，其中有美国的哈佛、耶鲁，英国的牛津，还有中国的清华、北大等。借音频听演讲，感受现场的气氛，聆听名人之声，感悟世界级人物送给大学毕业生的成功忠告。同时，你可以借此机会跟世界顶级人物学习口语，听他们的声音，模仿地道的原汁原味的腔调。听着他们的演讲，你的心头一定会充满喜悦和激动。这本演讲书是原汁原味的英语集成，这本演讲书是智慧的结晶，这本演讲书是引领你走向成功的声音。让我们一起聆听演讲，让我们一起迈向成功！